Penguin Education

Penguin Modern Economics Texts
General Editor: B. J. McCormick

Political Economy
Editor: K. J. W. Alexander

The Economics of the Common Market
Third Edition
Dennis Swann

Dennis Swann

The Economics of the Common Market

Third Edition

Penguin Books

Penguin Books Ltd,
Harmondsworth, Middlesex, England
Penguin Books, 625 Madison Avenue,
New York, New York 10022, U.S.A.
Penguin Books Australia Ltd,
Ringwood, Victoria, Australia
Penguin Books Canada Ltd,
41 Steelcase Road West, Markham, Ontario, Canada
Penguin Books (N.Z.) Ltd, 182–190 Wairau Road,
Auckland 10, New Zealand

First published 1970
Second edition 1972
Reprinted 1973
Third edition 1975
Reprinted 1977
Copyright © Dennis Swann, 1970, 1972, 1975

Made and printed in Great Britain by
C. Nicholls & Company Ltd
Set in Monotype Times

Penguin Modern Economics Texts

This volume is one in a series of unit texts designed to reduce the price of knowledge for students of economics in universities and colleges of higher education. The units may be used singly or in combination with other units to form attractive and unusual teaching programmes. The volumes will cover the major teaching areas but they will differ from conventional books in their attempt to chart and explore new directions in economic thinking. The traditional divisions of theory and applied, of positive and normative and of micro and macro will tend to be blurred as authors impose new and arresting ideas on the traditional corpus of economics. Some units will fall into conventional patterns of thought but many will transgress established beliefs.

Penguin Modern Economics Texts are published in units in order to achieve certain objectives. First, a large range of short texts at inexpensive prices gives the teacher flexibility in planning his course and recommending texts for it. Secondly, the pace at which important new work is published requires the project to be adaptable. Our plan allows a unit to be revised or a fresh unit to be added with maximum speed and minimal cost to the reader.

The international range of authorship will, it is hoped, bring out the richness and diversity in economic analysis and thinking.

B.J.MCG.

To Barbara Claire

Contents

Editorial Foreword   9

Preface   11

1 The Evolution of the European Economic
   Community   13

2 The Decision-Making Institutions   33

3 Tariff Barriers and the Customs Union   48

4 Non-Tariff Barriers   79

5 Factor Movements   105

6 Common Policies   116

7 Regional and Social Policy   166

8 Macro-Economic, Medium-Term and
   Industrial Policy   195

9 The Community and the World   219

10 The Renegotiation Issue   242

References   251

Further Reading   253

Index   257

Contents

Editorial Foreword

Preface 11

Part I: Foundations of the Keynesian Economic Revolution 13

1. The Declining Status of Institutions 15

2. Keynes and the General Theory 38
and Paul Baran

3. Keynes Mr. general ...

4. ... 100

5. Keynes and Post-Keynesian 135

6. Macro-Economics, Inflation and Finance
Industrial Policy 181

9. The Consumer and the World 219

10. The Keynesian ... 235

References 251

Further reading 253

Index 247

Editorial Foreword

Economists are frequently criticized for being 'too theoretical'. Such charges are usually based on a misunderstanding of the methodology of economics, and sometimes on the anxiety of the economists' public to have cut-and-dried answers to practical economic problems. In their defence economists have to point out that the degree of abstraction in economic analysis must be high compared to the complexity of situations in the real world, and that anyway cut-and-dried answers usually rely on chancy assumptions about the future and on value judgements which would not be universally accepted. This defence is particularly relevant in the field of 'political economy', where social judgements, institutional influences, government objectives and economic cause and effect are all relevant but when, nonetheless, it is important to distinguish between them as far as possible. The character, performance and future of the European Economic Community, the consequences for Britain of having joined the Community, the extent to which the character of the Community could be changed by renegotiation of Britian's terms of entry, these are all issues in political economy. Indeed the issue of Britain's relationship with the Community remains one of the major and most far-reaching political decisions to be taken for a generation.

Before Britain joined the Community Professor Swann had established a reputation as the British economist most knowledgeable about the institutions and work of the Community. Despite the increased attention paid by economists to the European Economic Community in recent years Professor Swann's pre-eminence has remained unchallenged. This book, now in its third revised edition, has been the major single source of information to students and the general public on the nature and development of the Community. It charts a course through the complexities of Common Market institutions and policies, condensing a vast range of knowledge in a way which will be invaluable to the student of economics, the business man and the general reader. Successive revisions have kept the information and treatment up-to-date. Those who have only a general idea of the workings of the Community will find this an invaluable source-book, filling out the picture in a detailed yet concise manner. The student of economics will note how economic theory is used to explain developments and illumine problems, though the general reader will not find this use of theory obtrusive. The distinction between economics and politics is carefully maintained, yet the economic problems are not considered in a vacuum but against the background of political objectives and institutional influences. In writing on what is, *par excellence*, an issue in political economy Professor Swann has demonstrated the contribution which economics can make to decision-taking.

K.J.W.A.

Preface to Third Edition

On 25 March 1957, the Governments of France, West Germany, Italy, the Netherlands, Belgium and Luxembourg signed the Rome Treaty. In so doing they agreed to create what is now known as the Common Market, or, more accurately, the European Economic Community. The latter title indicates that the arrangement is an economic one although, of course, the political aspect is also of the highest importance. This statement is not likely to give rise to any dispute. A former President of the European Economic Community Commission, Dr Walter Hallstein, once said: 'We are not in business at all; we are in politics.' The political nature of the Community is evidenced by the fact that it has political organs such as the European Parliament and the Council of Ministers. The latter makes binding decisions on matters which were formerly a national prerogative, as in the case of agricultural policy. Moreover, although the Community is primarily concerned with economic integration, the ultimate aim of those who have been in the vanguard of the 'European movement' has always been that close economic ties would eventually lead to political unity.

However, the main burden of this book will be related to the economic aspect of Community policy. This should not be taken as a further indication of the British preoccupation with the economic, as opposed to the political, nature of the 'European movement'. Rather, it is a consequence of the need to achieve some specialization in the analysis of Community policy. Nevertheless, the reader will observe that in the opening chapter frequent reference is made to the political factors which surrounded the creation of the Community. Without an appreciation of the influence of these factors, it would be impossible to understand why in the late 1950s Western Europe divided into two blocs.

As the title emphasizes, the focus of attention in this book is the European Economic Community. The more important aspects of policy in the European Coal and Steel Community are also discussed and Euratom is dealt with, although only in passing.

The book has two overriding aims. One is to discuss some of the economic principles underlying the decision to create the Common Market and the policies which the Community has been following since its inception. The second is to discuss the nature of these policies critically. This does not mean that the economic pros and cons of British membership will be neglected. This topic is in fact discussed at length in chapter 10. It will, of course, be appreciated that many of the subjects treated in this book could be the themes of separate monographs. Because of this, the book seeks to introduce the most important economic features of particular areas of policy, and a reading list is provided for those who wish to delve deeper.

In writing this book I have once more been able to avail myself of the courteous and efficient assistance provided by the London Office of the European Community Information Service. I am greatly indebted to my secretary, Mrs Brenda Moore, who has again rendered a great service by getting the manuscript into a fit state for the publisher.

1 The Evolution of the European Economic Community

European unity in history

Although the actual steps which have been taken to achieve economic and political unity in Europe are mostly, if not all, post-1945 in origin, the idea of such a coming together is not unique to the last quarter of a century. Quite the contrary; history is littered with proposals and arrangements which were designed to foster European unity.

As early as the fourteenth century the idea of a united Christendom prompted Pierre Dubois to propose a European confederation to be governed by a European Council of 'wise, expert, and faithful men'. In the seventeenth century Sully proposed to keep the peace in Europe by means of a European army. In 1693, William Penn, the English Quaker, suggested 'a European Diet, Parliament, or State' in his *Essay towards the Present and Future Peace of Europe*. In the nineteenth century Proudhon was strongly in favour of European federation. He foresaw the twentieth century as opening an era of federations and prophesied disaster if such developments did not occur. It was only after the 1914–18 war that statesmen began to give serious attention to the idea of European unity. Aristide Briand – a Prime Minister of France – declared that part of his political programme was the building of a United States of Europe.

The achievement of a lasting peace has been the chief motivating factor behind the drive for unity. However, economic advantage also played a role. The free trade tradition, and Adam Smith's dictum that 'the division of labour is limited by the extent of the market' was a contributing element. The idea that European nation states were no longer large enough to hold their own in world markets was put forward by the German thinker Friedrich Naumann in 1915.

Despite the fact that there was no shortage of plans to create a united Europe, it was nevertheless not until after 1945 that there occurred a combination of new forces together with an intensification of old ones, which compelled action. In the first place, Europe had been the centre of yet another devastating war arising out of the unbridled ambitions of nation states. Those who sought, and still seek, a united Europe, have always had at the forefront of their minds the desire to prevent any further outbreak of war in Europe. By bringing the nations of Europe closer together it has always been hoped that such a contingency would be rendered unthinkable. The 1939–45 war also left Europe economically exhausted. This engendered the view that if Europe were to recover, it would require a conjoint effort on the part of European states. The war also soon revealed that for a long time Western Europe would have to face not only a powerful and politically alien USSR, but also a group of European states firmly anchored within the Eastern bloc. An exhausted and divided Europe (since the West embraced co-belligerents) presented both a power-vacuum and a temptation to the USSR to fill it. Then again the ending of the war soon revealed that the war-time Allies were in fact divided, with the two major powers – the US and the USSR – confronting each other in a bid for world supremacy. It was therefore not surprising that 'Europeans'[1] should feel the need for a third force – the voice of Europe. The latter would represent the Western European viewpoint and could also act as a bridge between the Eastern and Western extremities.

Europe – the East–West division

The Economic Commission for Europe (ECE) was one of the first experiments in European regional action. It was set up in Geneva in 1947 as a regional organization of the United Nations (UN), and was to be concerned with initiating and participating in concerted measures aimed at securing the economic reconstruc-

1. 'Europeans' – members of the 'European movement' – sought to break away from systems of inter-governmental co-operation and to create institutions in Europe which would lead to a federal arrangement in which some national sovereignty would be given up.

tion of Europe. The aim was to create an instrument of co-operation between all the states of Europe, Eastern, Central and Western. Unfortunately, by the time it began to operate, the Cold War had become a reality and the world had been divided into two camps. In the light of future developments in Europe, this was a turning point. Economic co-operation over the whole of Europe was doomed. Thereafter, Western Europe followed its own path of economic and political unity, and Eastern Europe likewise pursued an independent course. This in due course led to two blocs in Europe – the Common Market or European Economic Community (EEC), and the European Free Trade Association (EFTA) on the one hand, and Comecon on the other. Any attempt to build bridges between the Western and Eastern blocs therefore implies trying to break down a division which began to manifest itself in 1947.

The political division of Europe was further revealed in 1948 by the emergence of the Brussels Treaty Organization. The Brussels Treaty was signed by the UK, France, Belgium, the Netherlands and Luxembourg, and was designed to establish a system of mutual assistance in time of attack in Europe. Clearly the Western European states had the USSR and its satellites in mind. This organization in turn took on an Atlantic shape in 1949 when, in order to provide a military defence organization, the North Atlantic Treaty (NATO) was signed by the five states just mentioned, together with the US, Canada, Denmark, Norway, Portugal, Iceland and, significantly, Italy, which had been an Axis power.[1]

Division in Western Europe – the beginning

The creation of the Organization for European Economic Co-operation (OEEC) in 1948 and the Council of Europe in 1949 marked the beginning of a division between the UK and some of the countries later to become members of the EFTA, and the Six[2] who subsequently founded the EEC.

1. Greece and Turkey joined in 1952 and West Germany in 1955.
2. The Six were, of course, France, West Germany, Italy, the Netherlands, Belgium and Luxembourg. In discussing divisions between Western and Eastern Europe, and within Western Europe, it should be remembered that

The division was founded in large measure on the fact that the UK was less committed to Europe as the main area of policy than the six Continental powers. During the second half of the 1950s the UK was still a world power. She had after all been on the victorious side and had been a major participant in some of the fateful geo-political decision-making meetings such as Yalta. Moreover, she still had the Empire to dispose of. British foreign policy was therefore bound to be based on wide horizons. Relations with Europe had to compete with Commonwealth (and Empire) ties and with the 'special relationship' with the US. In addition, the idea of a politically united Europe (in some eyes the goal was a United States of Europe) was strongly held on the Continent – particularly in France and Benelux – but, despite the encouraging noises made by Winston Churchill both during the 1939–45 war and after, it was not a concept which excited British hearts.

The difference between British and Continental thinking about the political nature of European institutions was revealed in the discussions and negotiations leading up to the establishment of the OEEC and the Council of Europe.

The war had left Europe devastated. The year of 1947 was particularly bleak. Bad harvests in the previous summer led to rising food prices, whilst the severe winter of 1946–7 led to a fuel crisis. The Continental countries were producing relatively little, and what was produced tended to be retained rather than exported, whilst import needs were booming. Foreign exchange reserves were therefore running out and it was at this point that the US entered upon the scene and the Marshall Plan was proposed. General Marshall proposed that the US make aid available to help the European economy to find its feet and that European governments get together to decide how much assistance was needed. The US did not feel it fitting that it should unilaterally decide on the programmes necessary to achieve this end. Although it seemed possible that this aid programme could be elaborated within the ECE framework, the USSR felt other-

the Six were also members of the European Coal and Steel Community (ECSC) and members of the European Atomic Energy Community (Euratom).

wise. Russian reluctance was no doubt based on the fear that if her satellites participated, this would open the door to Western influence.

A conference was therefore convened, and a Committee of European Economic Co-operation (CEEC) was established. The attitude of the US was that the CEEC should not just provide the US with a list of needs. The latter had in mind that the aid it was to give should be linked with progress towards European unification. This is a particularly important point since it indicates that from the very beginning the 'European movement' has enjoyed the encouragement and support of the US.

The CEEC led in turn to the creation of an aid agency – the OEEC. Here the conflict between Britain and other Western European countries, particularly France, came to a head over the issue of supra-nationalism. France in particular – and she was supported by the US – wanted to inject a supra-national element into the new organization.[1] We should perhaps at this point pause to define what is meant by supra-nationalism. It can refer to a situation in which international administrative institutions exercise power over, for example, the economies of the nation states. Thus the High Authority of the European Coal and Steel Community[2] (the ECSC) was endowed with powers over the economies of the Six and these powers were exercised independently of the Council of Ministers. Alternatively, it can refer to a situation in which ministerial bodies, when taking decisions (to be implemented by international administrations) work on a majority voting system rather than by insisting on unanimity.

The French view was not shared by the British. The latter favoured a body which was under the control of a ministerial council in which decisions should be taken on a unanimity basis. The French on the other hand favoured an arrangement in which an international secretariat would be presided over by a Secretary General who would be empowered to take policy initiatives on major issues. Significantly, the organization which emerged was

1. It is, of course, ironic that whereas France was then in the vanguard of the supra-national movement she is still its most dedicated opponent.

2. Created under the Paris Treaty of 1951.

substantially in line with the U K's wish for a unanimity rule. This was undoubtedly a reflection of the U K's relatively powerful position in Europe at the time. In the light of subsequent events it is also interesting to note that the U S encouraged the European countries to consider the creation of a customs union. Although this was of considerable interest to some Continental countries, it did not attract the U K. In the upshot the O E E C Convention merely recorded the intention to continue the study of this proposal. For a variety of reasons, one of which was the opposition of the U K, the matter was not pursued further.

The creation of the Council of Europe also threw into high relief fundamental differences in approach between the countries who later formed the Common Market on the one hand and the British and Scandinavians on the other. The creation of the Council was preceded by the Congress of Europe at the Hague in May 1948. The latter was a grand rally of 'Europeans' which was attended by leading European statesmen including Winston Churchill. The Congress adopted a resolution which called for the giving up of some national sovereignty prior to the accomplishment of economic and political union in Europe. Subsequently a proposal was put forward, with the support of the Belgian and French Governments, calling for the creation of a European Parliamentary Assembly in which resolutions would be passed by majority vote. This was, of course, contrary to the unanimity rule which was then characteristic of international organizations. A Committee of Ministers was to prepare and implement these resolutions. Needless to say, the U K was opposed to this form of supra-nationalism and in the end the British view largely prevailed. The Committee of Ministers, which is the executive organ of the Council of Europe, alone has power of decision and generally decisions are taken on the unanimity principle. The Consultative Assembly which came into existence is a forum – its critics would call it a debating society – and not a European legislature. In short, the British and Scandinavian functionalists, who believed that European unity, in so far as it was to be achieved, was to be attained by inter-governmental co-operation, triumphed over the federalists who sought unity by the more radical method of creating European institutions to which national governments would surrender some of their sovereignty. The final disillusionment of the federalists with the Council of Europe as an instrument of federal unity in Europe was almost certainly marked by the resignation of Paul-Henri Spaak from the Presidency of the Consultative Assembly in 1951.

The Six set forth – success and failure

The next step in the economic and political unification of Europe was taken without the British and Scandinavians. It took the form of the creation in 1951 of the European Coal and Steel Community by the Six, and this creation marks a parting of the ways in post-war Europe – a parting which by 1959 was to lead to the creation of two trading blocs.

The immediate precipitating factor was the revival of the West German economy. The passage of time, the efforts of the German people and the aid made available by the US all contributed to the recovery of the German economy. Indeed the 'Economic Miracle' was about to unfold. It was recognized that the German economy would have to be allowed to regain its position in the world, and that Allied control of coal and steel under the International Ruhr Authority could not last indefinitely. The fundamental question was how the German economy in the sectors of iron, steel and coal (the basic materials of a war effort) could be allowed to re-attain its former powerful position without endangering the future peace of Europe. The answer was a French plan, elaborated by Jean Monnet and put forward by Robert Schuman in May 1950. The Schuman Plan was essentially political in character. It sought to end the historic rivalry of France and Germany and to do this by making a war between France and West Germany not only 'unthinkable but materially impossible'. This was to be done in a way which ultimately would have the result of bringing about that 'European federation which is indispensable to peace'. The answer was not to nationalize nor indeed to internationalize the ownership of the means of production in coal, iron and steel, but to create, by the removal of customs duties, quotas and so forth, a common market in these products. Every participant in the common market would have equal access to the products of these industries wherever they might be located, and, to reinforce this, discrimination on grounds of nationality was to be forbidden.

The plan had a number of attractive features. It provided an excellent basis for solving the Saar problem. The handing back of the Saar to West Germany was more likely to be palatable to the French if West Germany was firmly locked in such a coal and steel community. It was also extremely attractive to the Germans since membership of the Community was a passport to international respectability – it was the best way of speeding up the ending of occupation and of avoiding the imposition of dampers on German economic expansion. It was also attractive to the federalists who had found the OEEC as inadequate to their aspirations as the Council of Europe. The OEEC unanimity rule, and the fact that no powers could be delegated to an independent commission or commissariat, were extremely frustrating. Not only that, but the prospects for the OEEC were not good since by 1952 the four-year period of the Marshall Plan would be over and the UK attitude was that thereafter its budget should be cut and some of its functions passed over to NATO. As it emerged, however, the Community was much more to the federalists' taste since, as already indicated, the High Authority was endowed with substantial direct powers which could be exerted without the prior approval of the Council of Ministers.

The Schuman Plan met with a favourable response from West Germany, France, Italy, the Netherlands, Belgium and Luxembourg. The UK was invited to join but refused. The Prime Minister, Clement Attlee, told the House of Commons:

We on this side are not prepared to accept the principle that the most vital economic forces of this country should be handed over to an authority that is utterly undemocratic and is responsible to nobody. (quoted in Palmer *et al.*, 1968, p. 258)

However, the Six were undeterred and in April 1951 the Treaty of Paris was signed. The ECSC was brought into existence and the Community embarked on an experiment in limited economic integration.

The next episode in the development of European unity was also connected with West Germany. When the Korean War broke out in 1950 the response of the US was to suggest that West Germany be re-armed. However, this proposal was opposed by France which was equally opposed to West Germany becoming a member of NATO. However, the French approach to this problem was not a negative one. Instead, the French Prime Minister – René Pléven – put forward a plan. This envisaged that there would be no German army as such, but there would be a European army to which each participating state, including West Germany, could contribute.

The UK was not opposed to the idea but did not itself wish to be involved. The Six were positively enthusiastic and discussion began in 1951 with a view to creating a European Defence Community (EDC). It was envisaged that there would be a Joint Defence Commission and a Council of Ministers. In addition, there was to be a Parliamentary Assembly and a Court of Justice parallel to those created in connection with the ECSC. The Six made rapid progress in the negotiations and the EDC Treaty was signed in May 1952.

Having gone so far, there seemed to be a number of good reasons for proceeding yet further. The pooling of defensive and offensive capabilities inevitably reduced the possibility of independent foreign policies. It was therefore logical to follow integration in the field of defence with measures which would serve to achieve political integration as well. Other forces were also at work. One was the desirability of establishing a system whereby effective democratic control could be exercised over the proposed European army. The other was the Dutch desire that progress in the military field should be paralleled by more integration in the economic sphere. The foreign ministers of the Six therefore asked the ECSC Assembly, in conjunction with co-opted members from the Consultative Assembly of the Council of Europe, to study the possibilities of creating a European Political Authority. In 1953 a draft of a European Political Community (EPC) was produced. It proposed that, after a transition period, the institutions of the ECSC and the proposed EDC be subsumed within a new framework. There would then be one European Executive responsible to a European Parliament (the latter would consist of a People's Chamber elected by direct universal suffrage, and a Senate elected by National Parliaments). In addition, there would be one Council of Ministers and one European Court to replace the parallel bodies created under the E C S C and E D C Treaties.

This was undoubtedly a high watermark in the history of the 'European movement'. The Six had already successfully experimented in limited economic integration in the fields of coal and steel. They had now signed a treaty to integrate defence and were about to go further and create a Community for the purpose of securing political unity. Not only that; the draft treaty proposed to push economic integration still further since it called for the establishment of a general common market based on the free movement of goods and factors of production.

However, on this occasion the success which had attended the Six in the case of coal and steel was not repeated. Five national Parliaments approved the E D C Treaty, but successive French governments felt unable to guarantee success in asking the French Assembly to ratify. Finally, the Mendès-France Government attempted to water the Treaty down but failed to persuade the Five. The Treaty as it stood was therefore submitted to the French Assembly. The latter refused to consider it and in so doing killed the E P C also.

An amalgam of motives lay behind the refusal of the French Assembly to consider the Treaty. One was opposition to the supra-national element which it contained. Another was the refusal by the French Left to countenance the re-armament of West Germany and the refusal of the French Right to have the French army placed under foreign control. British aloofness was also a contributory factor. One of the arguments employed by those who were against the Treaty was that France could not take part in the formation of a European army with West Germany if Britain was not a member.

It is perhaps worth noting that the failure of the E D C was followed by a British initiative also aimed at dealing with the problem of re-arming West Germany in a way acceptable to the French. A series of agreements were reached in 1954 between the US, UK, Canada and the Six. Under these agreements, the Brussels Treaty Organization was modified and extended. West

Germany and Italy were brought in and a new inter-governmental organization – Western European Union (WEU) – was formed. The agreements also related to the termination of the occupation of West Germany and the admission of the latter into NATO. As a counter-balance to the West German army, the UK agreed to maintain specified forces on the Continent. As has been pointed out, the main purpose of the agreement

was to provide a European framework in which Germany could be re-armed and become a member of NATO, while providing also for British military participation to relieve French fears that there would be no check or balance to possible German predominance. (Palmer *et al.*, 1968, p. 32)

It should also be noted that the response of Eastern Europe to these agreements was a further hardening of the East–West division in the shape of the formation of the Warsaw Pact.

The *Relance*

Nineteen fifty-four had been a bad year for European unity. The supra-nationalist cause had suffered a reverse and the creation of WEU – an organization cast more in the traditional inter-government mould – had thereafter held the centre of the stage. However, such then was the strength of the 'European movement' that by 1955 new ideas were again being put forward. The re-launching initiative came from the Benelux[1] states. They produced a memorandum calling for the establishment of a general common market and for specific action in the fields of energy and transport. The basic idea behind the Benelux approach was that political unity was likely to prove difficult to achieve. It was the ultimate objective but it was one which could only be realized in the longer run. In the short and medium term the objective should be overall economic integration. Experience gained in working close together would then pave the way for the achievement of the political goal. The memorandum called for the creation of institutions which would enable a European Economic Community to be established. These ideas were considered at the

1. Belgium, the Netherlands and Luxembourg agreed to form a customs union in 1944; it came into effect in 1948 and is called Benelux.

meeting of the foreign ministers of the Six at Messina in June 1955. They met with a favourable response. The six Governments resolved that work should begin with a view to establishing a general common market and an atomic energy pool. Moreover, a committee should be formed which would not merely study the problems involved but should also prepare the texts of the treaties necessary in order to carry out the agreed objectives. An inter-governmental committee, presided over by Paul-Henri Spaak, was therefore created. The Messina resolution recorded that since the UK was a member of WEU and was associated with the ECSC,[1] it should be invited to participate in the work of the committee. The position of other OEEC countries was not so clear – the question of whether they should be allowed to participate was in fact left for later decision by the foreign ministers.

The Spaak committee held its first meeting in July 1955. British representatives were present and then and subsequently played an active part in the deliberations. However, as the committee's probing progressed, differences between the Six and the UK became evident. The latter was in favour of a free trade area arrangement, whilst the Six were agreed upon the formation of a customs union – the Messina resolution had explicitly called for this kind of arrangement. Then again the UK felt that little extra machinery was needed to put the new arrangement into effect. The OEEC, perhaps somewhat strengthened, would suffice. This view was bound to antagonize the federalists who laid stress on the creation of supra-national institutions which would help to achieve more than mere economic integration. These differences culminated in the withdrawal of the UK representatives from the discussions in November 1955. Meanwhile, the Spaak committee forged ahead, although not without internal differences. The French, for example, were anxious about the transition period allowed for tariff disarmament, about escape clauses, about harmonization of social changes and they desired a high tariff round the union whilst the Benelux states were in favour of a low one. In April 1956 the committee re-

1. The UK signed an 'Agreement of Association' with the ECSC in 1954.

ported and its conclusions were considered by the foreign ministers of the Six at Venice in May of that year. Attitudes among the six Governments were not uniform. The French liked the idea of an atomic community, but were cooler on the idea of a general common market. The other Governments held reverse views. However, despite all this, the Governments agreed that the drafting of two Treaties, one to create the general common market and one to create an atomic energy community, should begin. Intensive negotiations followed and the two Treaties were subsequently signed in Rome on 25 March 1957. These were duly ratified by the national Parliaments. The E E C (and the European Atomic Energy Community) came into being on 1 January 1958.

The free trade area proposal

As we have seen, at the end of 1955 Britain's attitude towards the Six cooled to such an extent that she withdrew from the Spaak committee. However, as the Six pressed ahead, the U K began to realize that it had severely under-estimated the determination which lay behind the *relance*. As a result, a reappraisal of policy took place. In July 1956 the O E E C, under British stimulus, embarked on a study of the proposal that the O E E C states should create a free trade area which would embrace the customs union of the Six. The British hoped that the negotiations for the free trade area, and those relating to the common market, could take place simultaneously, but the Six refused. The O E E C report was completed in December 1956 and published in January 1957. Its conclusions were that a free trade area with the common market as an element was feasible. The U K took this as a signal to take the initiative and proposed that discussions should begin in earnest with a view to creating a European Industrial Free Trade Area. Detailed negotiations on the terms of a Treaty began in March 1957 and continued from October 1957 in an inter-government committee under the chairmanship of Reginald Maudling. These negotiations dragged on until the end of 1958 when they finally broke down.

The negotiations were extremely complex and the reasons for their failure are equally complicated. However, basically the problems were as follows. On the political side, the 'Europeans' were suspicious of the UK's intentions. They suspected that the UK, after it had realized that it had under-estimated the impetus behind the *relance*, had decided to take the offensive by proposing a free trade area as a means of wrecking the common market. Furthermore, it was recognized that whilst the path to the achievement of a common market (and what lay beyond) was bound to be hard, a free trade area would confer somewhat similar benefits and yet would involve a relatively less onerous régime. Because of this some members of the Six might lose heart and decide to follow the easier course.

From the economic standpoint the major difficulty was the UK's insistence on a free trade arrangement for industrial goods. Under such a system she would remain autonomous in respect of tariffs on goods emanating from outside the free trade area. This would enable her to go on enjoying her tariff preferences on exports of industrial goods to Commonwealth markets. Agriculture would also be excluded – this was certainly the basis of the earliest British proposals. This left the UK open to the criticism that she wanted the advantage of free access to West European industrial markets without giving a reciprocal concession to Continental food producers. The Commonwealth Preference system also meant that the UK would be guaranteed a continuing supply of food at low world prices. If on the other hand agriculture was brought within the free trade area framework, this low-priced supply of food could be in jeopardy. Indeed, if the agricultural protection systems of the Six were adopted, cheap Commonwealth food would be excluded. The UK would have to buy food at price levels approximating to those paid to farmers in the Six, and the traditional British deficiency payments system would have to be abandoned. It did not escape the attention of the Six that cheap food could have an effect on industrial wages such as to confer an artificial advantage on British industries when competing in the industrial markets of the free trade area.

Another source of difficulty was the degree to which harmonization of such things as social security charges was necessary. The French, particularly, tended to play this up, much as they did in the common market negotiations.

Undoubtedly one of the greatest bones of contention was the problem of the origin of imports and the possibility of deflections of trade. In a customs union, since there is a common tariff level on the imports of, for example, raw materials coming from outside, competitive strength tends to depend on the ability of member states to transform such inputs into industrial (and agricultural) outputs. In a free trade area, however, member states are free to decide the tariffs on such imports. These tariffs can therefore differ from state to state and imports of raw materials are therefore likely to be deflected through the low tariff countries. Methods of dealing with this problem gave rise to much technical discussion, but a unanimously acceptable solution was never achieved.

The failure of the negotiations was also in considerable degree due to diplomatic postures, particularly those of the British and the French. The latter left an impression of a certain deviousness. It was difficult to know whether, when they took a stand on a point of principle, it was because they really believed what they said, or whether it was because they found it useful as a means of opposing progress along a particular path. For its part, the U K exhibited some diplomatic weakness. The British undoubtedly under-estimated the enthusiasm of the Six for their kind of arrangement. There was a failure to appreciate what the 'Europeans' hoped to achieve in the political sphere. Also there was a tendency to frame our proposals in too stark and provocative a fashion, as, for example, when the U K declared that agriculture should be totally excluded from the free trade arrangement.

The inter-governmental discussion at least served to create an identity of interest between the 'Other Six' – the U K, Norway, Sweden, Denmark, Austria and Switzerland. It was therefore decided early in 1959 that they should press ahead with a free trade area and in this they were encouraged by their industrial federations. Portugal joined the discussions in February 1959 and on 4 January 1960 the Stockholm Convention establishing the E F T A was signed.[1] Western Europe was now divided into two trade blocs.

1. Finland signed an association agreement with the E F T A in 1961.

The EFTA

The EFTA arrangement was one which admirably suited British interests. The institutional machinery was minimal. There was nothing to match the majority voting in the EEC Council of Ministers or the ECSC High Authority's[1] powers of independent action. There were absolutely no signs that the EFTA was a stepping stone to political unity – basically it was a commercial arrangement. The emphasis was on free trade in industrial goods; in a limited number of cases agricultural goods were treated as industrial goods and therefore tariff reductions were applied to them. In the main, agriculture was left out of the arrangement, each member being free to decide its own method and degree of support. There was absolutely no question of the agricultural systems of the member states being organized within the framework of a common agricultural policy. Members were free to determine the level of protection applied to goods coming from outside. This enabled the UK to maintain Commonwealth preference not only on industrial but also on agricultural commodities. The latter implied the continuance of a supply of cheap food and the deficiency payments system of agricultural support.

Two features of the EFTA arrangement deserve special mention. One is that because of differences in national tariffs on goods coming from without, it was necessary to elaborate origin rules and a customs procedure so as to determine whether goods could be accorded the full benefit of the EFTA tariff reductions. The other was that the EFTA Convention made few demands on members in the field of harmonization of taxation, social security charges and the like.

Reappraisal and entry bids

The ink of the Stockholm Convention had not long been dry before the UK began a major reappraisal of policy. As late as 1959 leading British Ministers went on record as saying that for a variety of reasons – our Commonwealth ties, the British agricultural support system, doubts about supra-nationalism – the UK

1. In 1967 the commission of the EEC and Euratom and the High Authority were merged into one commission located in Brussels – see chapter 2.

could never contemplate joining the EEC. However, it is clear that from 1960 a reappraisal of policy was under way. By 1961 the re-thinking had proceeded far enough for the Prime Minister – Harold Macmillan – to announce that the UK intended to apply for membership of the EEC and for its part would be willing to join provided the special needs of the UK, the Commonwealth and the EFTA could be accommodated. As we indicate in chapter 9 this attempt failed. Then in 1967 the Labour Government decided to raise the membership issue. Harold Wilson and George Brown carried out a series of high level soundings with the Six (see chapter 9). Having judged the conditions favourable, an application was dispatched. Again the UK was rebuffed by the French and the British application, together with those of Ireland, Norway and Denmark (who had also applied in 1961), was left on the table. Following the Hague Summit of 1969 France (now led by President Pompidou) agreed to open negotiations relating to the admission of new members. Negotiations were commenced in June 1970 and concluded in June 1972. The accession treaty between the Six and the four aspirant new members was signed in Brussels on 22 January 1972 and the UK Parliament subsequently ratified the treaty. However, following the Norwegian referendum Norwegian membership was not proceeded with and on 1 January 1973 only the UK, Ireland and Denmark joined the Six. The breach between the Six and the UK, which had opened in 1951, was closed and the division between the Six and EFTA[1] was significantly diminished. The decision of the Labour Government in 1974 to seek a renegotiation of the terms of entry has, however, thrown some doubt on the long-term position of the UK in the Community.

We have not in this account discussed the details of the negotiations of 1961–3, 1967 and 1970–72. Since a full appreciation of them requires an intimate knowledge of various aspects of Community policy, the details of the negotiations have been left over until chapter 9. However, the more knowledgeable reader can obtain a continuous account by now referring to pages 224–37.

1. In 1972, Austria, Finland, Iceland, Portugal, Sweden and Switzerland concluded industrial free trade agreements with the Six. Norway followed shortly after.

New bearings

A number of new developments are at this point worthy of record. The Community has held a number of important summits – the one at The Hague in 1969 (between the Six) and the one in Paris in 1972 (with both the Six and the three aspirant members present) have been particularly important, indeed crucial. As the E E C twelve-year transition period neared its end (it actually ended on 31 December 1969) the Six could have concluded a treaty outlining the future path of integration and co-operation. But they did not. Instead they chose to map out the future by means of summits, with the communiqués acting as a form of treaty. The Hague Summit was very important. It embraced the idea of an economic and monetary union among the Six – this was a fundamental new step and was not foreshadowed in the E E C Treaty. The Paris Summit underlined this goal (indicating the measures to be adopted) but also recognized the need for a Community Regional Development Fund and called for new programmes of action in a variety of fields including social, industrial, scientific, technological and external trade policy. It follows that the policies discussed in this book must be regarded as outcomes not only based on formal treaties but also of summits such as those of 1969 and 1972. Ardent Europeans may of course doubt whether summit agreements are quite as solemn and binding as treaties. They may well wonder whether the impetus to further integration in Europe is based on more slender foundations than the integration of the past.

We must also take note of some signs of greater political integration. Attempts at political integration are long-standing – as we have seen within the Six they go back to the E D C and E P C era. Since then there have been sporadic attempts to make progress in this field. For example, in 1960 General de Gaulle, following bilateral talks with the other five, proposed the setting up of a supreme authority to formulate common foreign and defence policies. A summit of the Six was held in Paris in February 1961. This in turn led to the establishment of a committee to examine the problem of political co-operation, initially under the chairmanship of Christian Fouchet (of France). A second summit was held at Bad Godesberg near Bonn in July 1961. The Bonn

Declaration issued at the end of the meeting contained three decisions. Political co-operation between the Six should be adopted on a regular basis leading in due course to a joint policy. Heads of State or Government should meet regularly to concert policies. The summit members also instructed the Fouchet Committee to submit proposals 'on means and ways which would make it possible to give a statutory character to the unification of their peoples as soon as possible'. Later in 1961 the French Government put a 'Draft Treaty establishing a Union of States' to the Committee. The institutions proposed were as follows: (a) a Council of Heads of State or Government and of Foreign Ministers whose unanimous decisions would be binding on members; (b) a European Parliament with power of interrogation and deliberation but having no decision-making role; (c) a European Political Commission, in Paris, to be staffed by senior officials of the Foreign Ministries of each participating state. The aim of all this was to achieve common foreign and defence policies. There was to be a general review after three years which it seemed could lead to steps being taken to bring the European Communities within the union.

Disagreements between France and the Six soon became evident, although the Dutch had been distinctly nervous about the implications from the outset. The other five were concerned because they saw the defence arrangements as being outside NATO and the ambit of the Atlantic Alliance. They also saw a threat to the existing communities – the supra-national elements of the Paris and Rome Treaties could be lost if they were subsumed within the new union which was clearly based on the unanimity principle. Although a later draft of the Fouchet plan went quite a way to allay fears, a third draft, drawn up by de Gaulle himself, went back on these accommodations and a reference to economic matters being within the competence of the union opened up all the old fears about a watering down of supra-nationality. The plan ultimately foundered on UK participation. Originally the Dutch and Belgians had indicated that their participation was contingent upon the British being involved in the discussions – it should be remembered that the UK was then negotiating for membership of the EEC and its sister bodies.

This the French refused to accept but a compromise was reached in December 1961. The UK was to be kept informed and membership of the union would be automatic for new members of the economic communities. However, ultimately the problem was raised again in April 1962 when the UK pressed its desire to take part in the discussions. This in turn precipitated a split within the Six. France, Germany, Italy and Luxembourg were willing to continue discussing the text of the treaty, to agree it, to communicate it to the UK and, if the latter did not have a major objection, to put it into effect. But Belgium and the Netherlands agreed only to examine the project and communicate it to the UK – they would not sign it until the UK had become a member of the economic communities. This was sufficient to provoke a termination of the formal negotiations.

Thereafter, despite minor developments such as the de Gaulle–Adenauer Franco-German treaty of friendship and co-operation, there was a distinct cooling on the political front. After the 1963 French rebuff to the British bid for membership of the three communities the other members showed their strong disapproval of de Gaulle's actions, temporarily bringing the Brussels machinery to a halt. By mid-1963 a formula for achieving progress on the economic plane was found and the EEC began to gain ground. The disappearance of Adenauer from the stage and his replacement by Erhard was a blow to further progress on the Franco-German front. The supra-nationality crisis by 1965–6 did nothing to cement trust between the Six. The coming of Pompidou in 1969 did, however, open up a more co-operative era. The participants at the Hague Summit agreed to instruct their Foreign Ministers to study the best way to achieve progress in respect of political unification – a report was expected by July 1970. The result was the Davignon Committee (named after the Belgian diplomat Vicomte Davignon), which in turn led to the establishment of twice-yearly meetings of Foreign Ministers serviced by a political committee made up of senior Foreign Office officials. The Paris Summit re-emphasized the desirability of political co-operation and raised the frequency of Foreign Ministers' meetings to four a year.

2 The Decision-Making Institutions

Since what we are concerned with in this book is the economic policy of the European Community it is clearly important that we should appreciate just how policy is formulated. The main bodies which have an influence on policy-making are the Commission, the Council of Ministers, the Court of Justice, the Parliamentary Assembly and the Economic and Social Committee. (In the case of ECSC products the equivalent of the latter is the Consultative Committee of the European Coal and Steel Community.) The above order of listing does not reflect an order of influence on policy formation – there can however be no doubt that the Commission and the Council of Ministers are the most important bodies. In addition to the five bodies specifically referred to there are several others that are part of the Community machinery – we can cite the EEC Monetary Committee and the European Investment Bank as just two out of a host of possible examples. Additionally we should not neglect the various interest groups which the Commission consults – for example COPA (the grouping of agricultural organizations) and UNICE (the industrial association). In this account we shall confine our discussion to the five main bodies – the role of other bodies will be made apparent in later chapters.

It should of course be emphasized that we are here defining policy-making as the evolving of policies on the basis of *provisions laid down in the treaties*. Obviously the main line of policy is in some cases contained in the treaties themselves and to that extent we can say that the member state governments who negotiated the treaties, and subsequent applicants who have negotiated accommodations, were themselves basic policy-makers. Actually the picture is variable. In some areas, such as EEC transport policy, the Rome Treaty said little more than that there should be a common policy. As a result it has been left to the Commission, the Council etc. to effectively make policy. On the other hand the main features of cartel and concentration policy were laid down in both the E C S C and E E C Treaties. However, we shall see that that has not precluded the Community institutions from putting a lot of policy flesh on basic treaty bones.

In the above context it is also important to stress that the policy-making role of member state governments has been emphasized by the fact that, since the E E C neared the end of its transition stage, there have as we know been two major summits (The Hague 1969 and Paris 1972) which have in broad terms laid down the nature of policy development in a number of important fields. Needless to say in the summits the main influence has been that of member state governments.

The Commission

Structure

The Commission is in effect the civil service of the Community. Originally there were three civil services – one for each Community. In the case of the E C S C it was the High Authority whilst the E E C and Euratom each had a Commission. However, by virtue of a treaty signed in Brussels on 8 April 1965 it was agreed that these three executives should be merged, or fused, as from 1 July 1967. It is perhaps worth mentioning that the three treaties remained separate (whether they will in due course be fused only the future will tell). The fused Commission was therefore left with the task of administering the provisions of three separate founding treaties.

Originally there were nine E E C Commissioners. This number was raised to fourteen in 1967 on the occasion of the fusion of the executives but in 1970 was slimmed back down to nine. Then at the beginning of 1973, on the occasion of the accession of three new members, the number was raised to thirteen. The United Kingdom, West Germany, France and Italy each nominated two Commissioners whilst the smaller states – Belgium, Netherlands, Ireland, Denmark and Luxembourg – nominated one each.

The top Commissioners are appointed by the member governments for four-year renewable terms, whilst the President (currently a Frenchman – François-Xavier Ortoli) and the five Vice-Presidents hold office for two-year renewable terms. The current (1973) Vice-Presidents are Wilhelm Haferkamp (West Germany), Patrick Hillery (Ireland), Carlo Mugnozza (Italy), Henri Simonet (Belgium) and Sir Christopher Soames (United Kingdom). Each of the Commissioners is responsible for one or more portfolios: thus Sir Christopher Soames takes responsibility for external relations whilst George Thomson is in charge of regional policy. It should be added that the sharing out of these portfolios is a matter of keen bargaining between the member states.

Each Commissioner has a private office or *cabinet*, the appointments to which are his private prerogative. Usually, but not invariably, the members of the *cabinet* are of the same nationality as the Commissioner. If the Commissioner is away the *chef de cabinet* will act in his stead at the weekly meeting of the Commission which is usually held on a Wednesday. Beneath each Commissioner there is usually at least one Director General in charge of a Directorate General, i.e. a broad policy area. A Directorate General will in turn be split into areas relating to various aspects of the broad policy problem. These are presided over by Directors and below them are Heads of Division. (Since some Commissioners have a number of portfolios, it follows that they will preside over more than one Directorate General and in turn will be served by more than one Director General.)

It is most important to note that Article 157 of the Rome Treaty requires that Commissioners 'shall neither seek nor take instruction from any Government or from any other body'. In other words Commissioners are supposed to act with complete independence.

Role

To the EEC Commission fell the task of taking steps to see that the Community, as envisaged by the Rome Treaty, was established within the twelve-year transition period laid down by Article 8. In short action was needed if the aspirations of Article 3 – that there should be common policies in agriculture and transport, that competition should not be distorted, that a customs union should be established and so forth – were to be turned into concrete realities. To this end the Rome Treaty conferred upon the Commission an important power – the right of initiative. It is the task of the Commission to draft proposals (for regulations etc.) which the Council of Ministers (representing the member state governments) has to consider. The Council of Ministers has to decide whether to accept the draft or not. In some cases there must be unanimity (for example on the subject of new members) whilst in others a qualified majority vote is sufficient (but see below). If the Council accepts the draft proposal it is promulgated in the Official Journal and becomes law. If the Council does not accept it, it can only alter the draft by a unanimous vote. Generally we may assume that the various ministers will not be in a position to agree on the alterations which will be necessary to secure the degree of unanimity required. In this case the proposal has to go back to the Commission for them to come up with some alternative which will command the necessary support. This brings us to the second role of the Commission – it acts as a mediator, trying by means of negotiations with the member states to find an acceptable compromise which at the same time, hopefully, does not mean that the overall Community interest has been obscured by the horse-trading which may have taken place.

In approaching the Council of Ministers the Commission feeds it with draft regulations and draft directives. An approved regulation is of general applicability and directly binding on all nationals. An approved directive is addressed to governments and leaves them free to introduce the appropriate legislation at national level which will ensure the achievement of the objectives set out in the directive. Additionally, the Commission, on its own initiative, issues notices, opinions and recommendations. These are merely designed to guide and are not binding. For example, in the field of anti-trust the Commission has from time to time issued notices designed to guide businessmen as to the status of particular business practices, in conditions where some uncertainty has been felt to exist.

The Commission, having secured the Council's agreement to a particular line of policy, has to see that it is carried out. Here there is an administrative task. For example the Council of Ministers, on a proposal of the Commission, fixes the prices of farm products for the coming agricultural year. These prices have to be achieved by various devices such as intervention at the common frontier and support buying. This is a task which involves the Commission but it is not one that it discharges alone. In practice a large proportion of the staff of national Ministries of Agriculture have become effectively the agents of the Community, operating the Common Agricultural Policy (CAP) in co-operation with intervention agencies set up in each country. However, the Commission is involved in that the functioning of the CAP is supervised by Management Committees staffed by both national and Commission officials. Since the Commission staff totals only about 5,000, whilst a larger ministry in the UK may employ about 20,000, it is not difficult to see that the Commission could not hope to be solely responsible for the administration of all the policies which it helps to initiate.

Finally the Commission discharges a very important policing task. It has to see that individuals, companies and member states do not act in ways which clearly run counter to the treaty or to specific policies laid down by the Council. For example, groups of firms may enter into agreements which restrict competition and are clearly contrary to Article 3f (which calls for the achievement of conditions of undistorted competition) and Article 85 which prohibits agreements (subject to exceptions in clearly defined circumstances). The Commission may begin by seeking a voluntary termination of such an agreement but if necessary it has the power to issue formal Decisions prohibiting the agreement. By a Decision it can also inflict fines on parties to an agreement. Equally the Commission can take member states to task. In the case of state aids, for example, it will usually ask a state to voluntarily terminate an infringement, but if the state refuses the Commission can take the matter to the Court of Justice for a final determination.

Before we leave the subject of the Commission it is necessary to return to the subject of the Commission's role in respect of its right of initiative or proposal. A cursory glance at the Rome Treaty clearly indicates that this is well founded. For example in Title II on Agriculture Article 43 states

Having taken into account the work of the conference provided for in paragraph 1 of this Article, after consulting the Economic and Social Committee and within two years from this Treaty's coming into force, the Commission shall submit proposals for the working-out and putting into effect of the common agricultural policy, including the substitution for national organizations of one of the forms of common organization provided for in Article 40 (2) and for the putting into effect of the measures particularly mentioned in this Title.

In many other areas a similar right of proposal is evident. Whilst this is undoubtedly true, we have also to recognize that much of what was said earlier about the Commission's right of proposal is in a sense historical. It refers to the task of the Commission in making the E E C a reality within the transition period laid down. But the transition period ended on 31 December 1969 – where then does the Commission stand in the period after that date? In some degree the answer is – where it stood from the beginning of 1958 to the end of 1969. For example, the Rome Treaty led to the creation of the C A P, but having helped to create it the Commission still has to run it and modify it in the light of changing circumstances. To this extent the right of proposal therefore continues. Equally it must be recognized that at the end of 1969 there was a significant amount of unfinished business. For example Article 99 provides for the harmonization of indirect taxes and indeed the original Six have already agreed on, and introduced, a harmonized form of turnover tax. The harmonization of rates however has yet to be achieved. Since Article 99 gives the right of proposal to the Commission, it is a reasonable supposition that this right will continue in the post-transition period.

However, in this context we have to note the importance of the Hague and Paris Summits. As the transition period neared its end the member states could, if they had wished, have signed another treaty outlining the further forms of integration and co-operation they felt were desirable and appropriate. Instead we know that they chose to delineate the future by means of summit meetings, and the communiqué at the end of each has served as a kind of substitute for a treaty. As we have seen, the Hague communiqué was most important in that it embraced the notion that the Community should proceed further in the direction of economic and monetary union. We can safely assert that the EEC Treaty did not (certainly not explicitly) envisage such a move. Further we know that the Paris communiqué underlined the goal of economic and monetary union but also envisaged developments in other fields. For example, we noted earlier that it effectively embraced the idea of a Community Regional Development Fund and this is significant since the Rome Treaty does not contain provisions for such an institution. It is true that Article 92 permits state aids for regional development and gives to the Commission the task of vetting them. Equally it is true that references to the regional problem are explicitly and implicitly scattered throughout the treaty. But basically we must treat this as a new feature of Community policy which has effectively been opened up since 1969. It is therefore of paramount importance to know where the Commission stands in relation to these new areas of activity.

If we look at the Paris communiqué we see that in respect of regional policy the Commission has been placed in the position of proposer. It was charged with preparing a report on the Community regional problem and putting forward proposals. However, in other areas the communiqué often refers to the 'Community institutions' – a phrase which clearly can be taken to embrace the Commission but does not exclude the Council. At this stage it seems that we shall have to content ourselves with waiting to see to what extent the Commission in fact succeeds in retaining the right of proposal.

In this context it is also necessary to take note of Article 235 of the EEC Treaty. This Article reads:

Where action by the Community appears necessary to achieve, in the course of operation of the common market, one of the objectives of the Community, and where this Treaty has not provided for the necessary powers of action, the Council shall, by unanimous decision, on a proposal from the Commission and after the Assembly has been consulted, take the appropriate steps.

Effectively this amounts to saying that if powers are needed to achieve Community objectives and the powers do not exist, then the Community can create them. This is obviously a useful provision and could pave the way for a considerable expansion of policy falling within the Community ambit. It is therefore significant that the Commission enjoys the right of proposal in this context. It is also interesting to note that the Paris Summit observed that it was desirable 'to make the widest possible use of all the dispositions of the treaties, including Article 235 of the E E C Treaty'.

It would however appear that there is a limit to the possibilities under Article 235. Actions have to be necessary to achieve the objectives of the Community and there is room for argument as to how far the phrase 'objectives of the Community' can be stretched to accommodate new policies.

The Council

The Council is the only body which represents the member state governments. It is clearly the ultimate controlling body since draft regulations and draft directives only become the law of the Community if the Council is agreeable.

The Council is not a fixed body of individuals in the way that the Commission is. Where matters of agriculture are under discussion it will be the ministers of agriculture of the member states who will meet as the Council, and when transport is under discussion it will be the ministers of transport and so on. The ministers of foreign affairs and of agriculture normally meet once a month and sometimes more frequently when the pressure of business is heavy. The ministers of finance are regular participants and the ministers of transport, science and social affairs generally meet twice a year. The ministers of foreign affairs and of agriculture are in effect the senior body and the former tend to be called in when colleagues in specialist fields are locked in disagreement. The chairmanship of the Council also rotates – each member state holds it in turn for a period of six months. The chair is in fact passed on in alphabetical order – Belgium held the chair during the first six months of U K membership and it follows that the U K will not have its turn in the chair until 1977.

The E E C Treaty laid down important rules concerning voting procedure within the Council. Generally in the early stages (the transition period was divided into three four-year stages) decisions required a unanimous vote. However, in certain areas, such as agriculture, it was provided that a qualified majority of the votes in Council were adequate for a measure to be adopted. For this purpose France, West Germany and Italy had four votes each, Netherlands and Belgium two votes and Luxembourg one. Twelve votes were necessary for a measure to be passed. It was this which constituted much of the supra-national element of the EEC Treaty. Unlike the normal system of international organizations where unanimity is necessary, it was possible to evolve policies if only a qualified majority of the votes had been cast in its favour. This was a protection for the Commission since in its task of setting up the various Community policies it did not indefinitely face the prospect of having to achieve a unanimity among the member states.

Three observations are now necessary. Firstly, not all subjects were ones in which qualified majority voting was in due course envisaged. The admission of new members was one exception – hence the possibility that the French could, had they chosen, have blocked the admission of the UK indefinitely. Secondly, where the Council was acting on a proposal not initiated by the Commission, in addition to the twelve vote requirement four states also had to agree to the measure. This was a protection against the smaller Benelux states being overridden by the three bigger ones. Thirdly, in practice qualified majority voting has since 1966 ceased to have the significance which had been envisaged earlier. The issue arose in 1965 in connection with the Commission's proposals to tie into one package three elements: the completion of the farm finance regulations (desired by France), the independent financing of the Community out of its own resources (strongly desired by the Commission), and the granting of greater budgetary powers to the Parliament (desired by both the European Parliament and the Netherlands). France strongly disliked parts of this package and virtually absented itself from the Council for seven months. Much of the wrath of the French was directed against the Commission, which in their eyes was getting ideas above its station, and against qualified majority voting, due to apply amongst other things to agriculture in 1966, which France apparently feared might be used against it. The upshot was the famous Luxembourg compromise of January 1966. There was agreement to modify the status of the Commission, although the changes were not really of great significance. In respect of Council voting the Six agreed as follows:

I Where, in the case of decisions which may be taken by majority vote on a proposal of the Commission, very important interests of one or more partners are at stake, the members of the Council will endeavour, within a reasonable time, to reach solutions which can be adopted by all the members of the Council while respecting their mutual interests and those of the Community, in accordance with Article 2 of the Treaty.

II With regard to the preceding paragraph, the French delegation considers that where very important interests are at stake the discussion must be continued until unanimous agreement is reached.

The effect of this has been that by tacit agreement the Council hardly ever takes decisions by majority vote, except on budgetary items, despite the fact that the Rome Treaty provides for such a procedure on a wide range of issues.

With the admission of new members the voting system has been changed. France, West Germany, Italy and the UK have ten votes each, the Netherlands and Belgium each have five, Ireland and Denmark have three votes each and Luxembourg has two votes. Where the Council votes on a proposal of the Commission forty-one votes are needed. Where the Council acts on a proposal that does not emanate from the Commission the above voting rule must be accompanied by the support of six states.

When approaching the Council with draft proposals the Commission (after there has been consultation with various bodies which we shall discuss below) proceeds by way of the Committee of Permanent Representatives – known as 'Coreper' which is an abbreviation of its French title. 'Coreper' is made up of the heads of the member-state delegations to the Community and is located in Brussels. Proposals are discussed in 'Coreper' and its sub-committees before they arrive on the Council table. If 'Coreper' reaches full agreement the matter can pass through the Council without debate. In other cases it may be possible for the permanent representatives to agree on large sections of a draft proposal but areas of disagreement (either as between states or between states and the Commission) are placed in square brackets and left to be settled around the Council table. In some cases little headway may be made by 'Coreper' and the matter is then left to the ministers themselves to thrash out.

The Court of Justice

Whereas the Commission is located in Brussels, in and around the new Berlaymont building, and the Council meets (and its one thousand or so staff operate) in the Charlemagne building close by, the Court of Justice has its seat in Luxembourg in a new five-storey building on the Kirchberg. It has a staff which is expected to rise to about two hundred and fifty.

The Court of Justice originally came into being in connection with E C S C but it now dispenses a legal function for each of the three communities. There are currently nine judges, each appointed for a six-year term. Each member state has one of its nationals as a judge which seems to reflect some form of informal agreement since there is no formal provision for national representation. The U K has nominated Lord Mackenzie Stuart, a Scottish judge. Like the members of the Commission they are not representatives of national interests but are required to act as independent judicial officers. They are protected from pressure from member state governments by two procedural arrangements. Firstly, although hearings are in public the deliberations of the judges are in secret. Secondly, a judge can only be removed from office by a unanimous vote of his colleagues to the effect that he is no longer capable of carrying out his functions. The quorum for the full court is seven: in reaching its verdict there must always be an odd number sitting since decisions are reached by simple majority, the President of the Court having no casting vote. The decisions which the Court reaches are read out in the presence of the parties, usually some two to three months after the hearing. The Court produces its own reports containing the basic facts, the summing up by the Advocate General and the judgement. The latter individual is a stranger to English legal procedure. After the main hearing his tasks are to summarize the issues for, and to recommend a decision to, the Court. The Court is not bound by his views but great attention is paid to his arguments. The fact that the Court may not follow the Advocate General was well illustrated in 1973 in the *Continental Can* case when the Court took a fundamentally different line from that suggested by the Advocate General.

We have already given some indication of the kind of situations in which the Court is called upon to act. The Commission may call upon a member state to desist from some line of conduct which is contrary to the treaty, as for example the giving of state aid. If the member state does not desist the Commission can take the state to the Court. In the field of competition policy the Commission may by Decision forbid some action or impose fines. The enterprises concerned can appeal to Court of Justice. Thus in one case several aniline dye producers appealed to the Court against the fines imposed upon them for an alleged concerted practice in relation to dye prices, and in another Continental Can appealed to the Court against the Decision of the Commission forbidding its takeover of a Dutch can producer. We should also note the possibility that one member state can take another to the Court.

In addition to all these combinations of protagonists, mention should be made of the function of the Court in giving preliminary rulings for the benefit of national courts. Inevitably at national level issues arise which call for an interpretation of Community law and this is a major task discharged by the Court. Reference is obligatory when an issue arises in the highest jurisdiction in a country against which no judicial appeal is possible.

The European Parliament

The Parliament normally meets well away from the other three bodies in Strasbourg, in the building belonging to the Council of Europe. Parliament's secretariat (numbering about five hundred) is however located two hundred kilometres to the north-west in Luxembourg.

There are in fact 198 delegates to the Parliament – the size of the national contingents is shown below:

Belgium	14
Denmark	10
West Germany	36

France	36
Ireland	10
Italy	36
Luxembourg	6
Netherlands	14
UK	36

These delegates are nominated by the national Parliaments by a process called indirect election. Each member state adopts its own procedure of selection. It was intended that the Assembly should draw up proposals for elections by direct universal suffrage but no progress has been made in implementing this provision of the Rome Treaty. Except for the French Gaullists, the deputies do not sit according to nationality but arrange themselves in a semi-circle according to political grouping, with Left-wing parties on the Speaker's left and so on round to Right-wing deputies on the right. The largest group are the Christian Democrats (which the British Conservatives have expressed a long-term aim to join) followed by the Socialists and the Liberals.

The Parliament is consultative rather than legislative. A glance at the main policy areas of the EEC Treaty indicates that the Council has to consult the Parliament before deciding on a Commission proposal. In order to discharge its role the Parliament has a number of specialist committees (which representatives of the Commission may attend) and their reports are submitted to the House for debate and decision by vote in plenary session. Members can ask questions in the House and written questions can be addressed to the Commission. Representatives of the Council and the Commission attend the meetings and so it is possible to clarify matters on the spot.

The main power of the Parliament is that it can dismiss the Commission. For this to happen a motion of censure must be passed by a two-thirds majority of the votes cast, representing a majority of the members of the Assembly. This has never actually occurred but it was threatened at the end of 1972. The motion, which took the Commission to task for failing to introduce new proposals designed to increase parliament's powers of control over the Community budget, was withdrawn before it was put to the vote. The very size of the implications of a motion of censure may make it of limited practical significance. In any case there are other limitations. The Parliament may dismiss the Commission but it has no control over the selection of the new Commissioners who would replace the old ones. Also the villain of the piece may not be the Commission but the intransigence of the Council. At the end of 1969 the Council agreed to grant the Parliament powers over the Community budget as from 1975. These powers are limited. In respect of most expenditure (i.e. on the CAP and European Social Fund) the Parliament will still only be able to suggest changes, as has been the case in the past. However, in respect of the Commission's administrative budget Parliament will be able to increase the allocation to a limited degree.

The Economic and Social Committee

This body, which operates in respect of EEC and Euratom matters, and its ECSC counterpart, are purely consultative. The total membership of 'Ecosoc' is 144 and is made up as follows:

Belgium	12
Denmark	9
West Germany	24
France	24
Ireland	9
Italy	24
Luxembourg	6
Netherlands	12
UK	24

The membership is representative of the various categories of economic and social life and in particular includes representatives of producers, workers, farmers, merchants, the liberal professions, transport operators and the general interest. The members are selected by the Council from lists submitted by member states. A glance at the EEC Treaty indicates that on a range of issues, before action is taken by the Council, 'Ecosoc' must be consulted.

Commentators do not however assign any great weight to its advisory role. The truth is that, as indicated earlier, the main power in the Community lies with the Council and the Commission.

3 Tariff Barriers and the Customs Union

Within the E E C the free movement of goods has been stimulated by the action taken to dismantle tariffs and quota barriers and by attacks on those factors, non-tariff in character, which either prevent or distort intra-Community trade. In this chapter the focus of attention will be on those aspects of Community policy which relate to tariffs and quotas.

Forms of economic integration

Economic integration can take many forms and these can be ranged in a spectrum in which the degree of involvement of participating economies, one with another, becomes greater and greater. The *free trade area* is the least onerous in terms of involvement. It consists of an arrangement between states by which they agree to remove all customs duties (and quotas) on trade passing between themselves. Each party is free, however, to unilaterally determine the level of customs duty on imports coming from outside the area. The proposal put forward by the U K in 1957 typified such an arrangement, although it will be remembered that the initial British proposal related to industrial goods only and was therefore rather narrow in conception. The E F T A was of course an example of such an industrial arrangement actually in operation although, as noted in the previous chapter, some agricultural goods were treated as industrial goods and accorded tariff reductions under the Stockholm Convention.

The main problem of the free trade area is connected with the origin of goods. Since parties can apply differing rates of customs duty on goods coming from without, certain problems arise. Suppose, for example, that area member A applies a zero import duty while area member B applies a duty of 20 per cent. An exporter in a non-member country wishing to send goods to country

B will probably route them through country A. We say 'probably' because it will only pay to do so if the saving in import duty more than offsets any extra freight and handling costs arising from the deflection of trade through country A. There are a number of features of such a situation which are worth highlighting. Firstly, the non-member countries' goods will not only enjoy tariff-free treatment on entry into country A but (provided the free trade arrangement is fully operational) will benefit from the tariff-free entry into country B accorded under the free trade agreement. But the non-member will not necessarily have given country B any reciprocal trading concession. In effect country B's tariff has been undermined. Secondly, the deflection of goods through country A enhances the latter's prosperity at the expense of country B. Thus, if the import duty into country A was not zero, country A could raise extra revenue at country B's expense. Furthermore, country A will be able to develop extra freight and handling business out of the deflection of trade through its ports. Then again producers in country A who incorporate the imported goods into their exports to the rest of the free trade area would be at a competitive advantage as compared with similar producers in country B.

When drafting the Stockholm Convention the EFTA countries had therefore to devise origin rules which would enable the customs authorities to determine which particular goods could be accorded the advantage of tariff elimination. Such tariff treatment was granted if the goods were deemed to be of 'area origin'.The latter applied if they met any of three criteria. Firstly, that the goods in question had been wholly produced within the area of the Association. This was a most obvious criterion although in practice it was not always applicable to manufactured goods. It was pointed out that

in order to qualify under this criterion, goods must have been produced in the Area entirely from materials, parts or components which themselves are shown to have been 'wholly produced' in the Area. The use of any materials, parts or components, however minor, of non-EFTA or undetermined origin is sufficient to prevent a product from satisfying this criterion (EFTA, 1966, p. 76).

Secondly, that the goods had been produced within the area of the Association and the value of the materials imported from the countries outside the area (or of undetermined origin) which had been used in their production did not exceed 50 per cent of their f.o.b. export price. The latter was called the 'percentage criterion'. Thirdly, that the goods had been produced by a specified process of transformation. This was termed the 'process criterion'.

The next stage in economic integration is the *customs union*. Here tariffs and quotas on trade between members are removed but members agree to apply a common level of tariff on goods entering the union from without. Because of the latter factor, rules of origin are unnecessary. Article 9 of the Rome Treaty declares that the Community shall be founded upon a customs union, but in fact, the Community is more than just that. It is indeed referred to as a *common market* and the latter technical term implies that the free movement of factors of production – labour, capital and enterprise – exists alongside the customs union. This is in fact the case in the EEC, but the term 'common market' is still an inadequate description of the economic arrangement envisaged by the Rome Treaty. The latter calls for common policies in agriculture and transport and harmonization of policy in fiscal and other fields. These requirements push the Community beyond the level of a common market and in the direction of an *economic union*. We should of course add that if the aims of the 1969 Hague Summit are achieved then the EEC will eventually be transformed into an economic union. We are of course referring to the decision taken in 1969 to proceed to form an economic and monetary union. As we have already noted the Rome Treaty did not, certainly not explicitly, call for such a high degree of economic unification.

The basic theory of a customs union

We have seen that although in terms of economic integration the Community tends towards an economic union, its tariff and quota policy is based upon the creation of a customs union. It is therefore appropriate to consider what economic theory has to say about customs unions. Present understanding of the theoretical implications of such arrangements is based on the pioneer study of the subject by Professor Jacob Viner. The issues involved were subsequently developed by Professor James Meade and others. What follows is an elementary analysis based on Meade's basic theoretical formulation. This is designed for readers who do not have any knowledge, or only a limited knowledge, of economic analysis. Those who have some knowledge may prefer the somewhat more sophisticated approach which follows the elementary analysis and should regard the exposition immediately below merely as an introduction to the problem.

Elementary analysis

An important point which emerges is that the advantages of trade liberalization within the framework of such a union need to be kept in perspective. Customs unions *per se* are not so unambiguously beneficial as is universal free trade. Classical economists, such as David Ricardo, were able to demonstrate theoretically that the universal elimination of protection, particularly if it was at a high level, would lead to a great increase in world welfare. Each country would specialize in the production of those goods for which it was best fitted – in economists' language, countries would specialize in producing those goods in respect of which they have a comparative advantage. Taking the world as a whole, greater production would result than if countries insisted on protecting their industries and producing all or most of the goods which they needed. (The division of the increase of production would, of course, depend on the terms of trade.) But a customs union is not so unambiguously beneficial because it is not in effect universal – it represents free trade within a bloc and discrimination against the rest of the world. Thus in appraising the results of a customs union, two effects have to be distinguished. One is trade creation, which represents an improvement in resource utilization, and the other is trade diversion, which represents a deterioration. These two effects are illustrated in Table 1 (see p. 53). We assume the following:

1. The world consists of two countries, I and II, who wish to form a customs union, and a third outside country which we term country III.

2. Only three commodities are produced – A, B and C.

3. Prior to the customs union country I applied a 50 per cent *ad valorem* tariff to all imports, but after the formation of the union the tariff only applies to imports from country III.

4. Transport costs can be ignored.

Taking good A first, the lowest-cost producer is country III which lies outside the proposed union. Before the union, good A produced by country III (with duty applied) undersells A produced by country I, or A produced by country II (with duty applied). But after the union is created, A produced in country II no longer has duty applied to it and as a result undersells A produced in country III (bearing duty) and A produced in country I. This is called trade diversion. In the case of good B the lowest-cost producer is country II. But even prior to the union B produced in country II does not enter country I. This arises because the customs duty renders B produced in country II uncompetitive with B produced in country I. But after the union is created B produced in country II no longer has a customs duty applied and it enters country I and undersells B produced in country I. Here we have trade creation. In the case of good C, the lowest-cost producer is country I. It produces the good before and after the union. As a result neither trade diversion nor trade creation occurs.

It follows that in assessing the effects of a customs union we have to take into account that it can shift production away from the lowest-cost producer to a higher-cost member of the union. Such trade diversion is a departure from a previously more rational pattern of resource allocation. On the other hand, the creation of the union can shift production away from a less efficient to a more efficient member of the union and such trade creation represents a shift towards a more economic pattern of resource allocation. As a first approximation, therefore, we can conclude that whether or not a customs union is beneficial depends on the balance of these two effects.

How can the balancing be carried out? In the case of good A in Table 1, suppose that country I imports one million units first from country III and then from country II. The original cost was

Table 1 Trade creation and trade diversion (£)

Good	Cost or cost plus duty per unit	Country III exporting to country I	Flow of trade	Goods produced by country I	Flow of trade	Country II exporting to country I	Results
A	Cost	12		20		14	Trade diversion
	Cost plus duty prior to customs union	18	⟶	20	No trade	21	
	Cost plus duty after customs union	18	No trade	20	⟵	14	
B	Cost	14		17		12	Trade creation
	Cost plus duty prior to customs union	21	No trade: country I produces B	17	No trade	18	
	Cost plus duty after customs union	21	No trade	17	⟵	12	
C	Cost	16		10		12	Neither trade creation nor trade diversion. Country I is the lowest-cost producer and provides C before and after the union
	Cost plus duty prior to customs union	24	No trade	10	No trade	18	
	Cost plus duty after customs union	24	No trade	10	No trade	18	

therefore £12 million but is now £14 million. The cost of trade diversion – the extra cost incurred by virtue of obtaining supplies from the higher-cost source – is therefore £2 million. In the case of good B, suppose country I consumes half a million units; then the saving of trade creation is £2·5 million. On balance therefore, taking account of production effects only, the customs union is beneficial.[1]

This analysis is, however, based upon a number of simplifying assumptions. The first is that the demand for the goods in question is totally inelastic. This simplifies matters since in calculating the gains and losses we can assume that any changes in the price of A or B which result from the formation of a union will not cause the quantities consumed in country I, pre- and post-union, to differ. The second assumption is that supply curves are infinitely elastic. Clearly the absence of such an assumption would complicate the calculation of gains and losses since costs will change with movements along supply curves. It follows from all this that a union can have both advantageous and disadvantageous effects. Whether it is beneficial or not depends on the balance of the effects of trade creation and diversion.

More sophisticated approach

Basically what we shall attempt in this section is a demonstration, using the production possibility curve, of the benefits of universal free trade.[2] We shall then indicate how tariffs have an adverse effect on economic welfare. This will obviously underline the beneficial effect of universal free trade. In introducing tariffs explicitly we shall switch to micro-economic analysis. This has the advantage that it helps us to recognize that the effects of protection on economic welfare can in fact be separated out into production and consumption effects. The consumption effect has been ignored so far in the analysis presented in this book. We shall then use the micro-economic approach to analyse the trade creation and trade diversion effects of a customs union.

1. We can ignore good C since there was no change from pre- to post-union.
2. We ignore special arguments for protection, for example that relating to infant industries.

Let us begin with the production possibility curve analysis. For this purpose we shall adopt a two-country two-good model. We assume that there are only two countries in the world – country I and country II and they can produce only two goods – good A and good B. For each country we can construct a production possibility curve – the data on which they are based are shown in tabular form in Tables 2 and 3 and the curves themselves are shown in graphic form in Figures 1 and 2. In Table 2 we show the production possibility of country I. Assuming full employment of all its factors of production and a given state of technology it can produce any of the combinations of good A and good B shown. Thus if it devotes all of its resources exclusively to good A it can produce 100 units of A. Alternatively if it devotes all its resources exclusively to the producton of good B it can produce 30 units of B. But it can also devote its resources to producing both A and B and we show nine (out of an infinite number of possible) combinations.

Table 2

Country I production possibility data

	Units										
Good A	100	90	80	70	60	50	40	30	20	10	0
Good B	0	3	6	9	12	15	18	21	24	27	30

In Table 3 we show the data for country II. It can produce 150 units of A and zero units of B, or it can produce 120 units of B and zero units of A. Then again it can produce combinations of A and B and we in fact show two (out of an infinite number of possible) combinations.

Table 3

Country II production possibility data

	Units		
Good A	150	100	50	0
Good B	0	40	80	120

As we have said this data can be presented graphically in terms of the production possibility curves of countries I and II – see Figures 1 and 2. It will be apparent that in both cases the opportunity cost is constant. That is to say as we produce any given extra amount of one good the amount of the other good which has to be given up is constant. Thus in Figure 1 as we proceed from point A to point B we observe an increase of 10 units in the production of good A (from 10 to 20) and an enforced reduction of output of good B of 3 (from 27 to 24). The opportunity cost of the 10 extra units of A is the 3 units of B given up. Indeed all along the curve the opportunity cost rate is 0·3B for every extra 1A – examine, for example, the consequences of moving from point C to point D.

Suppose that each country is self-sufficient in terms of good A and good B. We could indeed assume that their self-sufficiency was

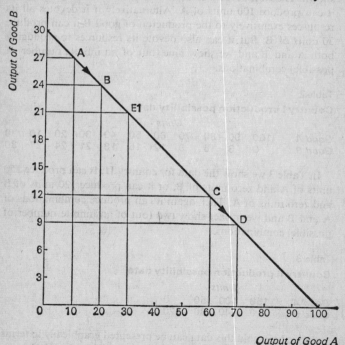

Figure 1 Country I production possibility curve

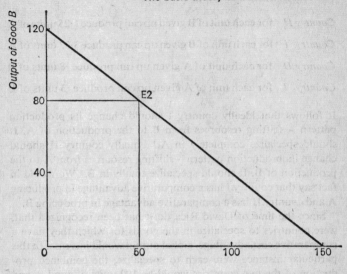

Figure 2 Country II production possibility curve

due to tariffs which were so high as to preclude trade from taking place between them. Just exactly what quantities of good A and good B each country would produce will at this stage have to be based on an assumption on our part. We will assume that country I produces for its own needs 30 units of A and 21 units of B (i.e. point EI in Figure 1) and country II produces for its own needs 50 units of A and 80 units of B (i.e. point E2 in Figure 2).

The next stage in the argument is to see how the two countries could gain were they to cease being self-sufficient – in other words were they to proceed to trade. We could in fact assume that the onset of trade was the result of an instantaneous sweeping away of tariffs – that is the creation of a free trade situation.

We must first note that from our previous data (upon which our production possibility curves were based) the following facts emerge:

Country II for each unit of B given up can produce 1·25 units of A

Country I for each unit of B given up can produce 3·33 units of A

Country II for each unit of A given up can produce ·8 units of B

Country I for each unit of A given up can produce ·3 units of B

It follows that ideally country I should change its production pattern – shifting resources from B to the production of A. It should specialize completely in A.[1] Equally country II should change its production pattern – shifting resources from A to the production of B. It should specialize totally in B.[1] We would in fact say that country I has a comparative advantage in producing A and country II has a comparative advantage in producing B.

Since the time of David Ricardo it has been recognized that, were countries to specialize in the goods for which they have a comparative cost advantage, global output would increase. In this particular instance were each to specialize, the combined production of the two countries would be 100 units of good A and 120 units of good B, compared with a combined total (before trade) of 80 A and 101 B (i.e. the combination of outputs at points E1 and E2 in Figures 1 and 2 respectively).

The gain from trade is then obvious and it springs from differences in opportunity costs or from the fact that one country has a comparative advantage in producing one good and the other has a comparative advantage in producing the other. But we should not immediately leap to the conclusion that trade will take place. In the first instance this depends on the terms of exchange in foreign trade between good A produced in country I and good B produced in country II. In other words whether trade will take place depends on what we call the terms of trade. Equally it is important to add that just how two countries share the production gain arising from specialization will depend on the nature of the terms of trade.

1. Complete specialization is a feature of constant opportunity costs but would not automatically follow if the opportunity cost curve was concave to the origin – i.e. if opportunity costs were increasing.

We can now proceed to illustrate these two propositions. We are saying that country I should cease producing B and should acquire B by exchanging its A for B produced by country II. Suppose that the terms of trading were that 10A commanded 2B then it would not pay country I to specialize and trade, since internally it can move along its production possibility curve and transform 10A into 3B. The terms of trade must be at least 10A or 3B – at which point country I is indifferent as between specialization and trade on the one hand and self-sufficiency on the other.

Let us now view the matter from country II's angle. We are saying that country II should cease producing A and should acquire its A by exchanging B for A produced by country I. If the terms of trade were that 10A commanded 9B, country I (as a potential specialist in A) would be delighted with such a favourable rate. But country II would not echo that sentiment – the reason being that a rate of 10A for 9B is the same as a rate of 10B for 11$\frac{1}{9}$A. However, by internal transformation (i.e. moving along its production possibility curve) country II can turn 10B into 12$\frac{1}{2}$A. Only if the rate was 10A for 8B (i.e. 10B for 12$\frac{1}{2}$A) would country II be indifferent as between specialization and trade, and self-sufficiency.

It follows that for there to be a *positive mutual desire* to trade, the terms of trade must lie between (but not at) 10A for 3B and 10A for 8B. For example, 10A for 6B would be mutually advantageous. Just where the terms of trade lay between 10A for 3B and 10A for 8B would determine which country gained most from the improvement of production consequent upon specialization. Thus as the rate moves from 10A for 3B to 10A for 8B country I gets more and more for its surplus of A which it sells to country II, whilst country II gets less and less for its surplus of B which it sells to country I.

We have of course been stressing the conditions necessary for *mutual* gain through exchange. It is true to say that irrespective of the terms of trade (i.e. whether they lie within the 10A–3B and 10A–8B bracket or outside it) specialization is bound to raise the combined or global output of A and B. Thus if the rate was 10A for 9B country I would be better off but country II would gain nothing – it would in fact be worse off. However, out of its gains country I could compensate country II and thus make country II willing to accept the policy of specialization and trade.

Before we proceed further it is necessary to note that although we have discussed the significance of the terms of trade in determining whether there is a mutual desire to trade, and in determining how much each country acquires of the increase of global output consequent on specialization, we have not offered any explanation of the way in which the terms of trade themselves are determined. Since such an explanation is not a necessary part of a proof of the gains from specialization we are not at this point including any analysis of the determination of the terms of trade. An offer curve explanation will, however, be found in Appendix I to this chapter (p. 74).

We have tried to explain how free trade can be mutually advantageous. We have suggested that a failure to specialize and trade may be due to tariffs. The stage has now been reached when we can introduce tariffs explicitly into the picture – showing (a) how a loss of economic welfare occurs and (b) how that loss of welfare springs from the production and consumption effects of the tariff. The analysis will be based on the use of supply and demand curves for the product of a particular industry – it follows that we shall be basing the argument on partial equilibrium analysis.

In Figure 3 we show country I's domestic demand curve dd, and country I's domestic supply curve ss, for good A. The supply curve ss has the normal positive slope – it indicates that the industry within country I supplying good A will be disposed to supply more per unit of time the higher the price of the good. The dd demand curve has the normal negative slope – it indicates that consumers in country I will be disposed to demand more per unit of time the lower the price of the good.

Since we are dealing with tariffs and trade we now have to recognize that there is a competing source of supply of good A in the form of imports from the rest of the world. This is represented by the supply curve S S(W)1. This is drawn as a perfectly elastic supply curve. The assumption here is that the imports of country I represent only a very small part of the demand for the good in question in the world market. Country I is therefore a price taker – it must take the price of imports of good A as being determined in the world market by world supply and

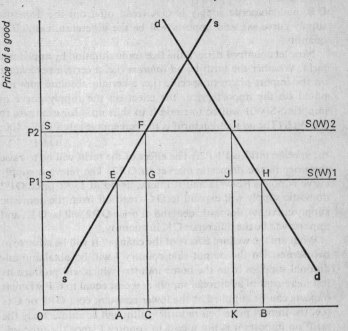

Quantity supplied and demanded of Good A

Figure 3 Welfare effects of a tariff

demand. Whether it imports a little or a lot of A it will not drive the price down or up by so doing. We are in fact assuming that there is no terms of trade effect arising from country I importing good A.[1]

If we assume that there are no tariffs then we can say that the price in the domestic market of country I will be OP1. This follows from the intersection of the supply curve sES(W)1 with the demand curve dd at H. The equilibrium price is OP1 (the price at which imports enter the domestic market). Domestic demand is

1. For an analysis of the conditions under which a terms of trade effect will arise see A. Myrick Freeman III, *International Trade: An Introduction to Method and Theory*, Harper & Row, 1971, p. 138.

O B, and domestic supply is O A (read off from the domestic supply curve ss), and imports will be the difference, i.e. A B in quantity.

Now let country I disturb the free trade situation by applying a tariff. Whether the tariff be *ad valorem* (i.e. a certain percentage on the import price) or specific (i.e. a certain absolute sum imposed on the import price) the effect on the supply curve of imports S S(W)1 will be to cause it to shift up – for example, to S S(W)2. (The *ad valorem* tariff is the percentage rate $\frac{P1 \ P2}{O \ P1} \cdot \frac{100}{1}$;

the specific tariff is P1 P2.) The effect of the tariff will be to raise the price in the domestic market to O P2. The relevant supply curve is now s F S(W)2 and it intersects dd at I. At price O P2 domestic supply will expand to O C (read off from the domestic supply curve ss), domestic demand at price O P2 will be O K, and imports will be the difference C K in quantity.

What are the welfare effects of the change? It will be adverse in two senses. On the output side country I will be obtaining additional supplies from the home industry which will produce its last increment of additional supply at a cost equal to C F whereas imports can be supplied at the lower constant cost O P1 or C G (i.e. the import price before tariff – although consumers pay the tariff on imports it is not a cost to country I since the proceeds of the tariff accrue to the national exchequer).[1] The production cost of protection is in fact represented by the triangle E F G (i.e. the difference between the cost of obtaining supply A C by import, which would be rectangle A E G C, and the cost of supplying A C domestically, which would be area A E F C).

There is also a consumption cost. Since consumption falls by an amount equal to K B, consumers will experience a loss of economic welfare. In this case although consumers were previously paying price O P1 for quantity K B (i.e. area B H J K) the

1. Although we shall not pursue it, there is of course a welfare effect arising from the fact that the tariff revenue has been collected by the government who will then presumably proceed to spend it. This second order welfare effect could not be analysed in the absence of information about the transfer, i.e. who paid the tariff and who benefited from the consequent government spending. This is just one of a number of effects which a truly sophisticated analysis would have to take into account – see Freeman, *op. cit.*, pp. 134–43.

actual utility enjoyed was equal to the large area BHIK under the demand curve. They will not, however, suffer a loss equal to the latter amount since they will be able to spend amount BHJK on other goods. If, however, as we must assume, they were in a state of consumer equilibrium prior to the tariff change, then we can assert that the utility they will thereby obtain will not exceed BHJK.[1] Thus the consumption loss will be BHIK minus BHJK, which is the triangle HIJ.

It follows that the welfare cost of the tariff is made up of both production and consumption costs – *the latter is a new element in our analysis*. Therefore, given knowledge of the rate of tariff and the elasticities of demand and supply, economists can seek to quantify the welfare cost of applying a tariff. What is of course crucial is that if the tariff is removed then by reversing the argument we can see that there would be welfare gains equal to EFG and HIJ. For example, EFG is a gain because a portion of domestic demand previously supplied from a high cost domestic source is now supplied by lower cost imports.

We can now proceed to apply this type of analysis to a customs union. This represents the application of free trade to two or more countries. Can we then echo the conclusions just drawn above and say that such an arrangement will be an unmitigated source of benefit in terms of production and consumption gains? The answer must be in the negative for the kind of reasons given previously in our discussion of trade creation and trade diversion. A customs union is not a perfect substitute for universal free trade – it is free trade within the participating bloc but it represents continued protection and therefore discrimination against the rest of the world.

Before we proceed to apply the analysis it is important to appreciate that trade creation and trade diversion effects may arise in connection with a particular good. This point is necessary in order to prevent a misapprehension which may arise from Table 1, where the analysis could lead to the conclusion that any

1. That is to say on other goods than A, with for example a price OP1 the last increment of utility derived (prior to the tariff) will also be BH. The redirection of an increment of money equal to price OP1 will therefore produce BH marginal utility. Thus the redirection of the amount of money BHJK will produce utility equal to BHJK.

2. This is in fact a result of the constant cost assumption of Table 1.

particular good displays only one of the phenomena but never both.[2] Having said that it is also necessary to say that a good will not inevitably exhibit both trade creation and trade diversion effects simultaneously – it may exhibit both effects, as we shall see, but it may not, as we shall also see.

In Figure 4 we show the usual domestic demand and supply curves dd and ss of country I. We now have to introduce the supply curves of imports from country II (who will be the customs union partner) and country III (who will remain outside the union). The relative position of the supply curves of these two latter countries is important, as will become clear. It will also be

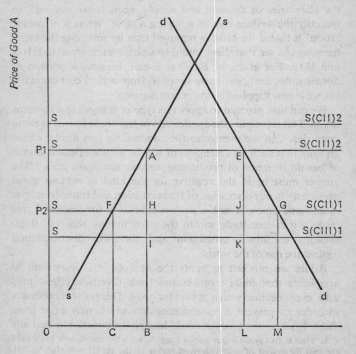

Quantity supplied and demanded of Good A

Figure 4 Trade creation and trade diversion

seen that we are employing infinitely elastic supply curves in respect of country II and country III. The idea that country I is a relatively small purchaser of goods from these two countries is *not* the reason for the horizontal nature of these supply curves: the horizontality is in fact based on the assumption that country II and country III are constant cost suppliers. This assumption renders the analysis a good deal simpler. We will explain why later.

In Figure 4, S S(CIII)1 is the supply curve of imports from country III and S S(CII)1 is the supply curve of imports from country II. Before the union a non-discriminatory tariff is applied to all imports into country I, and because country III is the lower cost supplier of the two outsiders it follows that country III's supply curve with tariff (S S(CIII)2) lies *below* country II's supply curve with tariff (S S(CII)2). It follows that before the union the relevant supply curve is s,A S(CIII)2 and it intersects dd at E. It follows that the equilibrium price level before the union is O P1. Domestic production is O B, domestic consumption is O L, and imports are B L. Note that since country III is the lowest cost supplier it is the sole source of import supply.

Now let us assume that a customs union is formed between countries I and II, whilst country III continues to face the old tariff. Country II can now supply at price O P2 since its supplies no longer bear tariff, whilst country III must go on supplying at price O P1 as previously. The effective supply curve is therefore s F S(CII)1. Equilibrium is at point G where s F S(CII)1 and dd intersect. The price level falls from O P1 to O P2. Domestic output now contracts to O C, domestic demand expands to O M, and imports are C M. *These imports now come from country II.*

We can now disentangle the welfare gains and losses. First we have trade creation effects which constitute a welfare gain. On the production side triangle F A H represents a production gain as more costly home production is supplanted by lower cost imports. The accompanying consumption gain is represented by triangle G E J. However, the new position does not represent an unmitigated welfare gain. The reason for this is that country I has now diverted imports from country III to country II and this is a switch from the lowest cost source of supply to a higher cost source of supply. The loss by switching is represented by the rectangle I H J K. Whether *on balance* the customs union leads to a welfare gain depends on comparing the gains (triangles F A H and G E J) with the loss (rectangle I H J K). In other words it depends on a weighing up of the trade creation and trade diversion effects. One thing is now clear: unlike the adoption of universal free trade a customs union does not inevitably lead to an increase in economic welfare.

The results are different if we assume that country II's supply curve before (and after) the application of the non-discriminatory tariff lies below that of country III. In Figure 5 we show such a situation. In this case the effects of the union are purely trade creation with production and consumption gains shown by

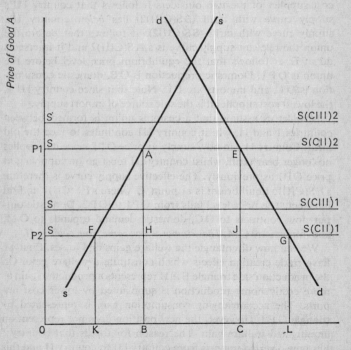

Quantity supplied and demanded of Good A

Figure 5   Pure trade creation

triangles F A H and G E J. Here the customs union leads solely to an increase in economic welfare.

Earlier we referred to the assumption that the supply curves of country II and country III were perfectly elastic. We indicated that this was a simplifying device. This requires elucidation. The device enables us to say that the net gain or loss of economic welfare sustained by country I (arising from the trade creation/diversion process) is also a net gain or loss for the world as a whole. In other words there are no other effects in, for example, country III that we need to take into account as well. This arises from the perfectly elastic supply curves of countries II and III. These reflect constant costs of production. Suppose costs of production were not constant. In the analysis relating to Figure 4 we note that country III will sustain a loss of exports to country I because the latter switches to country II for supplies. Suppose the supply curve of country III were a rising one (reflecting rising costs) then it would enjoy an efficiency gain by a reduction in output. But if country II was facing a rising cost situation it would sustain an efficiency loss by its expansion of output. Consumers in country III would gain by being supplied at lower cost whilst consumers in country II would lose by being supplied at higher cost. These would have to be taken into account in the final balancing process and obviously complicate the issue.

General conclusions

One thing is clear: the static analysis of customs unions does not of itself provide a basis for categorically commending or rejecting them. Whether they are good or bad depends upon the particular circumstances. However, some generalizations do emerge although it must be admitted that there is no substitute for measurement in deciding the actual results of a union. Firstly, a customs union is more likely to be advantageous on balance if the economies of the partners are actually very competitive but are potentially complementary. If they produce similar products but efficiencies differ, they will each contract their relatively inefficient industries and expand their efficient ones. There will be a beneficial increase in mutual trade without much diversion of imports or exports from other markets. If, on the other hand, their economies are already complementary, the prospects of gains on the production side would be correspondingly small. Secondly, a customs union is more likely to increase economic welfare the higher the initial duties on imports from partners. High duties imply high levels of inefficiency which are being protected. Thus the higher the inefficiencies the greater the gains from trade after such protection is removed. Thirdly, the production effects of a customs union will be the more advantageous the lower its tariff against the outside world. Fourthly, a union is more likely to raise welfare the greater the proportion of world production, consumption, and trade covered by it. The larger the union becomes, the greater the probability that trade creation will outweigh trade diversion, until, in the case of a union embracing the world, trade diversion ceases to exist.

Theoretical assessments

Predictions based on economic models reveal that the benefits of Western European customs unions are not great. Most of the studies which have been undertaken agree about one thing and that is that the gains are very small indeed – as little as 1 per cent of Community GNP. Why is the beneficial effect so limited? One answer is that a rather small part of total production is traded internationally. Thus services, building and much of the purchases of the public sector do not enter into international trade and the net gain from customs unions can only arise in connection with that part of production which is traded. Secondly, as has been pointed out by Nils Lundgren (1969, p. 52), if the removal of protection is to be significant it must have been costly to maintain. However, examples of really costly protection are rare since there is no great political support for such protection. For example, raw materials are normally duty free, largely because the production of them at home would involve astronomic costs. Much the same is true of more specialized commodities such as ships and aircraft. It is important to stress that we are not implying that the gains from international trade are small. On the contrary, because of the uneven geographical distribution of natural resources and so forth, they are enormous. But the fact is that these gains are already being substantially reaped since no one can afford not to reap them, and the existence of a substantial volume of international trade is a proof of this fact. As a consequence further gains from customs unions are bound to be limited.

Dynamic analysis

We may therefore legitimately ask why so much emphasis is placed on the creation of customs unions. The answer is partly political in that the process of economic integration prepares the ground for political unification. But the other reason is that the trade creation/trade diversion analysis of customs unions ignores many of the other advantages which can accrue to the participants. Firstly, a larger market gives rise to opportunities for the fuller exploitation of economies of large-scale production. National markets may not be big enough to enable firms to expand sufficiently to achieve the minimum optimal scale, and such a scale of plant or firm may require the sales area of the much larger Community market. (However, whether this is strictly a dynamic effect as opposed to the once-for-all nature of the trade creation/trade diversion static analysis is doubtful. It can be argued that once the economies of scale have been reaped the effect is exhausted and thus it is really static in character.) The much bigger Community market may also enable firms to expand and thus mount the research and development efforts which are necessary if European firms are to compete successfully with their American rivals. Secondly, there are some reasons for believing that the intensity of competition may increase as a result of the formation of a union. For example, industrial structures undergo a change. National monopolies become Community oligopolies and the situation in established oligopolies becomes more fluid, with a reduction of oligopolistic collusion and mutual awareness. Then again there is a possibility of a psychological change. Thus it has been argued that prior to the formation of the EEC relations between competitors in the relatively small national markets were personal and friendly. Competition manifests itself in the attempt of producers to expand at each other's expense. This was unlikely to happen under such circumstances. However, when trade liberalization occurred firms in one national market could seek to grow not at each other's expense but at the expense of producers in other national markets with whom relations are impersonal. Not only that but producers in those other markets would tend to behave likewise. As a result every firm would become aware of the fact that its own national market share could no longer be regarded as secure. Because of this they would tend to look less favourably on the preservation of less efficient compatriots. (The competition effect can only be said to be dynamic if it leads to a *sustained* higher rate of investment and/or technological improvement.) Of course, the much more aggressive business behaviour which now exists in the Community is due not only to the opening up of markets, but also to the infiltration of US investment which has brought with it more aggressive business strategies and better management techniques. But this infiltration was undoubtedly to a considerable degree the result of the bigger market, or the prospect thereof, which the Rome Treaty opened up, and is in effect another advantage of the customs union from the point of view of the members. Thirdly, although it is not strictly speaking a dynamic advantage of a customs union, it is necessary to point out that such an arrangement is likely to enable the members to extract better terms when they bargain together in, for example, international negotiations such as the Kennedy Round.

Tariff disarmament and trade expansion

The Rome Treaty requires that internal tariffs be eliminated. As we have seen, the French, particularly, were anxious about the transition period allowed for tariff disarmament to be accomplished. In the event it was decided that the period should be one of twelve years so that all tariffs would have to be eliminated by 31 December 1969. Table 4 shows a progress in tariff reduction on industrial goods and also indicates that the Community accomplished its tariff disarmament ahead of schedule. The Treaty also called for the abolition of quotas and this has been achieved, although the task was rendered relatively easy by virtue of measures of liberalization accomplished within the framework of the International Monetary Fund (IMF), the General Agreement on Tariffs and Trade (GATT) and above all the OEEC, prior to the coming into operation of the Rome Treaty.

This liberalization has been accomplished with relatively little trouble. We may well ask why this is so, particularly when we

Table 4 Internal tariff reductions of the EEC (per cent)

		Acceleration of		Acceleration of					
	1.1.59	1.7.60	1.1.61	1.7.62	1.7.63	1.1.65	1.1.66	1.1.67	1.1.68	
Individual reductions made on 1 January										
1957 level	10	10	10	10	10	10	10	5	15	
Cumulative reduction	10	20	30	40	50	60	70	80	85	100

Source: EEC Commission (1967), p. 34.

consider that countries are generally rather concerned about the level of their protection. The answer in some degree must be the obvious one that the liberalization process has been reciprocal. Then again too much should not be made of the idea that, because of differences in efficiency between states, the competitive process will lead to the absolute contraction or closing down of some enterprises. During a period of rapid expansion, such as has been experienced by the Six since 1958, it is more likely that competition will result in a smaller share of the overall development going to the less efficient and a larger share to the more efficient. There have however been some problems. For example, Italian kitchen equipment has caused considerable havoc in the French industry and led at one stage to the temporary levying of a tax on imports of Italian refrigerators. Mergers occurred in order to obtain the economies of large-scale production and to eliminate excess capacity. The other main occasion when anti-liberalization measures were introduced was 1968 when the French Government imposed quotas on French imports. However, this measure did not stem from the disturbances caused by trade liberalization but from internal political unrest. The quotas were approved by the EEC Commission, although after the event.

Simultaneously with the elimination of internal tariffs, the Community erected a common external tariff. According to the Treaty the external tariff was to be equal to the unweighted arithmetical average of the duties on imports from third countries which were operative on 1 January 1957. The annexes to the Treaty do, however, contain exceptions to this rule. For example, list B includes eighty commodities, mostly raw materials, with

Table 5 **The creation of the common external tariff (per cent)**

	Acceleration of		Acceleration of		
	1.1.61	1.1.62	1.7.63	1.1.66	1.7.68
Industrial products					
adjustment	30		30		40
cumulative adjustment	30		60		100
Agricultural products					
adjustment		30		30	40
cumulative adjustment		30		60	100

Source: EEC Commission (1967), p. 34.

respect to which the common tariff is not to exceed 3 per cent. Table 5 shows how the Community progressed towards the establishment of the common tariff.

The liberalization of trade within the Community has naturally given a considerable fillip to intra-Community trading. There has also been an increase in the rate of expansion of the Community's imports from third countries, though of modest proportions by comparison. The contrast between the rate of expansion of intra-Community trade and trade with third countries is highlighted by the fact that, taking the time periods 1953–8 and 1958–67, whilst the average annual percentage increase in imports from third countries rose from 9·4 to 10·0 respectively, intra-Community trade increased from 14·2 to 28·4.

Some attempts have been made to demonstrate the effect of internal tariff disarmament on intra-Community trade. One such piece of work by Williamson and Bottrill (1971) has shown some interesting results. (The student who wishes to follow the detailed

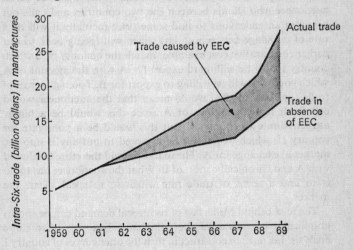

Source: *The Times,* 26 May 1971 (but see paper by Williamson and Bottrill in references at end of book).

Figure 6   Intra-Community trade effect of EEC

econometric argument should read the relevant paper mentioned in the references at the end of the book.) The study attempted to predict what would be the level of intra-Community trade flows in manufactures in the absence of tariff disarmament and compared this with the actual recorded flow. It showed that by 1969 intra-Community trade in manufactures was over 50 per cent higher than it would have been had the E E C not been formed. The results of the study are shown in diagrammatic form in Figure 6.

APPENDIX I

The basic question to be answered is: What kind of analysis can be employed to explain how the terms of trade are determined? One answer to this question was provided by John Stuart Mill and gave rise to what has been called the law of reciprocal demand.

Generally this is explained by assuming the existence of an auctioneer who stands between the two countries and calls out prices in an endeavour to find some price (actually it will be a rate of exchange between goods) which will (going back to our earlier comparative cost example) match the quantity of B which country II will be willing to export for A with the amount of A which country I will be willing to export for B. Too high terms of trade (i.e. 10A for 9B) would mean that the auctioneer would call forth large quantities of A since this would be a highly attractive rate to country I. But this would be a poor rate for country II, which would not be disposed to put any B into the market in exchange for A. The market would therefore be glutted with A and chronically short of B. What the auctioneer has to do is to find a terms of trade rate which so to speak clears the market.

The idea behind Mill's law of reciprocal demand can be shown graphically by means of the Marshall-Edgeworth offer curve analysis. Let us then construct in turn the offer curves of country I and country II. In Figure 7 below we assemble the data for the construction of country I's offer curve. On the horizontal axis we measure the A which country I will offer and on the vertical axis we measure the B which country II will offer. The lines drawn out from O represent different terms of trade between A and B. We

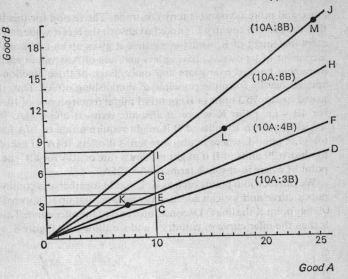

Figure 7 Data to construct offer curve of country I

recollect that a rate of 10A against 3B was the lowest rate country I was willing to contemplate – it was indeed one at which it was indifferent between specialization and trade, and self-sufficiency. We can plot a line showing such a rate by drawing lines joining 10A and 3B at C. A line then drawn from O, through C, represents the terms of trade 10A:3B. We can similarly represent terms of trade 10A:4B, 10A:6B and 10A:8B (which are progressively more favourable to country I) by a similar method – i.e. by joining 10A and 4B at E, 10A and 6B at G and 10A and 8B at I, and passing lines from O through E, G and I.

Let us now add the data which will enable us to plot the various points on country I's offer curve. This we do by asking what terms of trade country I would require in order that it be disposed progressively to absorb more and more B, offered by country II. The general principle lying behind our answers will be that as country I is asked to accept greater and greater quantities of B it will only be disposed to accept them at what are to it more and more favourable terms of trade. The reason for this is that the more B country I is asked to absorb the less it values any extra increment of B, whilst every time it gives up an additional increment of its own A, having less and less of A it values each increment handed over more and more. Each of these reactions springs readily from the principle of diminishing utility. Thus if asked to absorb 3 units of B country I might require a rate of 10A for 4B – i.e. point K where in absolute terms it offers 7½A. If asked to absorb 10 units of B it might require a rate of 10A for 6B – i.e. point L where in absolute terms it offers 16⅔A. If asked to absorb 20 units of B it might require a rate of 10A for 8B – i.e. point M where in absolute terms it offers 25A.

We can then join points such as K, L and M together as a continuous curve and we can additionally assume that up to approximately point K the line O D¹ constitutes part of the offer curve. This is then the offer curve of country I and we show it in Figure 8.

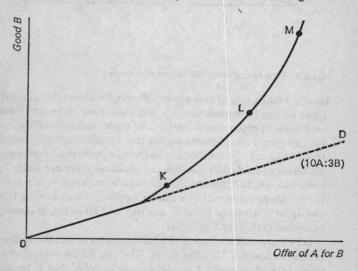

Figure 8   Offer curve of country I

1. i.e. the line representing a rate at which country I is indifferent between trade and specialization, and self-sufficiency.

We can carry out the same process in the case of country II, remembering that 10A for 8B represents terms of trade that leave it indifferent between specialization and trade, and self-sufficiency. Rates such as 10A for 6B, 10A for 4B are of course increasingly favourable to it. Following the logic employed in respect of country I we could construct the offer curve as shown in Figure 9.

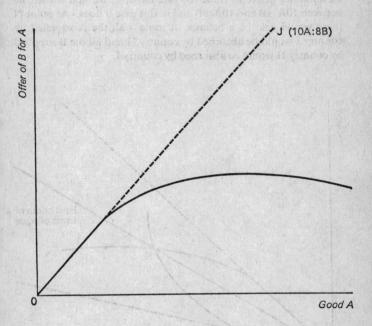

Figure 9 Offer curve of country II

In this case we should be considering the terms of trade rates at which country II would absorb increasing amounts of A supplied by country I.

In Figure 10 we superimpose country II's offer curve on that of country I. The point of intersection at N represents the equilibrium point, and if a line is drawn from O through N then that line represents the equilibrium terms of trade rate. (For there to be a mutual desire to trade the rate must, as we said earlier, lie between 10A:3B and 10A:8B and in this case it does.) At point N there would also be a balance of trade – all the A supplied by country I would be absorbed by country II and all the B supplied by country II would be absorbed by country I.

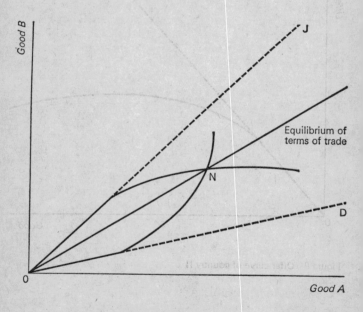

Figure 10   Equilibrium terms of trade

4 Non-Tariff Barriers

Although the EEC was able to complete its internal tariff disarmament by the middle of 1968, the task of creating a truly common market in which goods could move freely was not thereby achieved. There still remained other significant non-tariff barriers which could continue to prevent totally, or in some degree to restrict, or in some way to distort, the flow of intra-Community trade. Some of these factors pose considerably greater difficulties than mere tariffs. We shall discuss the nature of these non-tariff barriers (NTBs), what the Rome Treaty says about them and what specific actions have been taken by the Commission, Council of Ministers and Court of Justice. It is perhaps worth adding that in dealing with NTBs the focus will be on industrial goods – agricultural goods are of course subject to a separate régime.

Cartels and concentrations

These were an obvious device which could frustrate the process of integration through trade. There was plenty of evidence that prior to tariff and quota disarmament various forms of business arrangement, sometimes international in membership, existed which restricted trade flows and allocated and partitioned markets. It was recognized that where such devices did not exist initially, as the tariff barriers went down businessmen might resort to various practices in order to offset the effects of the removal of protection.

The anti-trust problem can be divided into two main compartments – (a) restrictive arrangements between otherwise independent firms and (b) the practices of dominant (or even monopoly) firms coupled with phenomena such as mergers which can create conditions of dominance or monopoly.

Instances of the former abound in Community case law. For example, there are price agreements whereby firms in one member state, when selling to another, agree on the prices which they will charge for exports. Sometimes indeed such firms may create a separate company which will conduct the export sales of all the participants – this is known as a common selling syndicate. These arrangements have been common in fertilizers: we can cite Cobelaz (Belgium – ammonium sulphate), C F A (France – ammonium nitrogenous fertilizers), Seifa (Italy – simple nitrogenous, phosphatic, potassic and compound fertilizers) and Supexie (France – phosphatic fertilizers) as instances of this practice. Parallel price behaviour may indeed be international in character. Thus in the *Aniline Dye* case the Commission and Court of Justice had to deal with a situation in which equal and simultaneous price movements were made by ten firms – six were from Common Market countries but three were Swiss and one was British. As a result of international agreements each home market may be reserved for home producers. Quota agreements may be entered into whereby home and foreign firms agree not to over-stock the home market. Firms supplying a home market may enter into reciprocal exclusive dealing arrangements whereby signatory suppliers will only supply signatory dealers, signatory dealers will only buy from signatory suppliers. If most of the dealers in a member state are locked in the arrangement, non-signatory suppliers, perhaps located in another member state, may have difficulty in penetrating the market. Firms in a member state may operate an aggregated rebate system in which domestic purchasers enjoy a progressive scale of rebate dependent on the (usually annual) volume of purchases from the signatory firms as a totality. The effect of this is to induce domestic purchasers to buy from the domestic firms rather than to import.

In respect of the concentration problem it is not difficult to see how a dominant firm would, for example, be in a powerful position to induce domestic dealers to deal exclusively with it and as a result importation would be reduced or even eliminated. Mergers and takeovers can have similar effects on the flow of trade. Thus in the now famous *Continental Can* case the burden of the Commission's case was that Continental Can, already dominant in the German market, had taken over one of its few remaining competitors in the shape of Thomassen & Drijver-Verblifa of the Netherlands.

Articles 85 to 90 of the Rome Treaty relate to the cartel and concentration problem. Article 85 states the basic law in relation to cartel agreements, and Article 86 does likewise in respect of concentrations – in this case the phenomen referred to is the firm which abuses a dominant position. We shall discuss the provisions of these two Articles in detail later. Article 87 is purely administrative – it provides for regulations and directives to be issued so that effect can be given to Articles 85 and 86. Article 88 is now of historical interest only since it provided that competent member state authorities should be able to apply Articles 85 and 86 pending action under Article 87 to set the Commission, and related institutions, in motion. Article 89 places the Commission at the centre of the stage in the application of E E C anti-trust law – this will be apparent when we come to discuss the implementation of the policy. Article 90 makes it clear that broadly speaking public sector undertakings are directly subject to the provisions of Articles 85 and 86.

Article 85(1) prohibits collusive practices subject to the possibility of exemption under Article 85(3). For an infringement under Article 85(1) three elements must exist.

(a) There must be collusion between undertakings. Such collusion may be by virtue of *agreements between undertakings* which may take the form of a contract but the word 'agreement' also relates to gentlemen's agreements. It may also arise as a result of the *decisions of associations of undertakings* – this relates to situations where trade associations issue recommendations that (whether they are said to be obligatory or not) in effect bind members to common lines of conduct. Collusion may also take the form of *concerted practices*. This phrase relates to a situation where common behaviour occurs in the absence of legal obligations.

(b) The collusion must be likely to affect trade between member states. This is a most important provision. It indicates that Community anti-trust law is not intended to root out all restrictions within the Community, but only those which impede the interpenetration of markets and thus the integration process. Restraints of purely local significance are left to the national anti-trust authorities.

(c) Collusion must also have the object or effect of restricting competition within the Common Market. This provision does not mean that Community law only applies to Community firms. Firms belonging to states outside the EEC can be subject to the anti-trust rules. Thus in the *Aniline Dye* case referred to earlier, British[1] and Swiss firms were fined by the Commission for their involvement with Community firms in activities leading to parallel price movements within the Common Market.

Although collusion is prohibited by Article 85(1) the possibility of exemption arises in Article 85(3). (Thus the law does not follow the American practice of treating restrictive arrangements as being *per se* (i.e. in and of themselves) illegal and not capable of justification; rather a more typically European stance is adopted which allows for the possibility that restrictions may be justified.) For exemption to be accorded a number of conditions have to be fulfilled. An agreement, decision or concerted practice must (a) contribute to an improvement in the production or distribution of goods, or to the promotion of technical or economic progress; (b) it must allow consumers a fair share of the resulting profit or benefit; (c) it must not impose on the participants any restrictions which are not indispensable to the achievement of (a) and (b) above; (d) it must not allow participants the possibility of eliminating competition in respect of a substantial part of the products in question.

Article 86 is somewhat simpler. It relates to firms in a dominant position. For their behaviour to be declared incompatible with the Common Market, and to be prohibited, three elements are necessary. Firstly, the firm in question must have a dominant position in the Common Market or a substantial part of it. (How large is substantial? A categorical answer cannot be given but it can be said that the territory of West Germany has been deemed

---

1. Before the UK joined the EEC.

large enough to qualify.) Secondly, the firm must exploit its dominant position in an improper manner – for example, by imposing unfair selling or buying prices. The important point to note here is that mere dominance is not proscribed – it is the abuse of dominance which falls foul of the law. Thirdly, as in the case of Article 85, trade between member states must be liable to be affected.

One of the key issues in connection with Article 86 has been its significance for mergers. Article 65 of the Paris Treaty provided powers for dealing with mergers. They have to be notified and can be prohibited if they give the parties to them the power to determine prices, to control or restrict production or distribution, or to hinder effective competition in a substantial part of the market for Paris Treaty products. By contrast an analysis of Article 86 seemed to some to indicate that it related merely to the conduct of an already dominant firm but not necessarily to mergers which could bring a position of dominance (or greater dominance) into existence. The Commission regarded the absence of merger controlling powers as a distinct weakness. It was, however, of the opinion that Article 86 could be applied to mergers. The importance of the *Continental Can* case lies in the fact that it explicitly tested this point. The Commission had issued a formal decision which prohibited the takeover of Thomassen & Drijver-Verblifa but Continental appealed to the Court of Justice to overrule the Commission on this point. In fact the Commission lost the case on grounds of inadequate detailed proof but the Court supported the Commission on the specific question of the applicability of Article 86 to mergers.

The position taken by the Court of Justice in the *Continental Can* case is extremely interesting. The Court laid great stress on Article 3f of the EEC Treaty. Article 3 lays down the specific tasks of the Community – i.e. the creation of common policies, a customs union and so forth. Article 3f requires the Community to create conditions in which competition will not be distorted. Taking this as its point of departure (and this underlines the importance to be attached to Article 3f) the Court noted that, unless Article 86 were to be interpreted as applying to mergers, competition policy would be seriously undermined in that firms which were precluded from gaining control over the market by collusion (by virtue of the prohibition of Article 85(1)) would seek that control by merger and takeover. Incidentally this interpretation of Article 86 indicates a capacity for flexibility of interpretation on the part of the Court. Article 86 was not viewed in the context of the question 'what do the words mean when strictly interpreted?' but in the light of the question 'what interpretation is necessary if the competition objective of the treaty is to be secured and protected?'. The Commission is currently seeking the approval of Council for a far-reaching regulation which would give it power to control mergers whether horizontal, vertical or conglomerate. The test to establish an offending merger would be that the parties to it acquire or enhance the power to hinder effective competition in the Common Market or in a substantial part thereof. An effect on inter-state trade would apply as usual. The proposed regulation would exempt concentrations below certain size limits. For certain sizes of concentration prior notification to the Commission would be called for. Powers to break up concentrations are envisaged. Interestingly the proposed regulation is not based on Article 86 but on the general enabling provisions of Article 87, and on Article 235 (discussed in chapter 2). The Commission is seeking a power to control mergers which does not require, as a prior condition of action, the existence of a dominant position. This would free the Commission from an inhibition clearly inherent in the very nature of Article 86.

We turn now to the implementation of the policy. How does the Commission get to grips with restrictive agreements and abuses of dominant positions? There is a fourfold mechanism.

The first is notification. Regulations have been promulgated which allow enterprises to notify agreements (and dominant positions) to the Commission. This has a twofold function: it helps the Commission to get its hands on practices which may impede the integration process and it also provides an opportunity for businessmen to clarify their position *vis-à-vis* the law. When notified (in conformity with the time limits laid down in Regulations) a practice enjoys a transitional validity until the Commission makes a decision concerning it. Firms may apply with a view to obtaining a negative clearance. That is to say in the light of the facts the Commission judges that the practice does not offend against Articles 85 or 86 and can therefore be allowed to continue to operate. A negative clearance may not be forthcoming unless modifications are made to an agreement. It might equally be the case that an agreement is so obviously restrictive that it is not possible to modify it in a way which would enable a negative clearance to be granted. In which case (if they decided not to terminate immediately) the notifying parties would have to follow a different path and seek to prove that the agreement had beneficial aspects which could allow it to be exempted under Article 85(3). But if the necessary conditions for exemption were not fulfilled the agreement would then have to be terminated. The Commission is responsible for the issuing of formal Decisions granting negative clearances, granting exemptions and prohibiting agreements. Once an agreement is prohibited the continued operation of it could lead to financial sanctions being imposed by the Commission.

Three further points need to be added at this point. The first is that the Commission has considerable powers to obtain necessary information – it can enter premises to this end. The second is that before Decisions are promulgated a committee, on which national experts serve, is consulted. The third is that *only* the Commission can exempt under Article 85(3), whereas competent member state authorities (as well as the Commission) can prohibit under Article 85(1), provided the Commission has not initiated a procedure in the case.

The second route for attacking agreements and abuses is that the Commission can operate *ex officio*. That is to say it keeps its eyes and ears open for information about practices which may contravene Articles 85 and 86. Procedures may as a result be initiated which could lead to formal prohibitions and possibly the application of financial sanctions. The third route arises out of the power of individuals (with a sufficient interest) to take advantage of the complaints procedure. Finally the Commission is empowered to observe the flow of trade and initiate investigations where it has reason to believe that the flow is either non-existent or sluggish because of the inhibiting effect of restrictions and abuses. Such sectoral investigations have occurred in the cases of margarine and beer.

So much for the rules and mechanisms. How has the case law developed? We must begin by observing that E E C anti-trust law is beginning to emerge as a force to be reckoned with. There is no doubt that the Community officials responsible for anti-trust policy believe in competition, and that spirit, harnessed to the basic Rome Treaty provisions, is beginning to make its mark. In earlier days the E E C Commission was seen to be deeply immersed in the administrative problems caused by a mountain of notifications. Then again the early cases were concerned with (vertical) distribution agreements – that is, agreements whereby a manufacturer agrees to deal in any national market solely through one distributor and bars all his sole dealers in other member states from supplying the market and undercutting the sole dealer. Some commentators felt that the Commission should have been attacking the big (horizontal) international cartels, concerned with price fixing and the allocation of national markets, which clearly restricted competition and struck at the unity of the market. Some observers felt that the previous experience of the E C S C held a lesson.

It is not unfair to say that the Paris Treaty provisions were more impressive on paper than in reality. It was therefore expected by some that Articles 85 and 86 would prove equally disappointing. But this has proved wrong. As an instance of this in the field of restrictive practices the Commission has levied some impressive financial penalties. Thus in the *Quinine* case six firms were collectively fined 500,000 units of account for being engaged in restrictions, international in scope, relating to prices, market sharing and quotas. On appeal to the Court of Justice fines on five of the firms were somewhat reduced. In the *Aniline Dye* case fines totalling 490,000 units of account were levied on the ten participating enterprises who were accused of having taken part in concerted practices relating to dye prices. On appeal the fines were not reduced. The most spectacular fines, however, were levied in the *Sugar* case when sixteen sugar producers were collectively fined 9,000,000 units of account for engaging in concerted practices designed to control trade in sugar between the member states, with a view to protecting national markets. We should not ignore the fact that for every spectacular formal prohibition, perhaps accompanied by fines, there have been a number of informal terminations and modifications.

The E E C rules have already begun to be interpreted in respect of the main categories of restrictive practice. In the horizontal category – price fixing, market sharing and quotas – we have as yet seen no cases where the Commission has been willing to exempt cartels which had a really significant control of the market. For example, the Commission has dealt with the series of fertilizer cartels mentioned earlier, which involved common selling syndicates. It has granted negative clearances but this was only because in respect of sales to other member states the firms ceased to sell through the syndicate and agreed instead to sell independently in competition. It does not follow that in respect of price fixing, quotas and market sharing the Commission has taken the American *per se* attitude. But we can say that the Commission attaches such importance to competition that it has not as yet encountered cases where it was convinced that the advantages of restriction outweighed the advantages of competition.

The Commission has attacked a series of practices of an exclusionary nature such as reciprocal exclusive dealing and aggregated rebates. The formal prohibitory decision in the *German Floor and Wall Tiles* case is particularly important since aggregated rebate arrangements have been common on the continent, especially, it seems, in West Germany.

As we have indicated quite early on the Commission showed itself to be concerned about vertical sole or exclusive dealing agreements. The key case seems to be *Grundig-Consten*. The West German firm Grundig had appointed the Paris firm Consten as sole dealer of its products in France at its particular stage in the distributive chain. Grundig had also banned its sole dealers in other states from delivering its goods in France and undermining Consten – this is known as territorial protection. The upshot of the *Grundig-Consten* and subsequent cases was that whilst sole dealing is capable of exemption, territorial protection, which buttresses the sole dealer's monopoly in the chain of distribution, gives rise to differences in prices for the same goods between national markets. It thus compartmentalizes the Common Market and offends against the anti-trust rules. Goods must be free to move across frontiers in the hope, not always realized, that inter-state price differences will be ironed out. Sole dealers are allowed to poach. It should also be noted that by regulation provision was made for the wholesale exemption of particular kinds of agreements – this is known as the block exemption provision. Regulations have been promulgated which allow sole dealing agreements, without territorial protection, to be subjected to the block exemption procedure.

The Commission has shown itself to be interested not only in maintaining and promoting competition but also in stimulating efficiency. A wide variety of group activities, particularly but not exclusively as between small firms, have been encouraged. Joint research and development and specialization agreements have been exempted provided effective competition has been allowed to continue.

It is also necessary to mention that the Commission has begun to attack the compartmentalization of the Common Market arising out of patents, copyrights and trademarks. Thus it is clear from the *Grundig-Consten* and *Sirena-Eda* cases that trademark rights cannot be invoked to prevent goods circulating freely over the whole territory of the Community.

It took the Commission longer to issue its first decision in respect of Article 86. However in 1971 in the GEMA case it prohibited some of the practices of a German company representing composers of music, and concerning itself with the exploitation of their copyrights, which had a dominant position in Germany since it had no competitors. This was followed by the *Zoja-Commercial Solvents* case when for the first time the Commission imposed a fine exclusively for the abuse of a dominant position under Article 86. This case centred on a refusal to supply a chemical used in the manufacture of a medicament for treating tuberculosis. The supplier held a worldwide monopoly of the chemical and cut off supplies to a competing supplier of the medicament. We have also seen that the Commission has shown great boldness in seeking to extend the ambit of Article 86 to cover mergers. In the test case involving Continental Can it succeeded.

Fiscal factors

Our primary focus will be indirect taxes. Within that area two forms of tax fall due for consideration. One is the turnover tax. The other is the excise duty.

It is not immediately obvious why indirect taxes such as the turnover variety should give rise to an NTB problem. The full import of that remark must, however, wait upon a discussion of two other issues. The first is the nature of turnover taxes as they existed in the Community at the time when the Rome Treaty was being drafted. The second is the traditional treatment of indirect taxes on goods entering into international trade.

Within the general category of turnover tax the Community operated two main kinds – the cascade and the value added systems. (The latter was of course adopted by the UK in place of purchase tax and selective employment tax in anticipation of British membership of the Community.) The French had opted for the TVA but the rest of the Community applied cascade systems.

The cascade tax was a multi-stage tax in that it was levied at each stage of the productive process. In practice it covered a broad range of products. It was therefore unlike the British purchase tax, which was a single-stage tax levied at the wholesaler stage, covering a relatively narrow range of goods. Cascade taxes were levied on the gross value of output at each stage in the chain of production. The important point to note is the cumulative nature of the system: tax is applied at each stage upon the whole selling value including tax. If the product is used in further production, the selling price of the resulting product upon which tax is charged will be inflated by tax paid at the previous stage. Under the cascade system the cost of producing a given item excluding tax (that is, the value added) will be the same whether produced by a vertically integrated firm or by a vertical series of independent enterprises, but the tax paid on the product of the latter will be greater than that levied on the former.

The basic feature of the TVA is that it is paid at each stage in the process of production upon the value added at each point in the productive chain. The final price of the product, in the absence of turnover tax, is equal to the sum of the values added at each point. Because of this fact it makes no difference whether the tax is collected at several points or as a single payment on the final product. The tax collected will be the same in either case – the tax is therefore neutral as between production which is carried out in a vertically integrated firm and production which is carried out by several separate firms with tax levied at the intermediate stages.

We turn now to the treatment of indirect taxes on international trade. (In practice we will assume that the trade takes place between members of a customs union.) Here we have to distinguish between the origin and destination principles. The origin principle can be explained as follows. Let us suppose that good X is manufactured in Country I and Country I applies a general turnover tax which amounts to 10 per cent on the cost of producing a good. If good X is exported to Country II it retains the 10 per cent tax and is thus delivered to consumers in Country II with the tax applied. Suppose that Country II applies a 20 per cent tax to good X which it produces itself, then, other things being equal, good X coming from Country I has an artificial competitive advantage. Indeed if producers of X in Countries I and II are equally efficient then producers in Country II will find their sales falling as they are undersold by Country I producers.

In the case of the destination principle, however, good X produced in Country I will when exported have the 10 per cent tax remitted. It would thus be exported to Country II free of the tax and Country II would apply to it its own tax at the 20 per cent rate. In other words the exported good bears the tax of the country of destination and not of origin.

The importance of the remark made earlier is now clear. In the case of the destination principle, *and this is the principle normally applied in international trade*, good X produced in Country I and good X produced in Country II are treated equally, in terms of the tax levied on them, when sold in Country II. *Differences in tax rates do not therefore lead to distortions of competition between the two countries*. Then why be concerned with the need to harmonize the tax *systems* and *rates* of the countries in the customs union?

In a large measure the answer lies in a consideration of the problems encountered in remitting turnover taxes on exports when a cascade system is operating. Specifically the problem is that it is extremely difficult to know with any accuracy just how much tax is incorporated in the price of the good and therefore how much should be remitted. Too little could be remitted, in which case exports are artificially disadvantaged. But too much may deliberately be remitted in which case an artificial export aid, and probably a concealed one at that, will operate. In this case we have an N T B which *distorts* trade and production.

Politically such artificial aids are divisive. There are, however, a number of other points which have also compelled action. From what has gone before it is evident that the cascade system gives an artificial incentive to vertical integration. This has several disadvantageous effects. Firstly, it may be more efficient to specialize in one stage of a productive process, but the tax discourages this. There may, of course, be no advantage as between vertically integrated and non-vertically integrated firms from the point of view of productive efficiency. But the vertically integrated firm enjoys an artificial competitive advantage. Secondly, although from the view of maintaining competition it is usual to regard horizontal concentrations as a main problem, there are reasons for fearing the vertical variety. A firm which is integrated backwards can control supplies of raw materials and semi-finished products to competitors and force them out of business or force them to conform to its wishes. However, this problem only arises if firms at an earlier stage in the production process are concentrated horizontally, and this is not inevitable since the tax does not bias industrial structures in this way. But it could be argued that by integrating vertically an enterprise could acquire financial resources which would enable it to concentrate horizontally. Such resources would enable it to endure the price wars which might be necessary to discipline non-vertically integrated firms. Thirdly, there are reasons for believing that vertical integration in industry tends to impede cross-frontier competition.

This argument is based on the proposition that in the absence of such integration firms at any stage of production have the alternative of buying the products of the previous stage either from domestic enterprises or from foreign firms. In effect an import gap exists. With vertical integration this possibility does not exist.

There were two other arguments favouring a change in the Community's tax structure. One was that in creating the Common Market the aim had been to produce within the enlarged market of the Six conditions which were analogous to those existing in a national market. But the destination principle meant that the administrative procedures for reimbursing indirect taxes and applying countervailing duties had to be maintained and this constituted a fiscal frontier not normally present when goods flowed within national boundaries. The other argument related to the obvious fact that a common market could hardly be said to exist when consumers in the various member states paid different prices for the same goods because national tax rates differed.

The need for action in the field of taxation was recognized in the Rome Treaty – Articles 95 to 99 are the relevant ones. It should, however, be noted that although Article 99 refers to harmonization of taxation it is only in respect of indirect taxes that specific action is contemplated. Article 99 requires that the Commission '. . . shall consider how to further the interests of the common market by harmonizing the legislation of the various Member States concerning turnover taxes, excise duties and other forms of indirect taxation . . . [and] shall submit proposals to the Council.'

In practice the Community has, as a first step, chosen to approach the problems discussed above by harmonizing turnover taxes on the value added model. In 1967 two directives to this end were adopted by the Council. All the member states were to adopt the TVA by not later than 1 January 1970 (subsequently Italy and Belgium were granted a time limit extension). The tax was to apply to goods and to certain services. The latter included freight transport but others, i.e. financial services, were excluded, and discretion was allowed in respect of a large number of services (such as those of doctors and hairdressers) who cater for private individuals. As a temporary provision a member state was allowed to limit the application of the common tax up to and including the wholesale stage and to apply a single stage retail tax of its own design.

The implementation of the provisions of these directives has meant that the distortion problem has been dealt with in the sense that tax remissions on exports can be fairly accurately calculated under a TVA system and the system can be more effectively policed. Also the artificial incentive to further vertical integration is checked but existing integration will not necessarily be un-scrambled.

Having harmonized the system the Community is still faced with the problem of harmonizing rates. When these are harmonized a shift can be made to the origin system. The problem of the fiscal frontier would then of course disappear and a truly common market in terms of level of tax would arise.[1]

The Commission has of course been responsible for making the proposals on the basis of which harmonization is achieved. But in addition it has been continuously responsible for policing the indirect tax system within the Community with a view to rooting out abuses. Abuses in respect of tax remissions on exports have been encountered on several occasions. Thus in 1965 the Commission brought an action against the Italian Government in the Court of Justice. The Court found for the Commission, holding that the Italian Government had infringed Article 96 by including company registration charges, stamp duty, mortgage charges, charges on licences and concessions, and taxes on motor vehicles and advertising in its arrangements for the refunding of internal taxes on mechanical engineering products exported to other member states. These charges were not charges on the goods in question. In the same year the Commission forced the Belgian Government to abandon a practice whereby Belgian goods supplied to the Government and to public bodies were exempt from turnover tax whilst foreign goods did not enjoy this privilege. This offended against the express provisions of Article 95 and the

1. There are two other problems. The tax base will have to be harmonized. The shift to the origin system will affect national tax revenues and member states may insist on some system of inter-state compensation.

Belgian Government was forced to apply equal treatment to home and imported goods.

Two points remain to be made. The first is that there are significant differences, qualitative and quantitative, in the field of excise duties as between the member states. The main products concerned are tobacco, alcoholic spirits, beer and mineral oils. But other products are also involved including sugar, wine, mineral waters, salt, matches, tea, coffee, cocoa, meat and margarine to mention some. Not all these products are subject to excise tax in every state and even when all the states tax a particular product they do not necessarily apply the same rate of tax. The current Commission proposals are that only five products should be subject to excise duty – tobacco, spirits, wine, beer and mineral oils (i.e. mainly motor fuel and fuel oil). The Commission proposes that the tax base be standardized as well as the method of collection. This would pave the way for an eventual harmonization of rates. The origin system could then be adopted and fiscal frontiers would be eliminated.

The second point relates to direct taxes. We shall assume that these do not give rise to an NTB. This assumption is in turn based on the further assumption that, for example, corporation taxes are not shifted forward. That is to say the tax is paid by the producer rather than being passed on to the consumer in the form of a higher price for goods. As a result any differences in national rates of corporation tax have the effect of distorting the allocation of factor of production capital. If entrepreneurs seek to maximize their returns net of tax, capital will flow to, and accumulate in, the low corporation tax states. In equilibrium returns net of tax will tend to equality between states. But if, when tax rates differ, net returns are equal, it follows that returns before tax must be unequal. Capital is misallocated. There is a problem (it is dealt with in the next chapter) but it is not an NTB problem since that relates to distortions in the flow of goods not factors. However, if corporate taxes are shifted forward then the matter is different. If differential shifting occurs a distorting effect on the flow of goods between states can be recognized. For example, suppose in State A capital goods producers shift the corporation tax forward to the fullest extent possible. Suppose in State B they do not shift forward at all. Producers of consumer goods in State A will be disadvantaged by the higher prices they have to pay for their capital goods.

State aids

It is not difficult to see that aids given to enterprises by states may distort competition between union members by giving some an artificial competitive advantage. Articles 92 to 94 of the Treaty are designed to deal with this problem.

Article 92(1) enunciates the basic principle. State aids which distort (or threaten to distort) competition by favouring certain enterprises, or the production of certain goods, are *in so far as trade between member states is affected* incompatible with the common market. Obviously aids with purely local effects are excluded – there is a parallel here with the law on cartels and dominant positions. With this as its general posture the Treaty then explicitly recognizes two categories of exception. One consists of a series of aids which are *definitely* excepted from the general ban (Article 92(2)). The other consists of a series of examples of aids which *may* be excepted (Article 92(3)).

The definitely-excepted category consist of aids of a social character granted to individuals. Aid granted to children in the form of free school milk would presumably fall into this class. The aid has, however, to be given without reference to where the goods come from. Discriminatory treatment whereby British milk was subsidized but other E E C milk was not would not normally be acceptable. Aids may also be given in connection with natural disasters and to areas in West Germany bordering on the German Democratic Republic which have been disadvantaged by that geographical division.

We come now to the second category. Clearly although there is no separate title in the Treaty relating to regional policy, those who drafted it were aware of pronounced differences in standards of living within the E E C and of the existence of regional problems which could only be dealt with if policies of (possibly intensified) regional aid were pursued. There is in effect a recognition of all this in the Preamble and in Article 2 which calls for the promoting '... throughout the Community [of] an harmonious development of economic activities, a continuous and balanced expansion . . .'. It was therefore inevitable that Article 92 would have to provide for the possibility of regional aids being deemed compatible with the common market. This is indeed the posture – they may be, but are not automatically, compatible. Clearly a blanket exception could not be given since regional aids might be excessive and thus become not a means of offsetting or overcoming certain locational disadvantages but a source of unfair competitive advantage. The theory that aids may be compatible applies not only to regional aids but also to assistance for the development of certain economic activities (i.e. industries). We have therefore the possibility of sectoral as well as regional aids. Aids may also be compatible if designed to promote an important project of common European importance or to remedy a serious disturbance in the economy of a member state.

Given that aids are banned but permitted in some cases, the Commission has the task (in conjunction with member states) of constantly examining state aids (Article 93). Following investigation the Commission may require an aid to be abolished or modified. Failure to agree on the part of a member state can lead to the matter being brought before the Court of Justice. The Commission has to be informed adequately in advance of proposals to alter existing aid schemes. We shall reserve the discussion of actual policy in respect of regional aids for chapter 7 below.

The other main area of the Commission's supervisory activity is sectoral aid. As already indicated, aids to specific industries can be compatible with the common market but the Commission has laid down certain criteria which must be respected. These are as follows:

(a) Aids must be selective and must only be granted to enterprises the development or reorganization of which justify the presumption that they will be competitive in the long run having regard to the expected developments in the industrial sector concerned.

(b) Arising out of (a) is the condition that aids must be degressive. Aid must eventually be phased out and the enterprises must then be able to manage without further assistance. Aids must therefore not allow indefinitely a continuance of a situation of less than optimum allocation of resources. Aids may, however, be envisaged as going on indefinitely if at the Community level it is decided to continue them in order to compensate for competitive distortions emanating from outside the Community.

(c) Aids must be as transparent as possible so that they can be evaluated by, amongst others, Community institutions.

(d) Aids must obviously be well adapted to the objectives in view and if there is a choice of method, then the method adopted should be that which has the least effect on intra-Community competition and the common interest.

A number of industries, in which sectoral aid has been granted, have been investigated by the Commission; the most important cases have related to shipbuilding, textiles, the film industry and the aircraft industry. The sulphur industry in Italy has also attracted the Commission's attention. In the case of shipbuilding aid has been a worldwide phenomenon and was particularly marked in the period 1960 to 1970 when what is termed an 'aid rush' occurred. The Commission has observed

... thanks to aid, some non-member countries have been able to build up an important, and in one case, a dominating position in the world market. (EEC Commission (1973), p. 132)

The member states of the EEC could not therefore stand idly by. Rather there was an escalation of aid as France and Italy were progressively joined by Germany, the Netherlands and Belgium. Apart from seeking a worldwide solution the Community recognized a need to prevent competitive distortions as between its member states (who of course compete not only in selling on the world market but in selling to each other). The Commission addressed a draft directive to the Council in 1965 but it was not adopted until 1969. It fixed an aid ceiling of 10 per cent of the selling price of a vessel – it was felt that this compensated for the competitive distortions facing Community shipyards through aid given in other parts of the world. More recently the position has eased and in 1971 another directive (valid for three years) was addressed to Council. Export credit aid was to be limited to the OECD limit (minimum rate of 7·5 per cent, deposits of 20 per cent, and duration eight years) whilst production aid would be limited to 5 per cent of the selling price in 1972, 4 per cent in 1973 and 3 per cent in 1974.

Finally we must note the other important form of state assistance – the export aid. The Commission has taken a very categorical stance on this topic: such aid cannot benefit from any exception whatsoever.

Official and technical standards

Member-state governments interfere on a very considerable scale in establishing official and technical standards. These are laid down for a variety of reasons but mainly to protect the public against physical harm and deception. As an example of the first we can cite the case of drugs and proprietary medicines. The need for government surveillance and control is all too obvious – experience with thalidomide leaves no doubt on that score. Then in the case of foods, standards have to be established in respect of flavouring, colouring and other additives; we can cite the ban on cyclamates as a case in point. But there are many others – electrical equipment and the emission of pollutants by road vehicles are two examples taken at random. Where the consumer is not likely to be harmed he may be deceived. For this reason there are rules on labelling designed to indicate to the consumer what certain designations, for example of textiles, really mean.

The desirability of such standards is not in question but to the extent that they differ significantly between states they do undoubtedly constitute a form of NTB. Either they mean that goods cannot be exported, or if they are exported they have to be adapted to the rules of each national market. Either way the economies of large-scale production, in the form of long runs of a standardized product, are in some degree sacrificed.

There are some interesting cases of differences in national standards. Ice cream is a good example. It may appear to be a relatively uncomplicated product but national laws concerning its contents vary and render what is legal in one country illegal in another. The main point of difference relates to the fats permitted to be used in manufacture. France, Germany and Luxembourg limit them to butter and cocoa butter but other countries allow the use of vegetable fats. Another example is beer. The Commission submitted its proposals for common beer-manufacturing rules to the Council in September 1971. One of its recommendations was that the use of unmalted grains in brewing beer should be allowed. Five of the six states agreed but Germany stood out against this because it would have meant repealing the country's 600-year-old purity law, the *Reinheitsgebot*, which restricts brewers to the use of barley malt, hops, yeast and water. This law also protects the 1,800 or so small German breweries from competition from the larger breweries in other member states, since the *Reinheitsgebot* makes most foreign beers illegal. In the field of textiles we can, for example, cite the differences in what is meant by the term 'pure wool'. Under Belgian law pure wool means 97 per cent pure wool whereas in France the law lays down a content of 85 per cent.

The need to harmonize standards was recognized by those who drafted the Rome Treaty, the relevant provisions being Articles 100 to 102 on the approximation of laws. Article 100 provides for the Council, on a proposal by the Commission, to issue unifying directives when laws, regulations or administrative actions of member states directly affect the setting up or operation of the common market.

Although there is much to be gained by harmonization (not only the economies of long runs but also the adoption generally of the best national practices available), it is only too clear that a massive administrative problem arises. A considerable amount of consultation is necessary – not only are producer and consumer groups consulted by the Commission but the proposed directive then has to pass under the scrutiny of the Parliamentary Assembly and the Economic and Social Committee before it finds its way to the Council table. There have been considerable delays at this last stage. For example, in 1972 the directive relating to chocolate was reported as having been on the Council table since 1963. Indeed such delays may mean that by the time the Council decides to act the directive is out of date. Even for those proposals which are approved by the Council there is a problem of obsolescence. Fortunately the Council has recognized that amendments to standards must be dealt with more flexibly and in 1969 remitted this task to the Commission in conjunction with an advisory committee. In 1969 the Council also agreed on a *status quo* arrangement – that is to say member states would refrain from issuing new national regulations in sectors covered by the then agreed Community harmonization programme. If a state found it necessary to introduce any regulations likely to create a technical barrier to trade, it would give the Commission a period of notice which would enable the latter to produce a harmonized set of requirements before the national regulations came into force.

The Community has made only limited progress in this field. Some harmonization directives have been issued in respect of manufactured products, several relating to motor vehicles and one to the labelling of textile products. In the area of food some progress has been made such as directives on colourants in 1962 and preservatives in 1963. A variety of approaches to harmonization have been adopted. For example, in the case of textile labelling total standardization was chosen: the national standards were abolished and a common Community standard substituted. Alternatively 'optional' harmonization may be pursued – Community rules come into force alongside existing national regulations. Manufacturers who produce in accordance with Community standards acquire access to all national markets whilst those who continue to apply only national standards have access to only their home market.

Public purchasing

The public sector – that is to say central and local government and nationalized bodies – is a major spender in the economic systems of western economies. Such public spending does not always take place in a non-discriminatory way. Rather than accepting the cheapest and/or best offers, the institutions of the public sector often adopt 'buy national' attitudes. The motives are various but include balance of payments considerations, the desire to build up particular industries (for example computers), prevention of unemployment and sheer prestige. Heavy electrical equipment (such as turbo generators for power stations and so forth) is a case in point. It was alleged before the Select Committee on Nationalized Industries in 1963 that Electricité de France was firmly wedded to French suppliers. (It was also alleged – though not proved – that Electricité de France allowed suppliers to recoup their research and development (R & D) overheads in the prices charged for home orders, thus allowing exports to be sold below full cost.) A report by the European Communities Commission in 1972 indicated that practically no electricity generators were imported into France and very few steam turbines – clearly the picture painted a decade earlier had not changed. The Commission also pointed out that only 8 per cent of the steel used for railways was imported, whereas in the case of steel used by private enterprise the figure varied according to the product from 21 to 34 per cent. A report of the European Parliament in 1965 indicated that in most E E C states the placing of building contracts took place on a discriminatory basis.

The E E C Commission recognized the seriousness of this problem early on and the *Third General Report* (1960) indicated that it had already begun to analyse it. The initial focus was on public works contracting; however, it is apparent that substantial problems were encountered and progress was extremely slow. Work was also begun on public procurement contracts. Draft directives were subsequently submitted to the Council of Ministers in respect of both these topics. The Council has not as yet adopted a directive on procurement but in 1971 it did issue three directives on public works contracting. The first swept away all obstacles to the freedom to supply services, the second drew up common rules for the awarding of contracts and the third established an advisory committee on the subject of public works contracting. The second directive relates to contracts of one million units of account and more but leaves those relating to energy and water for separate treatment. As a result of this directive contractors throughout the Community are guaranteed free and effective competition on all major public works contracts offered by member states. Contractors are informed of pending contracts through the Community's Official Journal. Competent authorities are obliged to accept tenders from all qualified contractors in the

Community and are required to award contracts on purely economic and non-discriminatory grounds. All discrimination of a purely technical nature was to be eliminated. A complaints procedure has been established.

State monopolies

In a number of the member states – France, Italy and Germany – the Commission has encountered problems raised by the existence of state monopolies. The main reason for such monopolies is fiscal – the monopoly revenues of the sales organizations accrue to the state as part of its fiscal revenues. Additional motives for the foundation of these monopolies have been the protection of national production and the assurance of supplies. From the point of view of the common market the main drawback of these organizations is that they have a discriminatory effect on the conditions of supply and marketing of goods emanating from other member states. These have consisted of the following: (a) refusal to import; (b) quantitative restrictions on imports; (c) the application of relatively more onerous marketing conditions on imported goods as compared with home produced goods; (d) discriminations against the advertising of foreign goods. These monopolies have also enjoyed exclusive exporting rights and, amongst other things, this has led to discrimination in the terms offered between home and foreign buyers. Table 6 opposite indicates the main state monopoly products as they existed when the E E C Commission first began to tackle the problem.

Conclusion

Progress in the field of N T Bs has been variable. Anti-trust policy, it is true, has been quite successful. Those who apply the anti-trust rules are dedicated believers in the virtues of competition and an impressive administrative machine has been set in motion. The pessimists have been confounded – the Commission has not proceeded to exempt restrictions wholesale. Quite the contrary, no cartel or practice involving significant control of the market has yet found favour with the Commission. The Commission has achieved a considerable psychological impact by levying some impressive fines. It has also shown boldness, and achieved suc-

Table 6 **State trading monopolies in the EEC**

State	Products	Type of monopoly
Germany	Matches	Fiscal
	Alcohol	Fiscal
France	Raw and manufactured tobacco	Fiscal
	Matches	Fiscal
	Gunpowder	Fiscal; public security and national defence
	Alcohol	Fiscal
	Potash	Common selling organization of purely commercial character
	Newsprint	Purchasing group of purely commercial character
	Petroleum	Complex system of import licences favouring franc-zone crude and state-owned Union Générale des Pétroles
Italy	Raw and manufactured tobacco	Fiscal
	Cigarette paper	Fiscal
	Matches, phosphorus, lighters, flints	Fiscal
	Salt	Fiscal
	Sulphur	Economic and social support for Sicily
	Quinine	Health policy
	Sweetening agents	Health policy
	Bananas	Relations with Somalia

Source: Information supplied by EEC Commission.

cess, in seeking to press its interpretation of Article 86 as applying to mergers. But we should not be carried away. The size of the Brussels staff is such that only a limited number of officials exist to carry out the competition policy – when pressed they will admit that they are really still only scratching the surface and much remains to be done.

In the field of taxation there are signs of some progress: the common form of TVA has been introduced but the formidable task of harmonizing the rates remains. There is still much to be done in the field of excise duties and the harmonization of corporation tax is still at the discussion stage.

In the case of state aids the picture is reasonably promising. The main weakness (as we shall see in chapter 7) was the escalation of regional aids, but the Commission believes its 1971 decision to put a ceiling on such assistance marks a real turning point – it may well be right. Sectoral aids have been more successfully contained and export aids have in the main been suppressed.

The harmonization of technical and official standards poses quite a problem simply because the administrative task is enormous. Whether the enormity of the task arises from a vast quantity of genuine cases or whether the Commission has an undue appetite for harmonization is an interesting question. (The latest 'victim' of the drive for equality is reported to be the British pickled onion.) The amount of work involved partly arises from the process of consultation with producer and consumer (some of the former have vested interests in continuing to be protected). Then there is the need to go through the whole Community process in the interests of democracy. If the procedure continues along present lines the task will take a long time to accomplish. If speed is deemed essential then something will have to give.

In the field of public purchasing we have clear signs of progress in public works contracting but as yet (1973) nothing has finally been decided in respect of public procurement. We can, however, be reasonably confident that a directive will eventually emerge in the latter field. Having said all that, it is necessary to add that it is not easy to legislate discrimination away. In the case of state monopolies we can only report limited progress.

5 Factor Movements

The free movement of labour

In keeping with the concept of a common market, as opposed to a customs union, the Rome Treaty provides for the free movement of labour. (There is a provision that freedom of movement can be limited on grounds of public safety, public security and public health.) Article 48 requires that free movement be achieved before the end of the transition period. In fact in this sphere of operations the E E C has registered a distinct success in that complete freedom of movement was achieved in July 1968, one and a half years ahead of schedule. It should be noted that free movement does not apply to employment in public administration. It has, however, been pointed out that this provision

is nothing like as restrictive as it sounds. No official regulations or codes of practice have been adopted and the position varies somewhat from one member country to another, but in actual fact virtually nobody is prevented from moving to another country even if he is a public employee. The onus is on the receiving country, which is usually happy to employ foreign manual workers in nationalized industries or local government. Professional and technical people are unlikely to be employed in a public service or nationalized industry of another country and no foreigner in any category is likely to be employed in national Government service. (Beever, 1969, pp. 27–8)

Article 48 complements the principle of free movement with a ban on discrimination based on nationality in regard to employment, remuneration and other conditions of work.

The Community approached the establishment of free movement of labour in stages. The first, which was provided for in Council Regulation 15 of 1961, operated between September 1961 and May 1964. During this period the movement of labour into another member state required the issue of a permit by the state of destination. Workers were permitted to renew the permit for the same occupation after one year of regular employment. After three years they were able to renew their permit for any other occupation for which they were qualified and after four years for any kind of paid work. In effect after four years discrimination ceased. During this first period a preference was given to national workers in that any vacancies in the national labour market were compulsorily notified for three weeks in the labour exchanges of the home country but after this period offers of employment were transmitted to other member states. But if, for example, an employer asked for a worker by name the temporary preference for home market supply could be waived. During this stage also a Community preference existed in that Community workers were to have priority over workers from third countries in filling job vacancies.

During the second stage, which extended from May 1964 to June 1968, progressive freedom under the permit system was speeded up in that after two years of regular employment a migrant worker could move to any job on the same terms as nationals. The national preference was abolished but a safeguard clause was inserted which enabled a member state to restore it for fifteen days when a surplus of manpower existed in certain areas or trades. If a member state operated the safeguard clause it had to be justified adequately. Apparently

the states have used this right infrequently. Germany, Italy and Luxembourg did not use it at all. The Netherlands and Belgium made use of it for three months during 1965 for show artists and musicians. France made use of this right for office workers and distributive trade employees. Finally both Belgium and France re-introduced the clause for some of their regions. (Yannopoulos, 1969, p. 229)

The priority of Community workers over non-Community workers was preserved.

In July 1968 complete freedom of movement became a reality. The principle of national priority was abandoned and so Community workers can now have the same access to jobs as nationals. Work permits have been abolished and as a result Common Market migrant workers can take up employment without having to comply with any formalities other than those for residence permits. The latter are issued for a period of five years and are renewable automatically. The priority of Community workers over non-Community workers has, however, been retained.

It hardly needs saying that complete freedom of movement could not have become a reality unless a lot of other problems had been dealt with. To take two examples, workers need to be informed of job opportunities in other member states and social security rights need to be transferable. In order to deal with the problem of job information the Community has established a European Co-ordinating Office (European Office for the Co-ordination and Balancing of Employment Supply and Demand). A system has been established whereby the member states inform each other about supplies of surplus manpower and offers of employment. The actual process of clearing is, however, very much a decentralized business carried out by the employment exchanges of the member states. The Commission has assisted by introducing advanced courses for government specialists in vacancy clearing activities. It has also helped to improve the clearing system by introducing a standardized terminology in respect of the description of occupations. The office produces quarterly surveys of the situation in and development of the labour markets in the member states. An annual report on vacancy clearing operations is also produced as well as a forecast for the coming year.

A generous level of social security benefits would be a considerable deterrent to labour mobility if a migrant worker had to sacrifice them on moving to another member state. At a relatively early date therefore the Community addressed itself to the problem of the social security of migrant workers. The main principles of the treatment of migrant workers are these. Firstly, a migrant worker is accorded similar treatment to a national. Thus if an Italian worker takes his family to Belgium, he receives family allowances at the Belgian level. Secondly, in determining the right to benefits and the calculation of them all insurance periods valid in the law of the various member states shall be added together.

It was also necessary to deal with other matters where migrant workers were discriminated against. For example, in the 1961 Regulation foreign workers were made eligible to vote for candidates to works councils in host firms. The Commission sought to render them eligible to be candidates but this did not prove acceptable. When a foreign worker moved from one state to another the 1961 Regulation allowed him to take his wife and minor children only and also required that he should have acquired 'normal' housing for his family. In the 1964 Regulation the Commission made some progress. A worker became eligible for election to a workers' council provided he had worked for three years with the firm and fulfilled the same conditions for eligibility as national workers. Not only that but the definition of family was expanded to cover not only the wife and minor children, but all children, parents and grandparents dependent on the worker. Although some of these issues seem to be relatively innocuous they were in fact the subject of keen bargaining and debate between the member states (see Dahlberg, 1968).

Migrant workers have of course to face the problems of adjusting to a new environment and obtaining housing accommodation. In 1962 the Commission sent a recommendation to member states to the effect that they should promote services to assist migrants on arrival in host countries. In 1965 in another recommendation the Commission drew attention to the need for improvements in the provision of housing. As will be seen later, in 1965 the Commission suggested that the tasks of the European Social Fund should be redefined so as to include assistance in connection with the provision of such accommodation.

Some studies have been undertaken of the trend and pattern of migration within the Community. One study (Yannopoulos, 1969), based on the years 1958 to 1965 inclusive, reveals the following facts. The number of work permits granted for the first time to foreign workers (intra-Community migration) rose from 156,000 in 1958 to 305,000 in 1965. In 1958 and 1959 the main recipient was France with Germany second. However, since 1960 Germany has been far and away the largest recipient. In 1965 80 per cent of all permits issued in respect of intra-Community migration were for movements to West Germany. Italy is the main provider of migrant labour – between 1958 and 1965 the Italian percentage of total Community workers migrating ranged from 75 per cent to 83 per cent. There was also good evidence that migratory flows were related to relative wage levels. Countries with the relatively highest wage costs per hour (manual workers) participated most in intra-Community immigration and vice versa. It is also interesting to note that as the differentials in hourly earnings progressively narrowed over the period, intra-Community migration became proportionately less important and the supply of labour from non-member countries became proportionately more important.

It could be argued that the free movement of labour would be distorted if levels of personal income varied from state to state. Labour would shift to low tax states. In practice this is not felt to be a problem. When the Neumark Committee reported in 1963 (*Report of the Fiscal and Financial Committee*) on various aspects of tax harmonization it pointed out that labour was less mobile than capital and therefore the problem of disparities in personal income tax did not pose a major problem. There is in fact no disposition at present to seek standardization of tax rates.

The free movement of capital

There are two main strands in Community policy in respect of the capital market. Firstly, as in the case of labour, the Rome Treaty calls for mobility of capital between the member-state economies. The Treaty explicitly provides for the abolition of controls on capital movements. Secondly, there are a whole series of other factors which affect the free flow of capital including some which can quite obviously give rise to serious distortions in the allocation of capital between member states. It is therefore desirable that such factors should be eliminated or harmonized as appropriate.

The Rome Treaty rules on capital movements

The Rome Treaty provisions in respect of the capital market are found in Articles 67 to 73. The basic provision is to be found in Article 67. It states that during the transition period, and to the extent necessary to ensure the proper functioning of the Common Market, member states will abolish all restrictions on the movement of capital belonging to persons resident in the Six. Also discrimination based on nationality, on the place of residence of such persons or on the place where the capital is to be invested shall be abolished. Article 67 also requires that current payments connected with the movement of capital should be freed of all restrictions by the end of the first stage of the transition period.

According to Article 68 national rules governing the capital and money markets must, when applied to freed capital movements, be exercised in a non-discriminatory manner. Article 71 contains a standstill requirement. Member states shall endeavour to avoid introducing within the Six any new exchange restrictions on the movement of capital and current payments connected therewith, and shall endeavour not to render existing regulations more restrictive. Article 73 contains a safeguard clause. If the movement of capital disturbs the capital market of a member state, the Commission shall, after the Monetary Committee has been consulted, authorize such a state to take protective measures in the field of capital movements. The Council may, however, revoke such a decision. A member state may, also, on grounds of secrecy or urgency, take measures without prior approval. In such a case the Commission and other member states must be informed of the measures not later than the date when they come into effect. However, the Commission, after consulting the Monetary Committee, may amend or abolish such measures. Whilst dealing with emergency measures we should also take note of Article 109 which relates to balance-of-payments policy. Briefly, that Article allows a member state in case of a sudden crisis to take necessary protective measures, which could include control of capital movements.

The directives on capital movements

With the formal rules behind us, the subject which now falls due for consideration is the degree to which the Community has dealt with those factors which hinder the free movement of capital. *The basic position is that the Community has introduced some liberalizing measures but a completely free capital market cannot as yet be said to exist.* In some degree this reluctance to free capital completely may be ascribed to a fear on the part of member states that the life-blood, capital, will ebb away if all controls are relinquished. However, in 1960 and 1962 directives were introduced which provided a significant degree of loosening up. The provisions in these directives can be divided into two categories. Unconditional freedom of movement was accorded in the case of direct investment, operations in quoted securities, personal capital movements, investment in real estate and short- and medium-term credits linked with commercial transactions and the rendering of services. Unconditional in this sense refers to the fact that freedom can only be revoked under the emergency provisions of Articles 73 and 109. Conditional liberalization was established for the issue of unquoted securities on capital markets and medium- and long-term financial loans and credits (i.e. those not connected with commercial transactions). Conditional in this sense refers to the fact that member states can apply restrictions to these types of transaction if the movements of capital involved are such as to impede the achievement of the objectives of a member state's economic policies. Three member states – France, Italy and the Netherlands – have taken advantage of this clause to maintain partial or total restrictions.

The UK as a new member of the EEC undertook to liberalize direct investments in both directions by the end of 1974 – and to make a start on easing the rules immediately on accession in 1973. The UK also undertook to liberalize capital movements of a personal kind by the end of 1974. For dealings in quoted securities the UK agreed to complete liberalization by the end of the five-year transition period. The same arrangements were made for the Irish Republic. The Danes have been allowed a somewhat longer period in respect of liberalization for quoted securities.

Restrictions and distortions

The above account refers to liberalization in the field of exchange control. In addition there are a number of other factors which affect the free flow of capital between states. Firstly, there are national rules affecting the directions in which capital can or cannot flow. Secondly, there are factors connected with the tax system.

In respect of the former there are, for example, restrictions governing the way in which banks may invest funds. In Germany they can put money into equities but in France and Belgium only certain banks may do this, and in Italy banks are precluded from equity participation. Savings banks in Germany and France can only buy the public sector bonds of their own countries. This is quite important since a considerable proportion of the savings in both these economies are gathered through the medium of the savings banks. Life Assurance companies are another important source of funds and again the national laws differ. Here we encounter rules which discriminate in favour of national – often government – issues. For example, in Luxembourg Life Assurance companies can only invest in Luxembourg government bonds. Examples of such rules and restrictions could be cited at length.

In 1964 the Commission attempted, by means of a draft directive submitted to the Council of Ministers, to deal with some of the main legal, administrative and regulatory obstacles to the free movement of capital; as yet this has not found favour.

It has been alleged that fluctuations in exchange rates and the possibility of loss have also had an inhibiting effect on capital movements – this point was made by the Segré Report of 1966 (*The Development of a European Capital Market*). The move towards monetary integration within the Community would ultimately deal with this problem since a narrowing of the margin of fluctuation around central parities leading to absolutely fixed exchange rates has been planned. However, when we come to review this aspect of policy in chapter 8 we shall note that progress has been disappointing.

Before discussing the distorting effects produced by the distribution of the Community's capital resources, we need to look at the different rates of corporation tax in the various states and analyse their effects. The Rome Treaty makes no explicit reference to the need for the harmonization of direct taxation. But Articles 100 to 102, dealing with the approximation of laws, provide the basis for a solution where discrepancies in the rate of tax, and its method of operation, produce distortions in the free movement of capital (or, as we saw in chapter 4, produce distortions in the free movement of goods). Let us first consider differences in rates. Such discrepancies can give rise to problems. Suppose that member state A levies a tax of 50 per cent whilst member state B is content with 25 per cent. Other things being equal capital will flow from A to B until the accumulation of capital in B leads to an equalization in the rates of return net of tax in both countries (in respect of investments of equal risk). But if the rates of return net of tax are equal then it follows that the returns *before tax* must be unequal. This in turn implies that the distribution of factor of production capital is distorted. Theoretically, it could be argued that there would, from a Community point of view, be a gain if capital was shifted from the member state where its return before tax was low to one where its return was high. (It should be emphasized that such an approach ignores a number of problems, and also assumes that businessmen seek to maximize returns net of tax.) A harmonization of rates would help to solve the problem but as yet no action to this end has been taken by the Council of Ministers. However, conventions between all the member states would be necessary, to prevent international double taxation. That is to say where an investor in one state invests in another he should not be taxed in the state where the investment has been made as well as in the state where he lives.

There are other problems concerned with the form of national corporation taxes. These arise in connection with the double taxation of dividends. The latter arises when distributed dividends have corporation tax deducted from them and then that taxed income is also liable for personal income tax. In the classic system, as has been operated in the UK, the Netherlands and Luxembourg, a single rate of corporation tax has been applied to both distributed and retained profits. This it is argued discriminates unfairly against the shareholder who is subject to this double taxation. It is said that it also distorts the system towards ploughing back profits when it might be desirable to distribute them in order that they be reinvested in other companies needing to grow. Some on the other hand argue in favour of the system in that it encourages retention and therefore investment, whereas dividends may be spent on consumer goods.

In some Community countries (France, Belgium and Germany), an attempt is made to compensate for the double taxation effect. The French and Belgians adopt the tax credit or imputation system which grants the shareholder a credit to set against his personal income tax liability. In West Germany there has been a split rate system – a lower rate of corporation tax is applied to distributed profits. (The tax credit system has, however, been under consideration in West Germany, and it should also be mentioned that although in the past the UK has operated the classic system, in July 1972 it decided to switch to tax credits.)

In deciding on the best form of corporation tax to adopt for the Community as a whole the Commission has seen some major drawbacks in the tax credit system. For example, the Belgian and French systems allow tax credits for residents only and only for companies registered in their own states. The latter restriction induces French or Belgian investors to invest in French or Belgian companies rather than in companies elsewhere in the Community. The former means that residents in other Community countries who invest in Belgian or French companies are discriminated against. It was for this kind of reason that Professor A. J. van den Tempel, when asked by the Commission to look at possible systems for taxing company profits, concluded that the classic system was the most suitable for the Community as a whole. But as yet the Council of Ministers has not decided what system will in fact be adopted.

The right of establishment and the freedom to supply services

The Rome Treaty also removed restrictions on the ability of nationals of one member state to set up in business in another, for the duration of the transition period. This is the meaning of the phrase 'right of establishment'. Just as, by virtue of tariff and quota disarmament, individuals and companies in one state have increased freedom to supply goods to another state, they should also be free to supply services, hence the concept of 'freedom to supply services'. In 1961 the Council of Ministers adopted general programmes designed to allow these rights and freedoms to be progressively enjoyed. Unfortunately difficulties have arisen in connection with different national standards. There is a parallel here with the problems arising in the goods sphere as a result of differing technical and official standards. In trade and industry liberalization has been largely accomplished but in, for example, the technical, medical and legal professions quite serious obstacles have been encountered and liberalization has been held back.

Because of the poor progress in the medical field Commissioner Ralf Darendorf, before he left Brussels, decided to hold a unique Common Market meeting. This occurred in 1973 when the Commission invited ninety-nine doctors to a public hearing to discuss the central problem of the mutual recognition of medical qualifications and the training which lies behind them. The doctors who attended were members of the Standing Committee of Doctors of the Common Market, and of Universities, and there were observers present from other professional bodies and from governments. Draft directives had been published in 1969 indicating the solution envisaged by the Commission but much criticism had been levelled at them. The public hearing is judged to have been a success and it is hoped that possibly by 1975 directives may be adopted. If the directives follow the lines of those published in 1969 then three requirements will be laid down: (a) where registration with a professional organization is compulsory (i.e. the General Medical Council in the British case) it would be open on equal terms to nationals of all member states; (b) each state would recognize the diplomas granted in other states; (c) a framework of minimum requirements for undergraduate and postgraduate medical education would be set up.

6 Common Policies

The Common Agricultural Policy

The logic of inclusion

First we must ask why such a policy is required at all. The Six could have adopted the approach of the EFTA and left agriculture out of the arrangement. However, a programme of economic integration within the Six which excluded agriculture stood no chance of success. It is important to appreciate that the Rome Treaty was a delicate balance of the national interests of the contracting parties. Let us consider West Germany and France in terms of trade outlets. In the case of West Germany the prospect of free trade in industrial goods, and free access to the French market in particular, was extremely inviting. In the case of France the relative efficiency of her agriculture (particularly her grain producers) as compared with West Germany held out the prospect that in a free Community agricultural market she would make substantial inroads into the West German market. This was obviously likely to result if the common price level of grain, for example, was set well below the West German level but at or above the French level. Agriculture had therefore to be included.

These factors do not, however, explain the emergence of a common policy. Agriculture could have been brought within the ambit of the Treaty without resort to common support systems and common price levels. Each member state could have operated its own agricultural support programme, with protection at the frontier and so forth in order to achieve predetermined price levels. Trade could have been fitted into such a system through the agency of bilateral agreements between members whereby they could have agreed to absorb certain quantities of each other's agricultural output. In practice the Six chose to go further than this since they agreed to free inter-state agricultural trade of all obstacles. This in turn implied uniform prices over the whole Community market. It also gave rise to the establishment of a centralized system for deciding what the common price levels should be and Community machinery for manipulating markets in order to bring them about. A Community system for financing the support policy was also clearly called for. The decision to establish free movement of agricultural goods within the Community was probably the result of two factors. Firstly, anything less than free trade in agriculture would have struck the French as discriminatory when compared with the treatment proposed for industrial goods. Secondly, if trade was not free, and national price levels could differ, then countries with low price levels would enjoy a competitive advantage in so far as low food prices give rise to low industrial wages.

In explaining the inclusion of agriculture within the Rome Treaty some account should also be taken of the sheer size of the agricultural sector in 1958. At that time farming occupied fifteen million persons – about 20 per cent of the working population of the Community. A process of economic unification, leading to eventual political integration, could hardly succeed if it failed to address itself to the problems faced by such an important section of the population. Within the Six agriculture is an occupation in which the problem of relatively low incomes is particularly acute. In any case the agricultural vote was so important that agriculture could hardly be ignored.

The system of price support

Although the machinery differs from commodity to commodity, the basic features of the EEC support system are as follows. The income support to producers is guaranteed by manipulating the market so as to bring about a high price – a price which in itself provides an adequate remuneration to farmers. The internal price level is partly maintained by a variety of protective devices at the common frontier. These prevent imports from the low-price world market[1] from eroding the internal price level. But in addition, provision is made for official support buying within the Community so as to take off the market the excess of supply over

1. The kind of situation which existed in the early days of the Community.

demand at the predetermined support-price level. The commodities so purchased may be later unloaded on the Community market when demand exceeds supply at the support level. Alternatively, they can be conveyed to other uses. Then again, and this is particularly important, they can be unloaded on the world market, usually at a loss.[1] As already indicated, in broad terms Community policy is a direct descendant of the policies pursued at the national level prior to the signing of the Rome Treaty.

It will immediately be recognized that this approach is the opposite of that adopted in the UK. At the risk of some oversimplification, it can be said that the British approach was to import food at low world prices. (This followed a long tradition in British policy. In the nineteenth century the free-trade policy of the UK involved the exchange of British industrial goods for the primary commodities which the Empire could most efficiently produce. The import of food at low prices found a further expression in the reciprocal Commonwealth Preference system.) In so far as the UK farmer could not make an adequate living by selling at market prices arising under conditions of free importation, British policy consisted of granting deficiency payments (financed out of taxation) sufficient to build up the price received by the farmer to a level set out in the Annual Farm Price Review.

A better appreciation of how the Community market support policy works can be derived from considering particular commodities. In the case of grain the Community operates a system of target prices. During the transitional stage the national target prices could and did differ because national markets were protected from each other. However, in 1967 all such protection was swept away and a common target price came into operation. In the case of soft wheat the common target price was DM 425 per ton in the area of greatest deficit in the Community. The latter is defined as the area with the least adequate supplies of soft wheat. The centre chosen was Duisburg in the Ruhr. It was therefore planned to manipulate the market so as to bring about a price of DM 425 at Duisburg. (Target prices in other main marketing

1. The kind of situation which existed in the early days of the Community.

centres were established which were essentially regional derivatives of the Duisburg price.)

Intervention prices for grain are set at 5–7 per cent below the target price. When the market price in the Community falls to the intervention price level, support purchases can begin. In this sense the intervention price represents the minimum support price for producers. This system prevents over-production within the Community from pushing the price level down.

In addition, the Community must protect the internal price level from imported supplies. This is done by applying a system of variable levies to supplies emanating from outside the Six. As part of this machinery, a threshold price level is determined. Imported supplies crossing the Community frontier at the threshold price level will, when they bear the further cost of transport, enter market centres at a price equal to the target price set for that centre. If imported supplies cross the frontier below the threshold price, a levy is applied equal to the difference between the price at the frontier and the target price. For example, suppose the target price of grain in the Belgian market centre of Brussels is $105. Suppose also that the cost of transport from Antwerp to Brussels is $5. Then the threshold price at Antwerp is $100. If supplies are imported at Antwerp at a price of $90 then a variable levy of $10 is applied. It should be emphasized that grain is an example of a fairly rigid system of price guarantee. In other cases, for example fruit and vegetables, prices can fall significantly before official support buying begins.

The evolution of policy

Between the signing of the Rome Treaty and 1968, by which time the common price systems had come into operation, the Community achieved three things. Firstly, it dissolved national systems of support. Secondly, the latter were replaced by Community support systems. These were operated during the transitional phase in conjunction with protection between member states and as a result differences in national price levels continued to exist. Thirdly, the protection between member states was swept away and thereafter the common support system was accompanied by common prices. The latter are of course agreed annually by the Council of Ministers in the light of proposals submitted by the Brussels Commission.

This evolution has not been achieved without considerable difficulty. Indeed the Community made progress through a series of minor crises. For longish periods the Six failed to resolve their problems. The solution of them was therefore left to marathon sessions of the Council of Ministers during which package deals were evolved. (It might be relevant to add that the ability of the Six to eventually agree was particularly due to the contribution of Sicco Mansholt, the Commissioner who between 1958 and 1972 was responsible for agricultural policy.) In December 1961 the Council embarked on a marathon which led to common policies in grains, pig meat, eggs, poultry meat, fruit and vegetables and wine, and to the laying down of the broad principles to be adopted in financing the policy. In December 1963 another marathon dealt with regulations relating to milk and dairy produce, beef and veal, rice and fats. In December 1964 the Council approached the extremely vexed question of the common target price for grain. It ought to be emphasized that progress up to this point had been concerned with support systems and not with the eventual common prices which those systems would produce. The common grain price was essentially the linchpin of the whole system. Once this price was adopted, all the others would tend to fall into place since they are all closely linked together. For example, grain is a major input cost in producing poultry, eggs and pig meat. But pig meat and beef prices are related by virtue of competitive substitution. In turn beef prices must stand in a certain relationship to milk prices if the raising of beef and dairy cattle are to be kept in line with evolution of the demand for these two products. The common grain price issue was also important because it brought France and West Germany directly into conflict. Relatively speaking, the West Germans were inefficient producers of wheat when compared with the French. The West Germans were reluctant to agree to a common price which represented a significant fall below their national price level. However, a common price at the German level (it was the highest in the Six in the 1964–65 season) would have done nothing to restrict German output but would have led to a considerable expansion of the output of other producers such as France and the Netherlands. The Community would have had huge grain surpluses on its hands which would have been costly to dispose of on world markets. In addition, since grain is an important input in the agricultural sector, the prices of other agricultural products would have been pushed upwards. The French for their part recognized that a relatively low common grain price would tend to cause a contraction of German grain output and the resulting gap could be filled by French farmers. In the end, after dire threats from the French, the Germans agreed to a common price for soft wheat of DM 425 per ton. This was to be operational from 1 July 1967. This represented a significant cut since the German farm lobby wanted DM 450. As a *quid pro quo* Germany, together with Italy and Luxembourg, received temporary and degressive subsidies from the fund set up to finance the Common Agricultural Policy. Agreement on common prices for other products followed. In the case of milk and dairy products, beef and veal, sugar, rice, oil seeds and olive oil, these were arrived at in another marathon session in July 1966 immediately following the end of the French boycott. It should perhaps be noted that although the common policy is protectionist and does not make sense economically, its creation was a remarkable administrative (and political) achievement. This is all the more true when it is recognized that the system covers about 90 per cent of farm output and the produce of more than ten million operatives.

Grants

In addition to assisting farmers by operating price-support policies, the national governments have given further assistance to farmers in the form of grants. These can be broken down into two kinds – capital and current. The former relate to assistance given to finance the improvement of farm structures, the provision of services such as water and electricity, and the installation of machinery. The latter refer to subsidies to reduce the cost of inputs.

Financing the policy

When in 1962 the Community established common support systems it also created a new organ for financing the Common

Agricultural Policy. This was the European Agricultural Guidance and Guarantee Fund. The Guarantee section deals with the cost arising from support purchases and export refunds. The Guidance section finances structural improvements in farming.

Since 1962–3 the tendency has been for an increasing proportion of the cost of financing the common policy to be borne by the Fund. In 1962–3 the Guarantee section of the Fund reimbursed member state governments one sixth of the relevant expenditure. In 1963–4 this rose to two sixths and in 1964–5 to three sixths. In respect of guidance the Fund made available in total a sum equal to about one third of the money paid out for guarantee purposes. Guidance expenditure took the form of grants to national governments to cover up to 25 per cent of approved schemes of structural improvement. The Fund itself drew its finance from national exchequers. Whatever sum was required for Fund payments under the guarantee and guidance heads was contributed in certain proportions by the member states. In 1962/3 the proportions were as for the general budget of the Community – that is West Germany, France and Italy paid 28 per cent each, Belgium and the Netherlands 7·9 per cent, and Luxembourg 0·2 per cent. In 1963–4 and 1964–5 these proportions were progressively changed. A diminishing part of each member state's liability was determined by the budgetary scale and a rising proportion was provided in relation to each state's net imports of agricultural products from non-member states.

In 1965 the Council of Ministers requested the Commission to produce a plan for financing the common policy for the remaining two years before unified markets began to operate (1967), and also for the period of market unification. Perhaps emboldened by its success in the previous three marathons, and under pressure from some member state governments, the Commission chose this as a moment to insert into its proposals measures which were controversial in character. The Commission proposed that all customs duties on intra-Community trade should be abolished by 1 July 1967. Simultaneously, the common external tariff should come into existence. This implied a shortening of the transition period by two and a half years since the Treaty did not require that it should expire until the end of 1969.

Since Article 201 of the Rome Treaty provided for the possibility that when the common external tariff was established the proceeds from it should accrue to the Community budget, the Commission proposed that from 1 July 1967 a progressive development should take place in this direction such that by the end of 1977 100 per cent of the customs duties should be paid directly to the Community. In addition, in the light of the decision taken in 1962 by the Council of Ministers that the levies on agricultural imports should accrue directly to the Community when the final stage of the Common Agricultural Policy was reached, the Commission proposed that this provision should also operate from 1 July 1967. Granted that the Community would have a huge income divorced from the control of national parliaments the Commission saw this as an excellent opportunity to extend the supervisory powers of the European Parliament. If the European Parliament could be given an effective voice over the Community budget, a step would be taken in the direction of a federal Community.

It is of course well known that General de Gaulle found this package very unpalatable. He had no sympathy with the proposal to enhance the power of the European Parliament. Nor did the prospect of a federal budget fed by direct revenues appeal to him. The French therefore decided to boycott the Community, ostensibly because of the failure to agree on new financial provisions by 30 June 1965, but really because of the reasons already referred to. In September 1965 the French President also revealed that he was seeking a revision of the Rome Treaty which would perpetuate the national veto in the Council of Ministers. This was connected with the fact that the Community was about to enter the third stage when most decisions would be made on a majority basis. The subsequent meeting of the Council of Ministers at Luxembourg in January 1966 ended in a twofold agreement. France and the other five agreed to disagree on majority voting.[1] The French agreed to return to the fold.

1. As a result, as we have seen, where a country's vital national interest is at stake the majority voting system will not be used. This has been attractive to British politicians and was reaffirmed at the Pompidou–Heath 'summit' of 1971.

The return of the French was accompanied by agreement on the method of financing the Common Agricultural Policy for the period up to the end of 1969. The budgetary proportions employed between 1962–3 and 1964–5 were dropped as was the principle of increasingly weighting national contributions according to net imports from non-member states. The proportions for 1965–6 were France 32·58 per cent, West Germany 31·67 per cent, Italy 18 per cent, the Netherlands 9·58 per cent, Belgium 7·95 per cent and Luxembourg 0·22 per cent. (In the 1964 marathon, Italy's contribution for 1965–6 had been reduced to 18 per cent and West Germany had for that year agreed to rise above the 31 per cent operating between 1962–3 and 1964–5.) In the year 1966–7 the proportions changed to West Germany 30·83 per cent, France 29·26 per cent, Italy 22 per cent, the Netherlands 9·74 per cent, Belgium 7·95 per cent and Luxembourg 0·22 per cent. From 1 July 1967 until the end of 1969 the financing method changed. Ninety per cent of all levies and customs duties on imports of foodstuffs were handed over by the member-state governments to the Fund. This was expected to cover about 45 per cent of the Fund's expenditure. The remaining 55 per cent or so was financed by the member states in the following proportions: France 32·0 per cent, West Germany 31·2 per cent, Italy 20·3 per cent, the Netherlands 8·2 per cent, Belgium 8·1 per cent and Luxembourg 0·2 per cent.

It should be noted that the agreement following the ending of the French boycott did not settle the direct revenue issue. The levies accrued to national exchequers and sums equal to them – but less 10 per cent to cover collection costs – were handed over to the Community chest. It should also be noted that the proposal that the proceeds of the common external tariff should accrue to the Community was tactfully dropped as was the idea of increasing the power of the European Parliament in budgetary matters.

On the expenditure side, from 1 July 1967 the Fund had paid the full cost of expenditure under the guarantee head. However, following the Luxembourg Agreement, West Germany insisted that expenditure on guidance should be limited to $285 million per annum. Capital grants from the guidance section were allotted up to a maximum of 25 per cent (in the case of Luxembourg and Italy up to 45 per cent in certain circumstances) of the total cost of improvement projects provided that the farms involved contributed at least 30 per cent and that some part of the balance was found by the member-state governments. The new agreement also included certain lump-sum payments to Italy and Belgium to compensate them for the fact that certain common market organizations had not come into operation in accordance with early decisions taken in the Council of Ministers.

In 1969 the question of the post-transition period financing of the Agricultural Fund, and indeed the Community's budgetary needs as a whole, fell due for settlement. Issues such as direct revenues and the powers of the European Parliament came to the fore once more. At the Hague Summit of December 1969 the French demanded and received satisfaction on the need to quickly devise a financial system for agriculture in the post-transition period. In return the French gave a boost to Community spirit by agreeing to the subsequent opening of negotiations with the four countries who had lodged applications in 1967. Later in December at yet another marathon session the Council of Ministers reached agreement on the financial issue.

The essence of the financial settlement was as follows. As an interim arrangement for 1970 only, the Six agreed to finance the farm policy by making contributions from their budgets – each member state had to pay a specified 'key' percentage of the cost involved. But from 1971 the Community would have its own direct revenues since member states would hand over all their receipts from levies and an increasing proportion of their customs duties. By 1975 100 per cent of all levy and customs revenues would be handed over. An administrative rebate of 10 per cent would be allowed. In 1975 the proceeds of a one percentage point of the value added tax (hopefully by then fully harmonized) would also accrue to the European Budget as part of the Community's own resources. Collectively, the 90 per cent of levy and external tariff proceeds plus the V A T contribution might in 1975 amount to 4,900 million units of account. These resources would feed the Agricultural Guidance and Guarantee Fund but would also be for other purposes such as the European Social Fund and European Regional Development Fund which we discuss in chapter 7.

Farm incomes

Article 39 of the Rome Treaty sets out the objectives of the Common Agricultural Policy. These include the increase of agricultural efficiency, the stability of markets, the guaranteeing of regular supplies and the ensuring of reasonable prices to consumers. The Treaty also refers to the need to ensure a fair standard of living for the agricultural population. Then again, at the time when the foundations of the Common Agricultural Policy were being laid, considerable stress was placed upon the need for a liberal trade policy since if the Community wished to export its own industrial products it had to be prepared to import other countries' agricultural produce. There is of course plenty of scope for conflict here. An obvious way to improve farm incomes is to raise the price of farm produce relative to the cost of producing it. Such a policy would increase farm incomes and, provided the price of consumer goods bought by farmers did not rise proportionately, their purchasing power would also go up. (In 1958 there was obviously a good case for such a development since farm incomes per head were only 43 per cent of those in the rest of the economy.) But a rise in the price of farm produce conflicts with the consumer's interest in low prices. Also, if a rise in prices stimulates greater home production then there will be less need to import. The latter conflicts with the need to maintain a liberal trade policy. If the Community does not buy from foreigners, why should foreigners buy from the Community?

Perhaps the most interesting of the objectives of the common policy is the one relating to the establishment of a fair standard of living for the agricultural population. This raises the question of what kind of farms are to enjoy this improvement. This was deliberated at length in the early days of the E E C and the Commission decided that the family farm would have a place in the European farm structure provided that it could occupy at least one or two workers full-time.

No policy of improving the relative position of the agricultural population, however, can achieve its end unless there is adequate data about farm incomes. Therefore in 1965 the Council of Ministers adopted a regulation for the purpose of marshalling evidence about agricultural incomes. This takes the form of a Community Farm Accounts Survey. The plan envisages covering ten thousand farms with an eventual build-up to thirty thousand. The survey will enable the Commission to produce comparative data on incomes in agriculture and industry and will form the main part of a 'Report on the Situation in Agriculture and Agricultural Markets in the Community' which will be addressed to the Council of Ministers and the European Parliament. It is worth noting that this version of the UK Annual Farm Price Review was the result of the 1961–3 UK entry negotiations.

Prospects

Having created this remarkably complex piece of machinery, the Six soon found it beginning to creak and groan under the pressure of mounting surpluses of agricultural products, particularly butter, grains and sugar. How did this come about? The answer is that the price levels established by the Community were relatively high. This result has emerged from the bargaining between member states. In order to achieve agreement the Commission, although initially proposing lower common prices, had subsequently to pitch the price levels well up so that the less efficient could shelter under them. This was clearly the case in milk. The surplus stocks of butter were a direct result of this since the common target price for milk is protected by support purchases of butter. But other factors were also at work. One was that whereas it was often the case under national systems that price guarantees were limited to a global output quota, the common prices under the common agricultural system applied to total production. The other factor was that as a reward for agreeing to particular aspects of the common policy, member states sometimes obtained agreement in the Council of Ministers for a more protectionist régime in respect of products in which they were particularly interested. For example, Italy obtained this type of concession in respect of fruit and vegetables.

Mounting surpluses were bound to raise the financial requirements of the Fund. A movement towards self-sufficiency or more than self-sufficiency leads to a reduction in revenue from levies on the one hand and an increased expenditure in the form of export refunds on the other. In December 1968, against this background, Sicco Mansholt put forward a new ten-year plan – 'Agriculture 1980'. It was obvious that the disparity between agricultural prices in the Six and the levels obtaining in world markets had to be narrowed. The cost of producing food in the Six had to be reduced. It also followed that if productivity per man or per acre was to increase, it would be necessary to have fewer men and fewer acres in production if output was to be prevented from outstripping internal needs. It was equally obvious that a policy of improving agricultural incomes by raising prices was likely to be extremely costly. A more acceptable way was to invest money in improving the farm structure. Bigger farms needed to be created which would eliminate the concealed unemployment that is characteristic of small farms. Strips needed to be consolidated so that time was not lost in proceeding from one plot to another. More mechanization would also help to increase labour productivity. In this way increased incomes could be paid to farmers without increasing the price of agricultural produce.

The Mansholt Plan therefore addressed itself to the task of increasing farm incomes and halting the spiralling cost of the C A P. To do this it aimed to shift the emphasis in the policy from market and price support to structural improvement.

The Commission proposed that farms of a more viable size should be created. The policy would be voluntary. Financial inducements and assistance would be used, but coercion was ruled out. Minimum size units were conceived as being two to three hundred acres for wheat production, forty to sixty cows for milk, and a hundred and fifty to two hundred head of cattle for beef and veal production. This larger size of farm would lead to more efficient use of labour and capital. Given that output had to be kept under control, the increase in productivity had to be balanced by a reduction in the labour force on the land and by a reduction in the quantity of land devoted to agriculture. Labour was indeed leaving the land but the Commission believed that if the standard of living of those remaining was to increase, the rate at which labour left agriculture would have to be increased. If its target was achieved, the actual farm population would fall to 6 per cent of the total working population by 1980; this compared with 20·7 per cent in 1960. As part of its plan of action the Commission called for a massive education and retraining programme. The Commission also envisaged that by 1980 the farming area in the Community would be reduced from 175 to 160 million acres. It was expected that if the whole programme could be carried through by 1980 then expenditure on supporting prices could fall from the existing level of about $2000 million to $750 million.

It is interesting to note that about a year after the Mansholt Plan was unveiled the French Ministry of Agriculture produced its own report on the structural problem in French agriculture. This was the Vedel Report. It too proposed radical solutions. According to Vedel the ideal conditions for 1985 required a reduction in the number of farms from 10·5 million to 250,000, each employing two to four people; a reduction in the active agricultural population from 3 million to 600,000–700,000; a cut of 12 million hectares in the 32 million hectares used for agriculture; an increase in the minimum farm size from 20 to 80 hectares. The report proposed to raise yields and labour productivity dramatically. The instruments to achieve this were price reductions (particularly grain and sugar); the conveying to other uses of 11 to 12 million hectares of land; retirement pensions for elderly farmers; retraining grants for young farmers; grants for equipment and restructuring; the creation of new sources of employment for displaced labour. Clearly in 1968 and 1969 radical ideas for Community farming were in the air.

The immediate reaction of the Community to the surplus problem was not to adopt the Mansholt Plan. This was an exceedingly complicated matter and time was needed to digest it. It was also bound to give rise to controversy. Instead the short-term response was to hold agricultural prices steady. Given the inflation of costs this was bound to render farm production less profitable, and this would tend to curb output and surpluses. Thus in June 1970 when the agriculture ministers met to decide prices for the 1970–71 season they elected to maintain prices at the level of the previous year (the Commission actually pressed for lower prices). This meant that prices remained largely unchanged for about four years, despite an inflation of costs of some 3 to 4 per cent a year.

As a result by 1971 some of the more critical aspects of the surplus problem (particularly butter) had at least been somewhat alleviated. However, a price freeze was not a policy which could be pursued indefinitely as the sole answer to the agricultural problem. Given the inflationary tendency of the period, stability of agricultural prices implied lower real incomes for farmers and this was bound to give rise to agricultural unrest. This was indeed manifested in 1971 – in February protesting farmers paraded three cows through the Brussels Council chamber, but altogether more serious was the mass demonstration by Community farmers in Brussels in March.

The Commission recognized that a thorough-going solution of the twin problems of overproduction and high prices required the implementation of measures on the lines indicated in the Mansholt Plan. Pressure for an increase in agricultural prices began to mount in the second half of 1970 and a difference of opinion between the Commission and the Council became apparent. Some members of the latter began to press for price increases, but the Commission refused to make such proposals unless accompanied by structural reform measures. In March 1971 a compromise was achieved – an increase in prices (not large in the circumstances) was agreed and a start was made on implementing the Mansholt Plan.

The new policy was essentially designed to get labour off the land, to increase the size and viability of holdings, and to shift agricultural land to other uses. Previously, as indicated above, governments had been giving grants on quite a significant scale, but these were national measures outside the ambit of the Council, which had mainly concerned itself with prices. Not surprisingly the grants and aids given were not harmonized as between states. A main feature of the new policy was that the Six were agreed on a series of common measures or joint projects which it was incumbent on them to adopt, though in a flexible manner according to national circumstances. These common projects would deal with the overproduction and inefficiency problem, whereas some previous national measures had either exacerbated it or at best had made no contribution to its solution. The Agricultural Fund Guidance Section was to contribute $285 million per year, which together with unspent balances meant that $1500 million would be available over a four-year period. Projects would qualify for 25 per cent assistance from the Fund, but in certain backward regions the contribution could be 65 per cent. Several common measures were agreed upon. For example, if farmers leave the land, and the land is conveyed to other users or to farms being modernized, those aged between fifty-five and sixty-five can receive a pension of up to 600 units of account per annum if single and up to 900 if married. (Other measures such as vocational retraining were also to be instituted, although these would be financed by the new-style European Social Fund – see chapter 7). The policy also provided for measures to modernize holdings. Here emphasis was laid on bringing vacated land into modernized holdings and creating a farm which would enable two units of labour to earn an income comparable to that earned in non-agricultural activities in the region. Various means of accomplishing this restructuring were envisaged, including interest rebates. The intention was that this policy would be reviewed after the first four years of operation.

Undoubtedly, these measures represented a first step on the road to structural reform of the Community agriculture. However, too much should not be expected from them since they seem to fall far short of the kind of massive programme which the Mansholt Plan originally appears to have envisaged.

Devaluation, Revaluation and Floatation

Under the Common Agricultural Policy the price of agricultural products is expressed in terms of the Community's unit of account which has a gold content equal to that of the US dollar. The automatic implication of this is that if a member state devalues, its farm prices in terms of the national currency rise, and vice versa if it revalues. It has always been a cardinal principle of the policy that the exchange rates of member states should remain unchanged. However, in August 1969 the French Government decided to devalue the franc by 11.11 per cent. This immediately created a minor crisis, since the common price arrangements were disturbed and there was a danger that French farmers would enjoy an increase in prices whilst farmers in other member states would not experience any improvement. More important, a rise in French prices would stimulate production and aggravate the already existing surplus problem. A Council meeting was therefore hastily summoned on 11 August. One possibility was that the unit of account could be devalued. However, although this could have offset the effect of devaluation on French producer prices and left them unchanged, it would have automatically worsened the prices received by producers in other member states. The policy was therefore rejected. Instead, a more complicated arrangement was adopted. During the marketing year 1969–70 the intervention or buying-in prices paid in respect of interventions in the French domestic market were to be reduced by 11·11 per cent with the intention of preventing a rise in prices. The devaluation would also give French food exports a competitive edge whilst imports into France would be disadvantaged. It was therefore decided that France should grant subsidies to imports from member states and levy compensatory duties on French exports in order not to distort the free movement of agricultural produce. In the 1970–71 period it was intended that intervention prices should be reduced by 5·5 per cent. Thereafter French agriculture was to be re-integrated into the CAP. In fact the re-integration took place in late 1972.

The decision to float the German mark and then revalue by 9·29 per cent also upset the working of the common policy. This had the effect of depressing German farm prices and incomes and making imports easier and exports more difficult. As a temporary measure until 31 December 1969 West Germany was allowed to increase its intervention or buying prices, to apply counterbalancing charges on imports, and to grant export subsidies. Thereafter the effect of revaluation upon farm prices was to operate, but since this would cause German farmers to be worse off assistance was to be paid to them. It was estimated that farmers would be worse off by $464 million per annum. An important problem then arose as to who was to foot the bill. In the event it was decided that the Agricultural Fund would bear a part and the rest would be found by the West German Government.

In the budget year 1971 the Fund would provide $96 million, in 1972 $60 million and possibly a further $30 million in 1973. The degressive nature of this aid meant that the West German Government would have to make progressively greater contributions. It was also agreed that by the end of 1973 the Council of Ministers would review the position. This was not of course the end of the travails of the agricultural policy – in 1971 the decision of the West German Government to allow the mark to float up and the decision of the Dutch Government to float the guilder threw yet further strains on the policy and gave rise to further protective measures. At the May 1971 Council, countries whose currencies were floating at least 2·5 per cent above their official parities were allowed to apply taxes on agricultural imports and to subsidize exports. In August 1971 further pressure led to Italy, Belgium and Luxembourg joining the float. The tax and subsidy system was then made available to them. There would be little point in continuing this chronicle of woe. The important point is that it has led to a situation of compartmentalization of the agricultural market with, for example, the result that by 1974 prices within the Community bore little resemblance to one another.

Reform of the C A P

We have discussed the nature of the original Mansholt Plan and the associated measures approved by the Council. It is, however, important to stress that they do not represent a reform of the C A P as a pricing system. Essentially the Mansholt proposals were concerned with structural improvements designed to increase efficiency and to deal with the overproduction problem. But the basic pricing system (primarily as a method of determining overall and relative outputs of the various agricultural products) was left intact. It is true that the system has shown some capacity for adaptation – subsidies for butter and for durum wheat, quotas for sugar, slaughter premiums for cattle and selective aid for hill farmers are examples. But these were really isolated and in some cases *ad hoc* deviations from the main theme, and the basic system devised in the early days of the Community still endures in 1974 despite all the strains we have detailed earlier.

It was not entirely surprising that thoughts should in due course turn to the question of the appropriateness of the price system itself. This became increasingly likely when the UK joined the EEC, since it had operated a basically different system of support and was expected to lose as a result of being integrated into the Community system. But doubts about the system were voiced well before British membership. The CAP market system was substantially completed in 1968 but in 1969 the first weaknesses began to become obvious, particularly the currency strains and the problems of surpluses. In seeking to reform the CAP attention tended to be focused initially on the Mansholt Plan but more recently agricultural economists have been suggesting major changes in the pricing or support system itself. It is also interesting to note that in 1973 the Commission decided to carry out a fundamental review of the system.

Before we consider some of the solutions which have been proposed, it would perhaps help if the basic problems of the CAP were recapitulated. We will, however, ignore the currency issue. A major weakness in the past has been the high price of some Community agricultural products as compared with the price at which they were available on the world market. We need to be rather careful here. The word 'some' is important. Also we need to recognize that there have been influences, such as the dumping of surpluses, which have artificially depressed world prices. Nevertheless there is little doubt that for a number of products (for example, grains and dairy produce) the EEC was a high cost supplier. However, during 1972 and 1973 we have been faced with a complication – namely that world prices of agricultural produce have shot up. In the case of wheat, barley and maize, for example, the 1973 world price was well above full Community price levels. Does this then modify the picture of the EEC as a relatively high cost supplier? The answer is no. Firstly, these world conditions may be temporary. But in any case the escalation of prices in the world market has been mainly a reflection of an excessive demand (pulling prices up) rather than inflation of the cost of actually producing supplies.

The high price of EEC agricultural products raised the cost of food to the Community consumer – in some cases above the level at which he could have obtained supplies on the world market. The consumer has been supporting what in the main could be described as a high cost system. (We should not of course forget that if output had been cut back in the earlier days of the Community the price gap between EEC and world prices would have narrowed as the Community began to draw more of its supplies from the world market.)

The high price of Community products has had two effects on the consumer. It has raised, more or less directly, the price of food products such as sugar and bread. But it has also *indirectly* raised the price of many other products – for example meat, dairy products and eggs – since high-priced grain has been an input in the production of these goods. The consumer has not only had to pay prices which in some cases were high by world standards, but the Community system has led to a growing self-sufficiency and, more to the point, surpluses in the case of sugar, grain and dairy produce. Here a real cost has been incurred by the Community since the surpluses have been sold off on the world market at give-away prices. The celebrated example of this occurred in 1973 when the Community sold 200,000 tons of butter to Russia, at a price of 8p per pound (16 per cent of its cost) – this cost the Farm Fund about £150 million in export subsidies. In other words the Community consumer has not only had to pay a high price for what he wanted but also a high price to dispose of what he did not want.

The price system of the Community, as opposed to that operated by the UK in the post-war period, tends to aggravate the surplus problem in that the higher market price implicit in the system reduces domestic consumption. The high price system has also, by virtue of greater degrees of self-sufficiency and indeed surpluses, led to reduced imports of food and thus to difficulties in trading relationships with the rest of the world.

The CAP has also been criticized because, although intended to raise farm incomes, it in fact failed to tackle the problem of the low income farmers. The price level needed to give low income farmers a reasonable standard of living would have been unacceptably high, but the price levels actually achieved have been higher than necessary to remunerate the larger and more efficient farmers. The benefits of the system have gone to the latter who have had most to sell and could have had quite adequate incomes on much lower price levels.

Plans to reform the system have sprung from many quarters and space does not permit us to review all of them in detail. Rather we will consider a few of the proposals and let an indication of the general logic of these schemes suffice.

One obvious measure, which does not involve a reform of the system but a more purposeful use of the present arrangements, would be to change relative prices. Products in short supply should enjoy price increases whilst those in surplus should have prices either cut, or held stable as general inflation proceeds. The Wageningen Memorandum of 1973 (produced by a group of distinguished agricultural economists who met at the Agricultural University of Wageningen in May 1973) suggested that the price of grains (particularly wheat) should be stabilized and this should be coupled with policy measures to stimulate beef production. The Commission in its 1973 report on the reform of the system seems to have accepted this idea but, taking account of developments since the Memorandum, they suggested holding the wheat price in order to discourage production (it was in surplus) but allowing coarse grain prices (barley and maize) to rise. The reason for the latter suggestion was that coarse grains were in short supply in 1973.

More complex proposals have been put forward involving reductions in the price of grains, and possibly dairy products, accompanied by indirect supplementation – in effect this would represent a return to a policy similar to the U K deficiency payments system. One advantage of this arrangement would be that, taking grains as an example, the cost of food would be more or less directly reduced in the case of bread and indirectly reduced in respect of a wide variety of other products where the price of grain is a significant input cost. Professor Josling has made proposals on these lines and what follows is a free interpretation of his ideas (Josling, 1973, pp. 95–8).

In Figure 11, in the case of histogram 1 area A represents the cost of producing grain to efficient farmers – that is, those in good geographical locations with well adapted farm structures. Area A

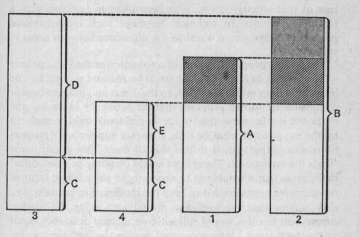

Figure 11   A reformed agricultural support system

in effect represents the price needed to cover the costs and provide a reasonable return for the efficient producer. In histogram 2 area B represents the higher cost of producing grain to farmers in less advantageous geographical locations with less well adapted structures. (We can in fact add some realism by assuming that a price represented by area B will in fact generate only a comparatively poor farm income – we know that the CAP price system has not solved the problem of the low income farmer.)

We know that the CAP protects Community farmers by, amongst other things, the application of protection at the common frontier. Thus in histogram 3, at the expense of some simplification, we could say that if area C represents the import price of grain into the Community then area D represents a variable levy to bring the market price of grain in the Community up to a level equal to area B – that is, a level just high enough to enable the inefficient to scratch a bare living. It should, however, be noted that whilst a price equal to area B may keep some only scraping along, it presents the efficient farmers with an income well in excess of that strictly necessary to keep them in business with a reasonable return. In technical language such intra-marginal producers derive a rent equal to the difference between areas A and B.

The Josling proposal consists of a reduction of the variable levy – for example, in histogram 4 it could be reduced to area E. The internal market price would fall, to the direct and indirect benefit of consumers. Josling proposes that the deficiency in the income of the efficient farmers (equal to the shaded area) could be made up by the payment of what he calls a market supplement (proportionate to output) equal to this shaded area. This would come 'from the exchequer'. The system would certainly be economical in the sense that it would not be necessary to pay efficient farmers the excessive prices needed to keep the inefficient in business. We may assume that the inefficient would also enjoy the market supplement but this would still leave an income deficiency equal to the dotted area. Josling suggests paying the inefficient a discretionary income supplement which could be equal to the dotted area.

The income supplement could be limited in duration – perhaps until the farmer retired or for a stipulated period of years. After that the farm would cease to operate and the land could be transferred to other non-agricultural uses. Clearly a policy of inducements in the spirit of the Mansholt Plan (including retraining facilities and new job creation) would help to ease the phasing out of income supplements.

Apart from reducing prices the policy would also reduce output. In the short run efficient producers would experience a change in price relativities – the price of grain would fall relative to other products and a switch of production (for example to beef) would probably ensue. In the long run the inefficient would be phased out. The Josling system also implies that price support and income support would no longer be indissolubly linked. The size of farm incomes, and the incomes of certain groups, would depend only partly on the supported price – the rest would derive from the exchequer.

The common transport policy

There are a number of reasons why a common transport policy was called for under the arrangements envisaged by the Rome Treaty. The first is that transport costs are an important factor influencing trade. Since the Community seeks to build up inter-state trade activity it is therefore desirable that there should be a cheap and well co-ordinated Community transport system. As an example of the impact of freight costs we can cite the estimate of the German Railways that in 1957 railway freight charges added 50 per cent to the producer prices of stone and building materials and 9–26 per cent to the prices of bulk goods. In the case of agricultural products it has been estimated that in 1955 in the UK the rail freight charges for a 400-mile journey added 28 per cent to the wholesale price of wheat and 22 per cent to the price of barley and oats. Secondly, it is necessary to recognize that transport on the Continent, as in the UK, has been subjected to considerable state intervention. Since these interventions have not been co-ordinated between states, considerable distortions could arise. But more important is the fact that transport has been manipulated so as to artificially aid exports and inhibit imports. Experience in the early days of the ECSC indicated that this would also be a problem in a general common market. But there is a third factor. As was indicated earlier in discussing agriculture, the Rome Treaty involved a delicate balance of national interests. In the case of the Netherlands it was clearly anticipated that since transport, particularly that along the Rhine, is a very important contributor to the Dutch GNP, a growth of intra-Community trade would be very advantageous to the Netherlands. It was therefore very obvious from the Dutch point of view that transport should be brought within the ambit of the Treaty and that, in so far as this could be accomplished, member states should be prevented from hiving transport activity off as a sphere where national interests would predominate. It is perhaps worth noting that in 1963 66·6 million tons of freight was carried to or from the Netherlands along the Rhine, a large part of this trade being transit in character. This constituted 61 per cent of all Rhine traffic, and 53 per cent of it was carried under the Dutch flag.

The Commission's original blueprint

The Rome Treaty itself is remarkably uninstructive on the nature of the common policy. It was left to the Brussels Commission to provide a basis for such a policy. In 1961 the Commission produced a memorandum which laid down what it thought should be the general principles of the common transport policy – this was known as the Schaus Memorandum (EEC Commission, 1961) after Lambert Schaus who was the Commissioner responsible for transport affairs. Then in 1962 the Commission produced its Action Programme (EEC Commission, 1962) which reviewed the measures which the Commission proposed should be implemented. The memorandum outlined three main objectives which the transport policy should achieve. One was to remove obstacles which transport could put in the way of a general common market. Another was that the policy should not merely aim to sweep away factors which delayed the creation of a common market, but should be a powerful stimulant to the growth of trade and the opening up of national markets. Both these were generally acceptable. The third was much more controversial. The Commission suggested that the Community should 'endeavour to create healthy competition of the widest scope'. In the light of the highly regulated nature of transport within the Community this was bound to be a controversial proposition, all the more so as the Commission proposed that the common transport policy should apply to national as well as international transport activity.

In working towards a basically competitive solution, the Commission had to deal with the fact that national authorities, in varying degrees, exerted two general kinds of control over transport activity. One was control over rates. The other was a quantitative control through the agency of licensing and quotas. The Commission took the view that a more flexible price system would have to operate in which enterprises would be free to operate on the basis of commercial criteria. This also implied powers to close down services if necessary. The Commission's proposal was that the Community should adopt a rate bracket or fork-tariff system. This was to apply to road, rail and inland waterway transport, whether national or international. Provision was also to be made for rate publicity. Own-account transport, as opposed to that for hire and reward, was to be exempt. Under this system the relevant authorities would specify maximum and minimum rates for particular types of traffic on the various routes, and consignors and carriers would be able to negotiate rates anywhere within the spread. The apparent logic of the arrangement was that the upper limit was designed to prevent monopolistic exploitation. The lower limit was designed to prevent the detrimental effects of excessive competition. The latter point requires some elucidation and what the Commission apparently thought was as follows. Freight transport is subject to undesirable rate fluctuations. This is due to marked inelasticities on both the demand and supply sides. Demand for transport depends on the general level of activity and in the short-term a fall in rates will not stimulate an extension of demand. On the supply side, because of the small-scale nature of much of the entrepreneurship, a fall in rates will not lead to a contraction of supply. Supply may indeed behave perversely in that vehicle owners may, when rates fall, seek to maintain their incomes by working longer hours. In so far as such conditions exist, a fall in demand would undoubtedly precipitate a steep fall in rates. Allied to all this is the fact that in a boom large numbers of new entrants may be attracted into the transport industry. This will be particularly the case in road haulage where capital requirements are relatively small. In a subsequent slump, however, capacity may not contract quickly. Instead entrepreneurs may for a significant period of time be prepared to accept rates which cover direct costs and make some small contribution to overheads. Under such circumstances rates may be dragged down for a substantial period. Such conditions may have a deleterious effect on investment in the industry and on road safety.

However, this argument is not wholly convincing. In the first place it seems possible that the adoption of the rate-bracket system was based not so much on economic considerations as on the need to achieve a compromise between the relatively free-rate system required by the Dutch and the rigid fixed-rate system which had been operational in West Germany. On the economic plane a number of criticisms can be raised. The first relates to the proneness of transport rates to marked fluctuations. More empirical evidence is needed here. It should be added that national experience indicates that the Commission's fears are not wholly justified. Secondly, as the Allais Report on transport pricing pointed out, there is much to be said for setting transport rates free and seeing what will happen. If monopoly or ruinous price cutting occurs, maximum and minimum brackets can be applied as and when required. It is in any case difficult to justify the simultaneous application of maximum and minimum rates (EEC Commission, 1965, chapter 32). This implies that monopolistic exploitation and ruinous price wars are likely to occur at one and the same time on a particular route! There is a third factor which should inhibit transport authorities from operating a rate-bracket system and that is the sheer magnitude of the administrative task involved. The costing effort called for is immense. This in turn gives rise to suspicion that the brackets will not be determined in any very scientific fashion. Rather, where a fixed rate already exists brackets may be set around it. Then again, where freer rates exist and the industry regards the going rate as adequate, the brackets may be set with reference to that figure.

The argument for calling transport a managed market partly arises from the administrative limits set to rate fluctuations by the brackets. How far in practice the Community solution is a managed one will depend on how much transport activity is placed under the rate-bracket régime and how wide the spread is between the brackets. If the brackets are sufficiently wide apart they may rarely exercise an influence.

Having proposed a system in which pricing freedom and competition between the various modes of transport would have a role to play, the Commission recognized that competition would not work in an undistorted fashion unless between the member states there was harmonization of the fiscal, technical and social burdens placed upon transport. Also, competition between the different forms of transport could not lead to the best use of resources unless action was taken to ascertain the costs of infrastructure, i.e. track costs, and an attempt was made to allocate these costs among the beneficiaries. The stress on a commercial approach to transport policy also required that where possible enterprises should be financially independent and should seek to balance their accounts without resort to state subsidies. If enterprises are burdened with such social obligations they should be compensated for the extra costs, and if they enjoy certain privileges they should pay for them. This latter process is termed normalization of accounts.

The second main area where the Commission has seen the need for change is licensing and quotas. Since this is a large problem we shall confine the discussion to the quantitative aspects of road transport. Let us consider the international aspect first. In respect of own-account transport the Commission took the view that there should be complete liberalization. This would imply that producers could carry their own products in their own vehicles anywhere in the Community and that no member state should be able to set a limit to the number of such foreign vehicles that could be admitted to its territory. In respect of hire and reward vehicles, however, the Commission's original proposals were more complicated. This form of transport has been governed by agreements between the administrative authorities of member states. They have been typically bilateral in character in that each state has laid down the number and load capacity of vehicles from the other state which it would allow on its territory at any one time. Broadly speaking, the Commission concluded that the quotas had not been expanded to the extent corresponding to the growth of trade between the member states concerned. The Commission therefore proposed, firstly, that bilateral quotas should be enlarged in conformity with the growth of inter-state trade. Secondly, that the bilateral licences should be progressively faded out. As the bilateral licences disappeared the Community licences would come into existence at a rate sufficient (a) to compensate for the disappearance of the bilateral licences, and (b) to cope with the growth of intra-Community trade. The new body of licences was to be termed the Community Quota. A French holder of such a licence could, for example, carry a load from Paris to Brussels. At Brussels he could discharge his load and take on another for Duisburg, and at Duisburg he could take on goods for Milan, and so forth.

In the case of national road transport for hire and reward

the Commission recognized that all member states limited entry by licensing. The Commission did not propose to eliminate the licensing system and to that extent it implied that a management element would continue. The Action Programme did, however, propose a harmonization and modification of national licensing practices. The modification would be designed to increase the flexibility of national licensing systems. In practice the Commission held the view that licence-quota policy had been restrictive and had given rise to relatively high rates.

Three further aspects of the transport policy require mention. The first is that Article 7 of the Rome Treaty requires that there shall be no discrimination on grounds of nationality, and in Article 79 this is reiterated in the case of transport. Secondly, we have already referred to the Rome Treaty's attack on state aids, and Article 80 reiterates this by prohibiting support rates. The latter are favourable transport rates designed to assist particular enterprises or industries (there are, however, exceptions to the prohibition of support rates). Thirdly, the Commission deems it important that there shall be some co-ordination of national transport network planning. In other words, it is desirable that member states constructing motorways to the same stretch of a common frontier should not end up with the roads terminating five miles apart!

Policy achievements

Progress in constructing a common policy in transport has been slow, particularly when compared with the vast achievements in agriculture. One of the first developments was the promulgation in 1960 of a Regulation relating to the prohibition of discrimination. This began to take effect on 1 July 1961. The ban on support tariffs came into effect in January 1962 with the entry into the second stage of the transition period. The Commission has, as part of its day-to-day activity, been exercising a continuous supervision over transport rates in order to enforce Articles 79 and 80. It is also relevant to mention the right of establishment which means, for example, that a firm in one member state can set up in the road transport business in another. A firm so setting up would of course have to face the fact that licences are not freely available on request.

In 1964 the Council of Ministers also issued a Regulation relating to infrastructure costs. This provided for an inquiry relating to the year 1966. The Regulation required that the Commission should submit to the Council of Ministers a report together with a study of the way infrastructure costs were met and proposals for a uniform system of assessing and distributing them.

In the case of own-account road transport, when the Commission came to review the situation, it found national road transport arrangements were fairly close to what it desired. In the case of international own-account activity, the situation was from the beginning relatively liberal and in 1964 the Commission was able to secure the Council of Ministers' approval to complete liberalization. Also in 1964 the Council of Ministers reached agreement on a Community Quota. The basis of the agreement was that the Community Quota and the adaptation of bilateral quotas were to come into operation on 1 January 1966. The Community Quota was to operate for the four years 1966 to 1969 and this was to be an experimental period. The quota for 1966 was to consist of 880 authorizations divided as follows: West Germany 210, France 210, the Netherlands 176, Italy 142, Belgium 118 and Luxembourg 42. The division of the total quota for the years 1967-9 was to be decided subsequently. Criteria to be applied in apportioning the licences included the development of trade and the use made of the authorizations. No state would suffer an absolute fall in its allocation. Simultaneously with the establishment of the Community Quota, existing bilateral quotas would be adapted to transport needs by means of negotiations between member states. No actual Council Regulation emerged as a result of this accord, since the agreement of the French was contingent upon a solution being found to the rate-bracket issue. Before leaving this subject we might mention that the Community Quota agreement departed from the Commission's original proposals in a number of ways. One was that whereas the Commission envisaged the disappearance of the bilateral quotas, the

1964 accord envisaged their retention and adaptation to current needs. The Community content was therefore whittled down.

In 1965 the Council also reached agreement on tariffication and thus appeared to bring to an end a long period of stalemate. The French abandoned the principle that tariff brackets should be applied to all forms of transport and the Dutch agreed to a system of publicity. The agreement was as follows. During stage one, which it was proposed would last for three years from 1 January 1967, the rate-bracket system would apply to international transport only. There would in fact be two forms of rate-bracket system – compulsory and reference. International road traffic, that is, for journeys of more than fifty kilometres, would come under the compulsory system. The latter system would also apply to international rail transport. In respect of rail traffic, however, it would be possible to conclude special contracts where these were required to counter competition from other transport media. For international inland waterway traffic, on the other hand, the reference system would apply. The reference bracket was so called because it would serve as a guide to enterprises as to the rates they ought to charge. It would not, however, be compulsory to charge rates equal to or within the brackets. If enterprises charged rates outside the brackets details would have to be published, whereas if they charged rates within the brackets no publication would be required. Both compulsory and reference brackets were to be published. In stage two, which would last from 1 January 1969 to 1 January 1972, the bracket system would be applied to domestic transport as well. The arrangements for international traffic would be the same as in stage one, with the important difference that the reference-rate system would be applicable to heavy merchandise. For the rest of domestic transport, member states would be able to choose between the compulsory and reference systems. The publicity arrangements would continue to apply. During the final stage, beginning in 1972, the whole system of rate brackets would be reviewed.

Ironically, this agreement was concluded just before the French decided to boycott the Community. No formal regulation therefore emerged, and as a result the accord on the Community

Quota was not implemented either. But the return of the French did not lead to progress. The discussion of details arising out of the 1965 agreement lead to deadlock, mainly because of continuing differences between the Six on the degree of market regulation required. The Dutch wished to see a more liberal régime than some of the other member states. However, in December 1967 the Council met and decided that the stalemate could not continue any longer. It decided that regulations covering important areas of policy should be agreed by mid-1968. The Council was probably galvanized into activity by signs that at least one member state was proposing to take action which was likely to create even greater divergences between national policies. Late in 1967 the West German Government published the Leber Plan which was aimed at reducing road congestion and drastically reducing the German railway deficit. In January 1968 the Commission urged the West German Government to modify the plan. In particular the Commission considered that the proposed tax on road haulage and the ban on the road carriage of certain goods should be abandoned.

In July 1968 the Council adopted a series of regulations. One related to the Community Quota, or Community Passport as it is now called. The Council agreed that up to the end of 1971 1,200 Community licences should be issued. These licences would be divided as follows: West Germany 286, France 286, the Netherlands 240, Italy 194, Belgium 161 and Luxembourg 33. Secondly, the Council adopted a regulation introducing for a limited period a tariff-bracket system for international road transport. The appropriate authorities were to publish fixed upper and lower brackets with a maximum spread of 23 per cent below the ceiling level. Goods had to be carried at these rates. Private contracts could be concluded outside the published brackets. These private contracts, which had to be immediately notified to the authorities, could be concluded for limited periods of time for consignments exceeding 500 metric tons per three months. Competitive conditions had to exist. If there was a disturbance in the transport market all private contracts could, for a set period, require the prior approval of the authorities. Both of these arrangements have been renewed – the Community

Passport provision has been extended to include the new Community members.

Regulations have also been adopted in the field of harmonization. One relates to tax-free entry of fuel in vehicle tanks. The other relates to conditions of employment of lorry drivers and specifies the age of drivers in relation to the size of vehicles, as well as maximum driving hours, and rest periods.

The Council also declared that the rules of competition contained in Articles 85 and 86 should apply to transport. (From 1962 to 1968, despite the Commission's view that the competition rules applied to transport, the Council refused to bring such activity within the ambit of the anti-trust rules.) In line with the Treaty, the Council regulation envisages situations in which agreements can be permitted. For example, agreements may be upheld if they bring stability to markets subject to major fluctuations.

In 1969 the Council took a further step towards establishing a common policy. It adopted a regulation providing for the normalization of railway accounts under common rules for the granting of subsidies. The Council also decided that some categories of subsidy should be progressively eliminated. The Ministers also agreed on a common definition of the obligations that governments could impose on road, rail and inland waterway transport in return for subsidies.

It is thus apparent that in 1968 the Six began to make some progress towards a common policy. But it is equally evident that much still remained to be achieved.

A new policy approach

The enlargement of the Community has provided the conditions for a change of policy. As a result of changes within the Commission itself arising from the accession of three new members there is now a new Commissioner and a new Director-General in the Transport Directorate. Not surprisingly a new policy has begun to emerge. The nature of the new policy was revealed in 1973 when the Commission adopted its 'Communication from the Commission to the Council on the Development of the Common Transport Policy'. The Communication concedes that the 'common transport policy has not made striking progress in recent years ...' and notes that the original conception of the 1961 Memorandum was that transport users should benefit from the advantages of competition. This is an interesting statement. To a degree it is true but a truly free competition system as between modes and undertakings is hardly consistent with the rate-bracket system. We may therefore take it that this statement is a piece of policy designed to reassure the Council that there will be some continuity between the approach of the future and that of the past. In fact the future policy is intended to be much more oriented towards competition than hitherto. A number of statements in the Communication seem to indicate that prices should progressively be left to find their own level under conditions of inter-modal and inter-undertaking competition. Intervention at the market level should progressively decline over time and be undertaken only in times of real crisis. The main intervention of the authorities should be designed to see that competition achieves the proper results. This can only be achieved (a) if infrastructure costs are brought into the pricing decisions of modes and undertakings; (b) if conditions of competition (hours of work, size of crews, taxation etc.) are harmonized; and (c) if environmental factors in the broadest sense are taken into account.

At this stage, since the policy has not yet unfolded, only two comments will be ventured. The first is that the policy has much to commend it as a logical economic approach. It clearly disassociates itself from such doubtful devices of the past as rate-brackets which, in terms of economic analysis, were never fully justified. The other point is that although it has a logic to it, the policy, with its emphasis on infrastructure costs and marginal social cost pricing, will not be easy to implement.

The common energy policy

Progress in this field has been limited. There are four reasons for this. Firstly, the responsibility for energy matters has been a divided one. The Paris Treaty placed responsibility for coal fairly and squarely on the shoulders of the ECSC. The Rome Treaty established that oil, natural gas, hydro-power and electric current were the province of the EEC. The task of dealing with nuclear power was assigned to Euratom. Secondly, none of the three Treaties contains a word about a common energy policy or even lays down a timetable for its elaboration. In some degree this fact is a reflection of the circumstances of the time when the Treaties were drafted. They all belong to the period when coal was the major source of energy in the Six. (In 1950 it met almost 75 per cent of the primary energy needs of the Community.) The main problem then was guaranteeing that the supply of coal was available, firstly on non-discriminatory terms to all Community purchasers, and secondly at reasonable prices. The latter meant the Six had to address themselves to the problems of the coal cartels, in particular the Ruhr cartels of which Georg was the most notorious. The decline of coal, the emergence of associated regional difficulties, together with the growing dependence on imported sources of energy, were problems of the future and were not then foreseen. The third reason for lack of progress is the involved nature of the problem. Governments, even in liberal economies, tend to get caught up in regulating the energy market. The Six were no exception – the regional problem, state monopolies, nationalized undertakings and fiscal policy are just a few of the complicating elements. The fourth reason has also been connected with governments. Their pursuit of national self-interest has made it difficult to achieve a common policy. This concern to defend national interests has been evident from the beginning but it became even more marked in the oil crisis of 1973 which we shall turn to later.

The need for a common policy – 1956–1973

One of the most frequently quoted arguments about the issue of a common energy policy related to the distortions which arose in the absence of such a policy. National energy policies exhibited significant differences and these affected the price of energy in national markets. For example, member states differed in the taxes which they imposed on fuel oil and in respect of the tariffs and quota arrangements for imported coal. Because energy constituted a significant proportion of the total cost of producing some goods, these differences could and did lead to serious distortions of the competitive process. An illustration of the possibility of distortion is provided by the fact that in steel production direct and indirect energy procurements constitute 26 per cent of the total value of the product. In chemicals, nonferrous metals, transport and building materials (including glass), the figures are 16, 15, 14 and 12 per cent respectively (European Coal and Steel Community, 1967, p. 11).

The second reason for a Community policy was connected with the increased competition which coal encountered, particularly from oil. This threw up a series of issues including unemployment and regional decline, the problem of the security and stability of energy supplies as the Community became steadily more dependent on imported sources, and the likely long-term evolution of the price of imported energy sources.

An appreciation of this set of interrelated issues requires that we go back in time to the first half of the 1950s. In this period there was a coal shortage, which in turn prompted users to do two things. They sought to economize in the use of coal; for example, the steel industry succeeded in developing techniques which curtailed heat losses. They also began to turn to substitutes – in practice this usually meant oil. However, this tendency to take decisions against coal was masked by the rapid economic growth of the period. Indeed, when in 1956 the O E E C produced the Hartley Report (*Europe's Growing Needs of Energy – How Can They Be Met ?*), the essential message was that there was a danger of a possible shortage of energy in Europe. Stress was also laid on the balance-of-payments problems inherent in dependence on imported energy. The Suez crisis appeared to vindicate this view since the immediate effect was rising prices stemming from high ocean freight rates for imported oil and coal. But the picture soon changed. The major oil companies, in order to cope with the growing demand, embarked on a programme of expanded production. They also began to diversify the areas in which they were prospecting and in so doing discovered substantial new reserves. In addition, the majors were joined by new companies who sought to carve out a place for themselves in the world market by offering low prices. The U S Government also played a part. In order to protect the home market it applied import quotas and as a result the bulk of the increased supplies flowed to markets such as Western Europe. Moreover, the Soviet Government decided during this period to resume selling Russian oil in the world market. Then again, imported oil gained the advantage of lower freight rates arising from major economies in transportation as a result of the use of bigger and faster ships.

The result of all this was that coal's competitive position deteriorated drastically. After 1956 the price of oil fell and there-after stayed low, whereas the price of domestically produced coal (despite a great increase in mechanization and in output per manshift) climbed steadily upwards. The position in 1956 and 1965 is shown in Table 7.

The effect of oil (and natural gas) on coal's position was dramatic. As we have indicated, coal was responsible for almost three quarters of the Community's primary energy supplies in 1950 and petroleum contributed 10 per cent. By 1966 coal had fallen to 38 per cent and petroleum had risen to 45 per cent. The rapid rise in the energy requirements of the Community was met by oil, whereas between 1957 and 1966 coal production fell by 12 per cent, the mining labour force below ground fell by 24 per cent and the number of pits in operation by 42 per cent.

Table 7 **Comparative price movements of imported coal and oil and community coal ($ per ton)**

	Community coal*	Imported US coal†	Imported crude oil‡
1956	12·53	21·60	20·30
1965	16·68	14·20	16·40

*Ruhr bituminous (schedule ex-mine).
†American coking fines c.i.f. Amsterdam/Rotterdam/Antwerp.
‡Kuwait crude c.i.f. Naples.
Source: European Coal and Steel Community (1967, pp. 27–8).

This evolution presented the Community with three main problems. Firstly, there was the resulting unemployment. The problem would not have been so difficult if the employment in coal mining had been evenly spread; unfortunately it was con-centrated in pockets and this gave rise to the threat of a severe regional problem. The unemployment problem would of course have been more tractable if the rate of decline of coal had even been merely arrested. Secondly, there was the fact that unlike other major economic blocs (the USSR and USA), the Community was highly dependent on imported supplies of energy and was becoming more so. This raised the question of the stability and security of supplies. Had there been a major political upheaval in areas mainly responsible for the supply of energy to the Community the consequences could have been disastrous. The need for security and stability of supplies provided an argument for supporting indigenous sources. There were, of course, other approaches to the problem such as stockpiling oil and diversifying oil supplies. (The discovery of oil and gas in the North Sea did promise to help to alleviate this problem.) Thirdly, there was the question of the long-term evolution of the world energy market. In 1962 the West European coal producers and the National Coal Board produced a memorandum (*Meeting Europe's Energy Requirements*) which argued that by the mid 1970s there would be a world shortage of energy and that in this light the prices ruling in the early 1960s were only temporarily low. They argued that it would therefore be prudent to keep mines in production. Subsidies would be required in the short term but in the longer term the energy price-level would rise and coal mining would become economic. There could be no question of closing the mines down in the short run and opening them up later since mining communities would have dispersed and the source of labour would be lost for ever. Also the mines would flood and the cost of bringing them back into production would be extremely high. Sinking new pits would be extremely costly, and it has to be borne in mind that there could be a gap of ten to fifteen years between starting to sink a pit and reaching a high rate of production.

A common energy policy: the first steps

In 1964 the ECSC took the first step along the road to a common energy policy when the Council of Ministers formally adopted the Protocol of Agreement on energy policy. This laid down certain broad objectives – cheapness of supply, security of supply, fair conditions of competition among the different sources of energy, and freedom of choice for consumers. The Protocol did not generally lay down details of policy but in the case of coal it did call for the speedy implementation of a co-ordinated system of state aids or subsidies. It is perhaps worth noting that in the case of coal the Community chose subsidies whereas in agriculture the task of rendering Community production profitable was achieved by a different route. In other words, it was decided that coal would be rendered competitive not by raising the price of imported oil to meet the price of coal but by enabling Community producers to supply their output at a price less than would otherwise be the case. The Community has indeed opted for a low-cost energy policy. There can be no doubt that this was the easiest path to pursue. Firstly, the Community was merely recognizing what was already happening, namely that as coal felt the impact of the competition from oil, member states were, in the interests of security and regional policy, granting their collieries half-concealed subsidies. The Protocol was therefore an open recognition of what had been happening anyway. Secondly, states such as Italy, which relied heavily on imported oil, would have strongly resisted any policy which raised their industrial costs.

It will therefore be appreciated that the Protocol envisaged a Community system of state aids or subsidies to the coal mines. This implies some co-ordination. Since subsidies were explicitly forbidden by the Paris Treaty it also required the invoking of Article 95 which allowed the High Authority to take special decisions 'in all cases not expressly provided for in the Treaty' when this appeared 'necessary to fulfil one of the Objectives of the Community'. The basic principle of co-ordination was that measures of aid by member states should be scrutinized by the High Authority. The latter would have the power to authorize them on the basis of Community criteria. These criteria included assessment of the degree to which the aids enabled the mines to adjust to the new market situation, the degree to which they assisted in preventing unemployment and economic disturbance and the degree to which competitive behaviour between mines was distorted. In particular, the High Authority had to direct its scrutiny towards two kinds of aid. One was contributions towards the social security costs of mining firms. The change in the manpower situation had led to these becoming excessive and the High Authority had to ensure that assistance did no more than defray the abnormal costs of social security and did not act as a positive subsidy which would put some mines at an advantage as compared with others. The other kind of aid was that made available for rationalization. The High Authority was given the power to authorize such subsidies in so far as they enabled mines to adjust to the new market conditions and did not distort competition between mines. Rationalization aid could take the form of assistance to enable mines to be closed, to improve the efficiency and productivity of mining enterprises and to help meet the cost of recruitment, training and retraining. The possibility was also envisaged that mining areas might be so badly affected by the competition from oil that serious disturbances were possible. In such cases extra aid was possible.

Two points are worthy of note. Firstly, although a Community aid system was envisaged this did not extend to Community financing. The cost of subsidies was to be borne by national exchequers. It could be argued that Community finance was appropriate. For example, in so far as keeping coal mines in production is dictated by the security-of-supply argument, why should Italy be able to enjoy the advantage of cheap oil imports and be allowed to avoid the cost of coal subsidies and yet be able to turn back to coal on non-discriminatory terms if oil supplies became inadequate or oil prices rose steeply? The second point is that at no time did the Council of Ministers take a decision on the amount of coal which was to be kept in production. However, the High Authority did in 1966 propose that the Community should guarantee outlets for 190 million tons of coal in 1970. By so doing the Community would keep the proportion of energy requirements met from Community sources close to 50 per cent. One way of doing this was to place quantitative restrictions on coal imports. Another was to subsidize domestic coal used by the iron and steel industry.

In 1966, however, a Community element did creep into the subsidy system. This arose in connection with coking coal. The impetus for this move were the difficulties arising from the import of cheap American coal. Because there is no common external tariff or common commercial policy under the Paris Treaty, member states are free to protect their coal industries, or alternatively to import coal at world prices. To the extent that member states tended to import American coal two effects were apparent. One was that countries such as the Netherlands and Italy which had sited their steel plants on the coast were in a good position to take advantage of these cheap supplies. On the other hand, West German iron and steel enterprises were highly dependent on the higher-priced domestic supplies. This distorted conditions of competition within the Community iron and steel market. The other effect was that cheap imported coal contributed towards a further erosion of the position of Community coal producers. The High Authority therefore proposed a subsidy for Community coking coal and coke. It was argued in justification that if no subsidy were given intra-Community imports would dry up as industry switched to imported supplies, and that the subsidy would help to buttress the domestic industry. Opposition was encountered from the French but in 1967 the Council of Ministers agreed to a subsidy system. Where coking coal and furnace coal produced in a particular member state was delivered to the steel industry of that state, the subsidies would be paid by the member state Government concerned. For coking coal and coke entering into intra-Community trade the subsidies (which were to be limited in size) were to be financed from two sources. The producing country had to meet 40 per cent of the cost; the other 60 per cent was borne by a common fund. The Six contributed to the latter as follows: West Germany 28 per cent, France 28 per cent, Italy 14 per cent, Belgium 11 per cent, the Netherlands 10 per cent and Luxembourg 9 per cent. The ceiling for subsidies on intra-Community trade was to be twenty-two million units of account.

The 1968 initiative

In December 1968 the new fourteen-man Commission presented a memorandum to the Council of Ministers entitled 'First guidelines for a Community energy policy' (EEC Commission, 1968a). This was an attempt to put new impetus behind the search for a common policy. The document was extremely detailed and the following description should be taken as an account only of its most striking features. The policy sought to achieve the same aims as the Protocol. Apart from freedom of choice for consumers and fair competition between energy suppliers, the essential aims were stability, security and cheapness of supplies. The memorandum implicitly admitted that up to a point there was some conflict between these latter aims.

The Commission recognized the existence of distortions. It therefore proposed that the solution to this problem was the full implementation of the Rome Treaty in the energy field. Freedom of movement of supplies should be achieved within the Community; this meant the elimination of impediments, whether they were state monopolies or technical obstacles. Differences in taxes were one distorting factor; the specific solution was the harmonization of consumer taxes on energy products and of taxes on hydro-carbon fuel, in conjunction with the elaboration of the common transport policy. Whilst on the subject of the establishment of a real common market in the energy sector, we might note that the Commission called for the full implementation of the freedom of establishment and the freedom to supply services.

Security of supplies called for action in a number of energy fields, particularly coal and oil. The memorandum recognized that the domestic coal production necessary to ensure security could not be achieved without a co-ordinated import policy. In the light of past High Authority pronouncements this probably meant that the Community needed a common commercial policy which set quantitative limits to coal imports. The memorandum also noted the need for aids to the coal mines, while recognizing that production needed to be concentrated in the most efficient mines. It called for the introduction of Community aid arrangements (since Community co-ordination already existed this probably referred to the need for Community financing) and for better co-ordination of existing Community aid with national aids. In the field of oil, adequate stockpiles were one way to achieve security. The memorandum also called for a Community supply policy and programme. Undoubtedly the intention here was that the Community should watch the pattern of oil imports in order to guarantee that it was sufficiently diversified. If the Community was not satisfied with the pattern, the memorandum proposed that suitable procedures for remedying the situation should be evolved. The Community would also be constantly considering the supply possibilities open to them, the risks of interruption and the methods of coping with them.

The Commission also proposed that the ECSC principle of drawing up general objectives (i.e. forecasts of the evolution of demand) should be applied not only to coal but to the whole of the energy sector, particularly in order to guarantee that investment kept pace with the rapidly rising demand for energy. The ECSC principle of notification of investment projects (which has been operational since the inception of the Paris Treaty in respect of coal and steel) should also be generally applicable in the energy sector. Opinions should be rendered on investment projects, and Community control would be tightened if experience showed that recommendations were being ignored.

The Commission also saw the need to maintain competition in energy supply. Since some enterprises already occupied a dominant position in the market for oil, natural gas and nuclear fuels, the Commission proposed that there should be a notification system, together with a period of suspension of action, where mergers were contemplated. This would enable the Commission to voice an opinion. The possibility of preventive control was contemplated in this field. The Commission also suggested *a posteriori* notification of the prices obtaining in the market for energy. This was, no doubt, particularly intended to put the oil industry on a par with the coal industry which, under the Paris Treaty rules, was required to publish its price lists.

In November 1969 the Council of Ministers approved the basic outlines of the 1968 memorandum and asked the Commission to submit the most pressing proposals as soon as possible. In practice not a great deal emerged. In December 1968 the Council adopted two directives requiring member states to hold oil stocks equal to 65 days' consumption. (The Commission proposed that this should be increased to 90 days as from 1 January 1975.) National governments, and not the Commission, can commandeer these stocks if a crisis arises. In December 1970 the Commission submitted a draft directive to the Council designed to bring into line taxes on petroleum fuels in the various states. This has not yet been adopted. In January 1972, as a result of the pressure of oil-producing countries for substantially higher prices, the Council adopted two regulations under which member states must notify the Commission of investment plans for oil, natural gas and electricity, and of import programmes for oil and gas. The Commission sought direct notification but in practice, other than in periods of crisis, the process takes place through the member states. These two regulations do not give the Commission any power of action in the energy field but they are designed to provide the necessary information on which a common policy could be built – given the goodwill of the member states. These are the main fruits of the 1968 initiative.

The oil crisis of 1973

Even before the crisis of 1973 there were signs that a new energy situation was about to emerge. This was apparent from the activities of the oil producers organized in the Organization of Petroleum Exporting Countries (O P E C) who, as we have noted above, were pressing for a higher price for oil. This posed a danger to the Community since it had become increasingly dependent on imported oil. By 1971 the Six derived only 20 per cent of their energy from coal and 60·8 per cent from oil. (The position of the Nine in the year prior to enlargement was very similar, the figures being 24·8 per cent and 58·4 per cent respectively.)

It was, however, the Yom Kippur war of 1973 which precipitated the crisis. The war involved the Arabs using their control over oil supplies as a weapon to force other states, including the Nine, the United States and Japan, to bring pressure to bear on Israel. Supplies of oil were reduced and in the case of the Netherlands (and the U S) supplies of Arab oil were totally cut off. This precipitated a crisis within the Community since the threat was that if the other eight countries supplied the Netherlands and undermined the blockade they themselves were likely to be exposed to blockade treatment. The conception of a free market in oil and oil products within the Community was a major victim of the Middle East conflict. The answer of the Nine seems to have been not to call the bluff of the Arab oil suppliers by openly declaring their intention to supply the Dutch, but rather to adopt what may be termed a 'low profile' policy – it was anticipated, particularly by the French and British, that patient diplomacy would be more productive of a satisfactory resolution. It is noticeable that the Nine in their November 1973 statement on the solution to the Israeli–Arab conflict adopted a stance which was distinctly favourable to the Arab cause.

The use of supply cuts as a weapon was accompanied by dramatic increases in the posted price of crude oil. Gulf crude oil which had been $3.01 per barrel up to October 1973 was marked up to $5.11 in the same month but by January 1974 it had escalated to $11.65. Libyan oil rose from $4.60 in October to almost $9.00 in the same month and by January 1974 this had become $18.76. The posted price of oil from the major producing areas had increased by very approximately 400 per cent. Initially this was taken to be a temporary problem – a device to secure a satisfactory settlement in the Middle East after which prices would return to normality. However, it soon transpired that these new price levels were to be maintained in the long term. The argument ran that this was a fair price – oil had not previously kept pace with the inflation in the price of industrial goods produced by countries in Western Europe, North America and Japan. It was the fact that major OPEC producers (the Middle East alone possesses about three fifths of the world's proven oil reserves) intended to maintain permanently this high price level which constituted the revolution in the facts facing energy policy-makers in the Nine. At the same time the view gained ground that the whole world was in any case moving into a period of energy shortage – even oil had a limited life as a major source of energy. It should be added that some of the factors which had helped to create the glut of oil in the sixties were no longer operative. For example, the US was now a net importer of oil.

At this point we may pause and consider the kind of response which the Community could have made to the new situation. First we must note the fundamental change in the problem. The facts of the sixties were that oil was getting cheaper and coal dearer, in absolute and relative terms. A central feature of energy policy was the subsidizing of coal and the emphasis in Community policy was on the harmonization of subsidies to avoid distortions, at least gross distortions, of competition. This did not prevent coal production in the Six from falling, contrary to what the West European coal producers (with their forecast of a world energy shortage in the mid-seventies) wanted. Coal production fell from 239,000 metric tons in 1960 to 165,000 in 1971. Nevertheless the policy of subsidization helped to limit the decline of coal production and the associated increasing dependence on imported energy. But in the new circumstances of late 1973 the protection of coal ceased to be a problem. Coal became highly competitive. In calorific terms the cost of coal was probably only one third that of oil. It could therefore be argued that the output of coal should be increased. New pits should be opened up. Capital should be invested in the industry in order to increase output. Since coal is a *Community* energy resource (under the Paris Treaty), if those countries with the coal reserves need capital to expand and modernize the industry then the capital-providing agencies of the Nine should be set to work to provide the funds.

The policy of diversification of supplies would obviously have to be maintained. At this point it is worth noting how well founded that policy has proved to be. In the past the main threat was seen to be the potential instability of the Middle East. Two wars – the Six Day and the Yom Kippur Wars – vindicated the fear of vulnerability. What was perhaps less clearly seen was the danger of being in the hands of a monopoly supplier of oil in the shape of OPEC. The fact that OPEC and its influence embraces producers outside the Middle East makes diversification more difficult. To be successful diversification of supply would require that a substantial supply of energy be obtained not from outside the Middle East but from outside OPEC. Obviously the main thrust of a diversification policy would be (a) the development of indigenous sources – coal, North Sea oil, natural gas, and atomic energy, and (b) access to oil supplies which emanated from, for example, North America (on the assumption that such supplies were independent of OPEC influences). The development of more advanced forms of atomic energy generation was also imperative in the long run given that oil has in any case a limited life. Active collaboration to speed research in the atomic energy field would seem an obvious priority. The third element should consist of seeking to match the monopoly power of OPEC by some form of equivalent buying or monopsony power.

A common energy policy would also involve a policy of maintaining adequate stocks of oil (and coal) – the decision to hold stocks of oil equal to sixty-five days' consumption had been vindicated and the ninety day proposal of the Commission ought to be adopted as soon as possible. A common policy would also address itself to the elimination of distortions arising from differences in taxes, pricing rules etc. – this was referred to at the beginning of this account and would continue to be an essential element of policy.

Against this possible common energy policy scenario, how has the Community responded? The Copenhagen Summit (December 1973) marked the first step. This was to be a meeting designed for quiet reflection but the energy crisis supervened and the Foreign Affairs Ministers of six Arab oil-producing countries descended on Copenhagen. The Summit communiqué declared as follows:

The Heads of State or Government considered that the situation produced by the energy crisis is a threat to the world economy as a whole, affecting not only developed but also developing countries. A prolonged scarcity of energy resources would have grave effects on production, employment and balances of payment within the Community.

The Heads of State or Government therefore agree on the necessity for the Community of taking immediate and effective action along the following lines:

The Council should adopt at its session of 17/18 December 1973 the Community instruments which will enable the Commission to establish by 15 January 1974, comprehensive energy balance sheets covering all relevant aspects of the energy situation in the Community.

The Commission should on this basis proceed to examine all present or foreseeable repercussions of the energy supply situation on production, employment, prices and balances of payments as well as on the development of monetary reserves.

The Heads of State or Government ask the Commission to present by 31 January 1974, proposals on which the Council will be invited to decide as quickly as possible and in principle before 28 February 1974, to ensure the orderly functioning of the common market for energy.

In this context the Commission is asked to submit to the Council as quickly as possible for rapid decisions, proposals aimed at resolving in a concerted manner the problems raised by the developing energy crisis.

For the same reasons they asked the Council to adopt provisions to ensure that all member states introduce on a concerted and equitable basis measures to limit energy consumption.

With a view to securing the energy supplies of the Community, the Council will adopt a comprehensive Community programme on alternative sources of energy. This programme will be designed to promote a diversification of supplies by developing existing resources, accelerating research into new sources of energy and creating new capacities of production notably a European capacity for enrichment of Uranium, seeking the concerted harmonious development of existing projects.

The Heads of State or Government confirmed the importance of entering into negotiations with oil-producing countries on comprehensive arrangements comprising co-operation on a wide scale for the economic and industrial development of these countries, industrial investments, and stable energy supplies to the member countries at reasonable prices.

They furthermore considered it useful to study with other oil-consuming countries within the framework of the OECD, ways of dealing with the common short- and long-term energy problems of consumer countries.

The Council should establish at its session of 17/18 December 1973, an Energy Committee of Senior Officials which is responsible for implementing the energy policy measures adopted by the Council.

The Council at its meeting later in December immediately took up the problem of energy referred to it by the Summit but quickly encountered a difficulty – the UK decided to block the formal approval of measures in the energy field (this was lifted in January 1974). It elected not to co-operate until adequate action had been taken in the field of regional policy in connection with the setting up of a Regional Development Fund. Nevertheless agreement in principle was recorded in respect of the production by the Commission of energy balance sheets and the establishment of an Energy Committee.

On the question of harmonization the Commission proposed

(January 1974) a system for supervising oil prices. This was thought necessary because in some states oil price-control powers exist whilst others operate under free market conditions. Under conditions of shortage two possibilities could arise: prices in the free market states would rise without limit and cause distortions of competition; and speculative movements of oil could occur, with supplies shifting to high-price markets with a consequent shortfall of supplies in controlled markets. The Commission proposed that it should be notified of price levels and if exaggerated price differences or speculative movements occurred the Council could take appropriate action.

These represent the main *internal* policy responses by the Nine up to the end of January 1974. We turn now to the external aspect. The day before the Copenhagen Summit the American Secretary of State Dr Henry Kissinger had made a suggestion to the effect that the European countries, North America and Japan should create an 'Energy Action Group' to work out a policy of collaboration on energy – the Nine could participate as the Community. Later, in January 1974, President Nixon followed up the Kissinger initiative with an invitation to the members of the Community to attend a conference of Foreign Ministers in Washington. It was proposed that collaboration would in the first instance be established between industrialized oil consumers, but the President suggested that developing countries would also in due course be brought into the picture and this would then pave the way for discussions with the OPEC states. The Nixon letter indicated that one of the objectives would be 'to develop a concerted consumer position for a new era of petroleum consumer–producer relations which would meet the legitimate interests of oil-producing countries while assuring the consumer countries adequate supplies at fair and reasonable prices.' The Council of Ministers of the Nine responded by agreeing to attend: the Community would be represented by the Presidents of the Council and Commission – member states could also attend as individuals.

The Nixon initiative draws attention to a noticeable weakness in the Community's approach to the power of the OPEC producers, where the Community has not reacted as might have been hoped or expected. In the past the presence of an external threat has served to induce a high degree of common action. Indeed the early history of European integration was a response not only to the need to prevent internal strife but also to meet a potential threat from the East. But the pressure of the OPEC countries has not had the same effect; the Community has not sought to match OPEC's monopoly with a Community monopsony. In defence it could be argued, perhaps not wholly convincingly, that the Community does not constitute the sole buyer of oil and that a more cohesive arrangement would be one which included, for example, the US and Japan.

Critics of the Community have indeed pointed to a lack of cohesiveness in the Community's approach to the OPEC states. They criticize the blatant pursuit of self-interest evident in the French and British individual initiatives with Iran and Saudi Arabia, involving barter exchanges of industrial goods, technology, and in some cases arms, for oil. This has been widely condemned not least because such individual deals are likely to bid up the price of oil as compared with the terms likely to be obtained if a common and cool stand is maintained.

7 Regional and Social Policy

Regional policy
The rationale

Basically it can be argued that at the time when the E E C Treaty was drafted two broad sets of reasons could be adduced in favour of the Six pursuing an active regional policy. (Whether this was to be a Community or national responsibility we will discuss later.) The first was that prior to the effects of establishing the E E C substantial regional problems existed within the national economies of the Six. The second was that once the process of integration was under way it was not difficult to see that it was likely to exacerbate the already existing problem of regional disparities. (It could of course be added that if economic integration led to greater regional disparities then the process of political unification, which it was hoped would arise from economic integration, might be jeopardized. This political aspect was recognized in the formative days of the E E C and it is interesting to note that in the 1973 Thomson Report on regional problems this point was again highlighted.)

We shall not pursue in any great depth the nature of the regional problem as it existed in the early days of the E E C. Clearly this is largely a matter of history. The under-development of areas which were primarily agricultural was the main regional problem facing those who drafted the Rome Treaty. There was also the problem of older industrial regions where a decline of staple industries was taking place. It is however important to emphasize that whilst such problems existed when the Treaty was drafted this source of structural unemployment became more pronounced in the early sixties for reasons given below. A third problem also began to manifest itself in due course. This was the problem of congestion in certain regions – for example that around Paris.

The original and emerging problems

The classic under-development problem of the Community was the Italian Mezzogiorno. This was a region with a population of eighteen million (38 per cent of the Italian total) which comprised about half the land areas of the country. The Mezzogiorno consisted of the south (the regions of Abruzzi-Molise, Campania, Basilicata, Apulia and Calabria) together with the islands of Sicily and Sardinia. The 'southern problem' is best illustrated by statistics of income *per capita*. Within Italy itself there is a significant difference between the north and the south: Professor Saraceno (1965, p. 4) estimated the *per capita* income in the south to be 50 per cent of the national average and 40 per cent of the northern region's. The contrast with the Community as a whole was of course even starker. Professor Levi Sandri, writing in the same year, but referring to 1958, stated that the *per capita* income of the most favoured region in the Community (Hamburg) was about seven times the figure for the least favoured Italian region (Calabria) (Levi Sandri, 1965, p. 2).

Basically, the Mezzogiorno economy was founded on low-productivity subsistence agriculture. A considerable amount of effort and money has now been devoted to industrialization. The Cassa per il Mezzogiorno (Development Fund for the South) channelled vast sums into agricultural improvement and infrastructure investment and the state holding companies IRI and ENI were obliged to channel at least 40 per cent of their investment into the south. In spite of all this the regional take-off into sustained industrial growth had not taken place in the Mezzogiorno. The rapidly growing population has had to find much of its opportunity through emigration to the north and to other Community countries.

France provided the other example of persistent regional imbalances and major areas of under-development. These areas included central France (Massif Central), the south-west (Languedoc, Roussillon, Pyrenees and Aquitaine), Brittany and Lower Normandy, Corsica and the Alpine region (Savoy). It should be noted that whereas the Italian South was heavily populated, all these French regions (except Brittany and Lower Normandy) were lightly populated. The migration of population from these areas had brought little benefit to the local economies. The farms remained under-capitalized and migration had indeed deprived these regions of the more energetic citizens who were indispensable if progress of any kind was to be made. (By contrast the Paris region was prosperous. Its congestion and the resultant social costs were such that measures had to be taken to arrest its growth in order to channel development to the less favoured regions. Much of this was accomplished through the medium of the successive Plans.)

The other main problem of the Community, becoming more apparent in the sixties, related to the difficulties experienced in areas such as the Ruhr, the Sambre and Lorraine. These were areas which had been heavily industrialized for many years. Their prosperity was founded on iron ore reserves and coal, and the industries which were founded on these resources began in due course to feel the effects of competition. The domestic iron ore industry had to meet the competition from cheap imported supplies. The domestic iron and steel industry had to meet the competition from Japan and the newly industrialized countries. Coal of course faced the combined threat of oil and natural gas. Whether or not a severe regional problem develops depends on the rate of run-down of particular industries. In the Ruhr the relative efficiency of coal mining there meant a fairly small decline which could easily be offset by the growth of other sectors. In the case of the inefficient Belgian coal industries, however, where the pace of decline was rapid, severe regional problems were encountered, as for example in the Borinage.

Possible new problems arising from integration

When the process of economic integration began to operate a new set of forces were expected which could exacerbate some of the existing and emerging problems which we have already outlined.

A possible source of regional difficulty was the effects of competition. It was anticipated that the creation of the Common Market would stimulate greater efficiency, in that the more efficient enterprises would expand and the less efficient would contract. It was not inevitable that this would contribute to an aggravated regional problem in one country. A state might find one of its industries succumbing to international competition. But equally well it might have one or more industries which are simultaneously under the influence of the new opportunities created by the Common Market. Labour from the contracting industry would then move into the expanding industry or industries. Moreover, output per head in the expanding industry, particularly if it was a new one, might exceed output per head in the contracting industry, particularly if it was an old one. Employment prospects might therefore remain unchanged and income per head could rise. However, all this is based upon a number of assumptions which do not always hold. Industries are sometimes geographically concentrated either because of the existence of local supplies of raw materials and fuel or because of the external economies to which geographical concentration gives rise. Labour would therefore have to move to get new jobs and it has to be remembered that labour is not always highly mobile. Then again the unemployed labour force might be unskilled and unadaptable.

The classic case of the decline of a geographically concentrated industry within the Community as a result of competition was that of Belgian coal – this was, of course, an ECSC problem. The Belgian industry was divided into two zones, the Campine Basin in the north and the Southern Basin which was an extension of the French Nord/Pas-de-Calais field. The Southern Basin – the more important of the two – was particularly inefficient owing to a combination of poor geological conditions, old equipment and small pits. The pits of the Borinage were the most inefficient of all. Some indication of the inefficiency of the Southern Basin can be derived from the fact that in 1950 the output per man-shift (in kilogrammes) was 1075 whereas in the Ruhr, Saar and Lorraine the figures were 1486, 1676 and 2088 respectively. The Belgian coal industry was of course an extremely important source of employment. Not only did 10 per cent of the Belgian industrial labour force find employment in the industry but that employment was naturally concentrated on the coal fields. The decline in the fortunes of coal, particularly in the face of oil imports, therefore posed a grave regional problem for Belgium. Inevitably, if the Community coal industry had to contract, it was the high-cost sector which was most likely to bear the brunt. This is indeed what happened. Whereas between 1956 and 1966 German and French output fell by 16 per cent and 9 per cent respectively, Belgian output fell by 41 per cent. This development was somewhat ironic. Traditionally the problem area of Belgium was Flanders where agriculture was the predominant occupation and incomes relatively low. The Wolloon area on the other hand enjoyed a prosperity founded on coal and steel. But as a result of the decline of coal the Wolloon area suffered a setback whilst new industries moved into the Flemish region and greatly improved the local income levels.

A second way in which regional difficulties could arise out of economic integration was connected with factor price equalization. As we have already noted the EEC in principle called for the free movement of factors of production. As the Community achieved this objective a tendency was likely to arise for the earnings of factors to be equalized between states much in the same way that this takes place within states. Thus capital would tend to flow from areas where its remuneration was low to where its remuneration was high, and vice versa, until differences were eliminated. Labour, though much less mobile, might be expected to tend to do likewise. But in the case of labour, factors other than pure market forces might also operate. For example, just as within states we tend to find national rather than regional wage rates and bargaining, so in the Community there could be a tendency for wage rates to be equalized between states through the comparability principle. In so far as such equalization tends to take place, it has been argued that the earnings of capital and labour will approximate to what the most productive industries can pay. Whereas enterprises at the centre, where production conditions are favourable, will be able to pay the equalized rate, enterprises in the peripheral areas, away from the centres of population and sources of raw material, will find that costs of production are relatively high and they will not be able to pay the rate. As a result unless firms located in the peripheral areas received subsidies, the industries located there would tend to decline.

There were other factors which were likely to be important. A glance at the map of the original Six quickly reveals that the most highly developed regions formed a bloc of concentrated economic activity centred on the Rhine–Rhone axis extending from the Netherlands in the north to northern Italy in the south. In 1963 the Birkelbach Report to the European Parliament estimated that this area covered about 35 per cent of the land area of the Community but accounted for 45 per cent of its population and about 60 per cent of its Gross Product. Inevitably, the question arose as to whether a far-reaching process of economic integration would lead to an acceleration of this concentration to the detriment of the relatively peripheral regions. It was not difficult to recognize certain polarization factors at work. Thus some industries, in determining their location, would be drawn towards a market, and this could imply a position close to the Rhine–Rhone axis. Then again the central axis created external economies – for example, a skilled labour force and a disposition to accept the disciplines of industrial employment, not to mention the services of specialist commercial and financial institutions. It was easy to see these polarization factors at work but there was no evidence of any automatic balancing dispersal factor, except that full employment at the centre might eventually drive industry out into the peripheral regions. That is to say, the demand for labour might have an inflationary effect upon wage rates and earnings and land might become extremely scarce and expensive. However, the experience of the UK, with its growing concentration of industry in the Midlands and south east of England, gave little hope of any such automatic corrective tendency. The magnetic influence of the Paris region in France similarly suggested that a dispersal factor was not likely to arise spontaneously.

Earlier we stressed the role of regional policy in the process of interaction between economic and political unity. It was not difficult to see that the prospects for political unity would be severely jeopardized if the economic policy of the Community did not tackle the problem of the disparities in income per head between the member states and between regions within member states. To put it another way, the success of the Community as a durable political entity could not be guaranteed if the arrangement was seen as benefiting some states or areas at the expense, or to the exclusion, of others. The latter point gathers added force when it is remembered that economic difficulties could be accentuated by political, linguistic, cultural and religious divisions. Economic differences could then fan the flames of separatism based on these latter factors.

Community regional instruments under the Rome Treaty

When we consider such policies as agriculture and transport we see that there are separate Titles (i.e. groups of Articles relating to a policy problem) within the Rome Treaty devoted to these subjects. The Titles call for common policies (in some cases detailing their nature) and provide the powers for their implementation. But, as we have noted earlier, there is no separate Title relating to the regional problem and indeed no explicit call for a common regional policy. Rather there are a series of Articles scattered through the Treaty which relate to the regional problem and it is to these that we now turn.

First we should note the general provisions of the Treaty. The Preamble refers to the fact that the contracting parties were

anxious to strengthen the unity of their economies and to ensure their harmonious development by reducing the differences existing between the various regions and the backwardness of the less favoured regions.

This is the clearest indication in the Treaty of the need to tackle the regional problem. Regional policy is to address itself to narrowing the existing disparities – it is, however, not made apparent whether this is to be achieved by national or Community action. Article 2, which spells out the broad aims of the EEC, is much more vague.

The Community shall have as its task, by setting up a common market and progressively approximating the economic policies of member states, to promote throughout the Community an harmonious development of economic activities, a continuous and balanced expansion, an increase in stability, an accelerated raising of the standard of living and closer relations between the member states belonging to it.

And Article 3, which lists specifically the future policies which will have to be developed by the Community (i.e. the various common policies, the establishment of the external tariff, the internal tariff and quota disarmament etc.) makes no reference to regional policy. However, a European Social Fund and European Investment Bank are called for and as we shall see below they have made a contribution to the solution of regional problems.

There are also several provisions scattered through the Treaty which provide for the possibility of various policies being modified or developed with the regional problem in mind. Article 39(2) indicates that the CAP must have regard to 'structural and national disparities between the various agricultural regions'. Article 49d, concerned with free movement of labour, calls for machinery to supply information about job opportunities and thus to avoid threats to the standard of living and employment in various regions. Article 75(3) allows the common transport policy to be modified where it might lead to the standard of living and level of employment being adversely affected in a region. Article 80(2) provides for the possibility of allowing support tariffs (i.e. tariffs set at a level which involves selective aid to enterprises or industries) on grounds of regional economic policy.

The main provisions relating explicitly to regional policy are to be found in Article 90 relating to state aids. The general posture of Article 90 has already been discussed in chapter 4. Basically it says that aids for regional development may be permitted (this is a derogation from the general principle that state aid is prohibited) and that the Commission shall exercise a general supervisory role.

Regional aid schemes have indeed posed a very considerable control problem for the Commission. The basic problem is that the various regions have been competing with each other to attract footloose investment capital. Regional aid schemes became more costly as a result of competitive outbidding and this process of bidding did not appreciably increase the flow of investment. Rather it tended to give rise to reciprocal neutralization with unjustified profits for the beneficiary enterprises. Also aids tended no longer to correspond to the relative seriousness of the situation. In some cases the aid schemes applied were such that it was difficult to estimate just how intensive they were.

The Commission eventually succeeded in achieving a common policy in this field when in 1971 the Council of Ministers adopted a 'First Resolution on General Regional Aid Schemes', setting out certain general principles. There would be a gradual implementation of the Resolution, the general principles applying in the first instance to central regions. These would include the Community as a whole except (a) Berlin; (b) the eastern border of the German Federal Republic; (c) the Italian south (i.e. the Mezzogiorno) and (d) south and south-west France. These excluded zones were called peripheral regions and appropriate solutions would be worked out for them. In the central regions there would be an aid ceiling of 20 per cent. According to the Commission

This ceiling ... which takes into account all cumulative regional aid regardless of form is fixed at 20 per cent of the investment in net grant equivalence calculated on the basis of a common method of aid evaluation.

In order to compare various forms of aid and the different aid systems of the member states, it is necessary that this method, which is based on the relative amount of aid granted as against the amount invested, should only take aid after taxation into account, i.e. the net grant equivalence remaining to the beneficiary after deduction of profits tax.

Aid had to be transparent – that is, it should be possible to calculate its intensity. New aids would have to be transparent and existing aids would be progressively modified to make them so. Aids should also be regionally specific. That is to say they were not (except for Luxembourg) to cover an entire territory but should relate only to the regions really in need and these regions had to be clearly specified. Aids also had to be geared to the seriousness of the problem and graduation of aid by area had to be clearly indicated. This Resolution undoubtedly marked an important step on the way to the establishment of a common policy on the scale of aid.

As already pointed out the Commission has to supervise regional aid and in the past it has intervened in specified cases. We can, for example, cite the 1971 decision of the Commission requiring the West German Government to put an end to nonselective investment grants in the north-Rhine Westphalia region. These grants had been introduced in 1968 in order to assist in the creation of new jobs for those unemployed as a result of the closure of coal mines. The aid was originally intended to last for two years but was extended by the West German Parliament and this extension was opposed by the Commission. In its view the unemployment problem had virtually disappeared and there was no obvious reason why the aid should be continued.

Article 90 seemed to suggest that the role of the Community in regional policy would be largely negative. The Commission would vet aids but would not be involved in the business of giving them; the allocation of aids was a national responsibility. Ironing out the initial regional disparities and coping with the regional impact of integration was a job for the member states. In fact this view is only partly true. We have to recognize that three Community aid-giving bodies have been established whose assistance has had some impact on the regional problem. One of these is the European Investment Bank (EIB). This was established under the provisions of Articles 129 and 130 of the Rome Treaty. The Bank was devised to grant loans and guarantees on a non-profit-making basis within the Community for (according to Article 130) the following purposes:

(a) projects for developing backward regions;
(b) projects for modernizing or converting undertakings; or for developing fresh activities called for by the progressive establishment of the common market, where such projects by their size or nature cannot be entirely financed by the various means available in the member states;
(c) projects of common interest to several member states which by their size and nature cannot be entirely financed by the various means available in the individual member states.

(From 1963 the Bank's sphere of operations was extended to associated states.)

The loans and guarantees are extended to enterprises, local and regional authorities and financial institutions. These loans cover only a part of the cost of a project – the Bank rarely lends more than 40 per cent of the cost of fixed assets. Loans generally range from 2 to 10 million units of account and never exceed 30 million.

Between 1958 and the end of 1972 loan and guarantee contracts for 2,842·0 million units of account had been entered into. Of these 2,455·5 million units of account (86 per cent of all loans and guarantees) had been extended in respect of operations within the Community. Of the 2,455·5 million units of account devoted to internal purposes 74·4 per cent (i.e. 1,826·5 million units) were given for regional development; 2·4 per cent (59·3 million units) were made available for modernization and conversion of enterprises (the contribution to the structural problem has thus been small); 22·4 per cent (549·4 million units) had been employed in respect of projects of common European interest – this has been mainly in respect of infrastructure investments of interest to several member states (e.g. motorways, inland waterways etc.); 0·8 per cent (20·3 million units) had been disbursed on special investments in West Berlin.

It is really the 74·4 per cent devoted to regional development which is of prime significance in this context and it is worth noting that about three fifths of this has been applied to infrastructure improvements such as transport, energy and telecommunications, and the other two fifths to industrial investments and public utilities. The bulk of the aid has gone to Italy.

The current subscribed capital of the EIB (from the nine member-state governments) is 2,025 million units of account. Only 20 per cent has been paid up – the balance not paid up constitutes the Bank's guarantee for its borrowings on the capital markets of member and non-member states. Since the Bank raises its capital in the open market it has to gear its rates of interest on loans to what it has to pay. The EIB is therefore not in the business of lending at subsidized rates although the member-state guarantees allow it to obtain first class terms and to reflect these in its lending. Thus whilst the Bank channels aid to under-developed regions it is not strictly in the regional aid business. Indeed many of the regional aid weapons such as capital grants, rebates of interest, employment premiums etc. are clearly outside its scope.

Two other EEC bodies have made a contribution. One is the European Social Fund which has in the past reimbursed governments to the extent of 50 per cent of expenditure in retraining and resettling unemployed people and in supporting the wages of labour whilst enterprises converted to new lines of production. Clearly such assistance could help to alleviate the unemployment problem experienced in the regions and more will be said on the subject below. Since 1971 a reformed Social Fund has existed with new criteria for action which specifically enable it to intervene in order to deal with structural unemployment arising indirectly (rather than directly) from the working of the EEC.

The other fund which has potentially been able to make a contribution to the regional problem has been the Agricultural Guidance and Guarantee Fund. Its activities under the heading of Guidance have been directed to the structural improvements and modernization of farms. Considerable scope for improvement has clearly been evident in backward agricultural regions. However, it seems likely that improvements designed to deal with low labour productivity, though possibly raising *per capita* incomes, would probably create more unemployed agricultural labour. The need to create industrial jobs to absorb the surplus labour is therefore obvious. The Commission has indeed pressed the Council to broaden the rules for the use of the AGGF to allow its use for industrial job creation in backward agricultural areas. The desirability of using Guidance funds in this way was reiterated in the 1973 Thomson Report.

Before leaving the topic of the Community's initial approach to the regional problem we should note that the Brussels Commission has since 1967 also been responsible for operating the relevant provisions of the Paris Treaty. Redevelopment policy has consisted of loans made available to develop new sources of employment in areas where coal and steel industry employment has contracted. Readaption policy has been directed towards making grants to tide workers over until they could find new jobs, to assist with resettlement and to contribute to the cost of retraining.

The idea of a regional fund

Since the inception of the EEC the Commission has been striving towards a policy which would deal effectively with the regional problems within the Community. The Action Programme of

1962, and the Memorandum on Regional Problems of 1965 (with its stress on development poles such as that created at Taranto-Bari), were expressions of that concern. It was not, however, until 1969 that the Commission came into the open with the idea that it should itself be an active participant in regional policy – that is to say it should play a role in the actual process of aid giving and not just be concerned with negative controls and studies of the general problem. In documents attached to the 1969 Memorandum on Regional Policy it proposed the creation of a Regional Development Rebate Fund which would make grants by way of abatements of interest. This would be managed by the Commission and would be financed from the Community budget. The Commission proposed the creation of a Standing Regional Development Committee. This would be chaired by a member of the Commission and would consist of representatives of member states together with an observer from the European Investment Bank. If either the Commission or a member state so desired, a regional development plan could be discussed by the Committee. Any Community aid could only be granted after discussion had taken place within the Committee. A member state could proceed with a regional programme which was not scrutinized by the Commission but the plan would have to be independent of Community assistance. In the Memorandum the Commission noted the competitive nature of regional aids and there are good grounds for assuming that the Commission saw its ability to control the purse strings of the Rebate Fund as being a device which would enable it to exercise pressure to harmonize the aids given by various states. As we have seen above, in 1971 the Council was persuaded to set a specific ceiling to aids in the central regions of the Community. But the specific proposal for a Regional Development Rebate Fund was not implemented.

Also significant in 1969 was the Hague Summit. By calling for the achievement of economic and monetary union by 1980 (an aspiration endorsed by the 1972 Paris Summit) it paved the way for a new emphasis on the role of regional policy. The Werner Committee in its final report of 1970 (*Economic and Monetary Union in the Community*) recognized that regional policy would have a role to play but did not describe in detail the exact reasons why it would be necessary. Two arguments can, however, be deployed in favour of regional policy as an active and necessary ingredient of monetary union. Firstly, suppose that industrial unions in the UK sought Community pay levels but at the same time UK productivity lagged behind that of the Community. The United Kingdom would become uncompetitive in the Community market – exports would tend to fall and imports to rise. Both these factors would tend to create unemployment. Prior to the union this problem could be alleviated by a devaluation. But once an economic and monetary union was achieved this line of policy would be precluded. Exchange rates would quite possibly be fixed prior to the creation of a common currency. Within the Community the UK, for example, would be placed in the same position as Northern Ireland is currently in the UK. Northern Ireland has not been able to alleviate its unemployment problem by making its goods more competitive in the UK market by means of a devaluation against England, Scotland and Wales. It can therefore be argued that in an economic and monetary union such disequilibrium of a member state would have to be treated as a regional problem of the Community and an adequate regional policy would be needed.

While not doubting the logic of the argument, it might be observed that such a justification for a regional policy (consisting typically of subsidies to capital and labour) would be novel to say the least. Regional policy aids are really most appropriate to deal with structural unemployment. Thus in the UK some industries, such as coal and shipbuilding, have tended to be concentrated in certain areas. When such industries have been in a state of decline (as coal has been in the face of oil, as shipbuilding has been due to foreign competition, as linen has been as a result of man-made fibres and cheap textile imports, as agricultural employment has been in Northern Ireland due to mechanization) a regional concentration of unemployment has resulted. To attract new investment in order to absorb surplus labour a variety of subsidies has been offered. This seems to be an appropriate policy. But if the unemployment arising from factor price equalization is going to be used as the grounds for regional aids then a new era in regional policy will be opened up. Aids will be given not because society no longer requires certain products but because the labour producing them is demanding income levels which are inconsistent with its productivity. Such regional doles might grow continuously if income aspirations consistently rose faster than productivity. (This might ultimately provoke a revolt on the part of the aid donors.)

The second argument why economic and monetary union might give rise to a demand for regional action is related to capital movements. The Werner Report suggested that the union would require the establishment of a free capital market in the Community – we have seen in chapter 5 that such a market does not yet exist. Again it could be argued that if factor price equalization occurred, capital would leave the less favoured (possibly peripheral) locations of the Community. That is to say prices for particular products would tend to equality over the whole Community market but costs would be higher in the less favoured regions and the return on capital would consequently be lower than in more advantageous locations. Again we are giving a lot of significance to factor price equalization. We are also implying that subsidies to capital would be needed to compensate for the uneconomic wage aspirations of labour in the problem regions.

We have just indicated that factor price equalization might be a continuing process – would it be equally true to say that in the 1970s the competition and polarization arguments discussed earlier would also continue to be relevant? Given that internal tariff and quota disarmament was completed by mid-1968 the answer seems to be in the negative. On the other hand it can be argued that the process of industrial decline may be slow. Perhaps more to the point it could be argued that non-tariff barriers will be slower to come down. Additionally the accession of new members will mean that industries in the Six and the three new countries which have previously been protected will progressively be subjected to competition. As for the polarization factor this seems to be likely to continue to operate.

It was at the Paris Summit of 1972 that the Community took the next step forward. The British were successful in securing the agreement of the Nine to the establishment of a Regional Development Fund. There can be little doubt that factors other than the need for regional development inspired the British move. The terms of entry secured by the U K were such that, compared to other members of the Community, its ultimate contribution to the Community budget was likely to be high relative to the benefits it was likely to receive. The idea of a Regional Development Fund financed from the Community budget was therefore seen as a means of correcting the imbalance – that is to say it was expected that, given the problems of its economy, the U K could look forward to being a net beneficiary. The Regional Fund might do for the U K what the C A P had done for France!

The Summit agreed on three things: (a) the member states should co-ordinate their regional policies; (b) the Commission should prepare a report on the regional problem in the Nine; (c) the Community should set up a Regional Development Fund. This was to be set up before the end of 1973 – it would be financed from the Community's own resources. Interventions from the Fund should, in co-ordination with national aids, permit the achievement of economic and monetary union, and the correction of regional imbalances – particularly those of the backward agricultural regions and those arising from industrial change and structural unemployment. Clearly the Regional Fund was not intended to supplant national efforts. Rather it was to be joined with them and the national efforts should themselves be harmonized.

In 1973 the Thomson *Report on the Regional Problems of the Enlarged Community* was published and it, together with the report of 1971 (*Regional Development in the Community*), indicated clearly the continued existence of marked economic disparities between the regions. The 1971 report, breaking each of the Six into three or four regions, showed that gross domestic product per head in dollars in 1969 ranged from 3,411 in the Paris region to 965 in the south of Italy. There was, however, one encouraging trend in that the gap between these two regions had narrowed somewhat between 1960 and 1969. The Thomson Report, which brought the three new members into the picture, focused particular attention on three magnitudes – income per head, unemployment and net emigration in the regions. Income per head in 1970 ranged from approximately 4,200 dollars in the most prosperous region in France to 820 in the poorest region in Italy. The national average income per head was highest in West Germany (which was of course above the Community average), followed by Denmark, France, Belgium and the Netherlands (all of whose national averages were above the Community average). The national average in the UK lay below the Community average – even its most prosperous region lay just below it. The national average of Italy came next in descending order and last came Ireland – none of their regions were above the Community average. The best Italian region was not as high as the best UK region and the best Irish region lay below the best Italian one.

The Economist has produced a map showing 1973 income per head data – regions being classified as having average *per capita* incomes of below £700, £700–900, £900–1,100, £1,100–1,250 and over £1,250. The resulting picture is quite interesting. It shows that the three poor countries of the Community are Ireland, Italy and the UK. In geographical terms the richest areas lie in the heart of the Community, whilst the fringe areas (Italy and the British Isles) are the poorest. Within the fringe *per capita* income drops towards the extremity – thus in the British Isles there is, broadly speaking, a progressive deterioration from the London area to the south-east, to Scotland and Wales, then to Northern Ireland with the Irish Republic at the bottom. (The fact that the north-east and north-west of England fall into the same category as Northern Ireland slightly upsets the general progressive pattern.) In the case of Italy the tendency is, broadly speaking, much the same – income levels decline with the movement south from relatively prosperous Lombardy, through Emiglia-Romagna next to Toscana and Lazio and then to a group of regions, all at the bottom of the scale, extending from Marche on the Adriatic coast of Italy to Basilicata, Calabria and Sicily in the very south.

The Thomson figures on unemployment paint a similar picture. In the period 1969–1971 regions with more than 4 per cent unemployment were the whole of Ireland (north and south), and a significant part of the north and east of Great Britain; the whole of the lower half of mainland Italy and the associated islands, and including significant areas of the northern half on the

Adriatic side; the major part of Denmark – here there is a contrast with the income *per capita* picture; several Belgian administrative districts.

The picture in terms of net migration is less clearly defined. The *heaviest rates* are to be found concentrated in central and southern Italy, Ireland (north and south) except the region round Dublin, and Scotland. But net migration is also *noticeable* in northern and north-west England, the eastern zone of West Germany, north-west France and much of Denmark. In addition major zones of net migration are apparent in north-east Italy and in the frontier zone of Belgium, France and Germany.

Broadly speaking, taking all three criteria, Ireland (north and south), Scotland, north-east and north-west England and of course central and southern Italy are the prime regional problem areas.

The proposals of Commissioner George Thomson (who is responsible for regional policy), as adopted by the Commission, were published in 1973. He envisaged a Fund (financed as part of the Community budget) which in its first three years would amount to 2,250 million units of account – 500 million in 1974, 750 million in 1975 and 1,000 million in 1976. Criteria to be adopted in deciding which regions should benefit from the Fund were (a) a gross domestic product *per capita* below the Community average; (b) heavy dependence on agricultural employment; (c) heavy dependence on employment in declining industries (20 per cent of local employment to be in this category); (d) a persistently high level of unemployment (an average over a number of years of at least 20 per cent above the national average and at least 3·5 per cent); (e) a high rate of net emigration (at least 10 per 1,000 over a long period). The Commission has in fact published a list of regions and areas qualified to receive aid under its proposed criteria.

Community aid could be for industrial and service investments or investments in infrastructure. In the case of production of industrial goods or services the investment would have to exceed 50,000 units of account. The Fund's assistance for these goods or services would not be more than 15 per cent of the cost of the investment and would not exceed 50 per cent of the national aid.

In the case of infrastructure the Fund would not contribute more than 30 per cent of the expenditure incurred by the public authority involved. The Fund's aid for infrastructure could take the form of a rebate of up to three percentage points on loans from the European Investment Bank. An essential feature of the proposal is that aid from the Fund would be devoted only to investments which were part of a regional development programme. Aid would complement rather than be a substitute for national action and would therefore help to implement regional development policies faster than the member state alone could.

The Fund would be administered by the Commission assisted by a Fund Committee (consisting of representatives of the member states and chaired by a representative of the Commission). The regional development programmes which the Fund aided would themselves be examined by a separate Committee for Regional Policy. The proposed tasks of this Committee would be multifarious but study of the co-ordination of regional aids and the problems of dealing with areas of heavy industrial concentration would be high on its list.

At the time of writing the Fund has not been established. Failure to set it up was due to disagreement between the member states over its size. The U K wished for a sum larger than that proposed by the Commission – the West Germans called for one which was markedly smaller. The West Germans were perhaps more concerned over the way in which the aid was distributed, wishing to see it concentrated in areas of real need.

Social policy

The original conception

There are four strands to Community social policy. The first is really contained in Article 2 of the Rome Treaty which lays down the tasks which the Community has to achieve. These are said to be the promotion of

... an harmonious development of economic activities, a continuous and balanced expansion, an increase in stability, an accelerated raising of the standard of living ...

The main preoccupation of the E E C is with the enlargement of the Community cake. Such an enlargement has social as well as economic implications. The question of the distribution of the cake, and in particular the question of the level of social services and the like, is largely left to the member states in the first instance. In the longer term the influence of harmonization may be felt; this is discussed below.

The second strand of social policy relates to labour mobility. As we have already noted, under the Rome Treaty social policy is not confined to those spheres of activity which involve financial hand-outs. It also covers those policies which enable people to better themselves by virtue of the removal of restrictions on their freedom. The establishment of conditions in which a worker can move from one member state to another without loss of social service benefits and so forth, are acts of social policy. In a significant number of individual cases such opportunities almost certainly provide a more powerful means of social improvement than mere doles to the unemployed. The subject of freedom of movement of labour has, however, been dealt with in chapter 5 and we shall not discuss it further here.

The third strand relates to social security harmonization and closely related issues, such as equal pay for equal work. The harmonization issue was a feature of the negotiations leading up to the Paris and Rome Treaties. It should perhaps be stressed at this point that in the original Six, as compared with the U K (and Scandinavia), the employer contributed a much higher proportion of social security revenue. Thus in 1962 French employers contributed 69 per cent whereas the state contributed 7 per cent and the insured 20 per cent. (This contrasted with the U K where the figures were 21 per cent, 52 per cent and 27 per cent respectively.) Because of the fact that within the Six the burden on French employers was particularly severe the French Government attempted, at the time when the Paris Treaty was being negotiated, to include provisions for the immediate harmonization of social costs of production. In practice the High Authority was not given the power to harmonize social conditions and Article 3 merely refers to the general intention to harmonize conditions in an upward direction. In negotiations leading up to the Rome Treaty the issue was again raised by the French. They argued that the higher rate of social security payments – very approximately 50 per cent on top wages – raised their costs of production and placed them in a competitively vulnerable position. They also cited other examples of exceptional burdens, such as the law on equal pay for equal work and paid-holiday schemes. Once again the French did not succeed in obtaining an explicit agreement and powers to harmonize social security burdens within a given time-span. Article 117 states that the member states agree on the need to promote better conditions of living, work and employment so as to lead to their progressive harmonization and improvement. The Article also enunciates the belief that the operation of the Common Market will favour the harmonization of social systems. The Community position may be said to be that harmonization in an upward direction is desirable. In order to achieve the objectives of Article 117, Article 118 lays upon the Commission the task of promoting close collaboration between the member states in a number of fields including employment, labour law and working conditions, basic and advanced vocational training, social security, protection against occupational accidents and diseases, occupational hygiene, the law of trade unions and collective bargaining between employers and workers.

It should be emphasized that the relatively high burden of social security and other charges laid upon Community employers has continued to exist. Not only that but this burden as a ratio to wages continues to vary between states. Also the contrast between the light burden borne by UK employers as compared with their counterparts in the Community has remained. It should perhaps be added that social security is not the only burden – to that has to be added the cost of family allowances, holidays, bonuses, bounties and other fringe benefits. In the Six in 1968 the ratio of all such charges borne by employers as a percentage of wages was: Italy 91·9 per cent, France 70·0 per cent, Belgium 54·5 per cent, Netherlands 49·9 per cent, Germany 44·5 per cent, Luxembourg 40·8 per cent and (for a comparison) the UK figure was 22·2 per cent. Significantly France was not at the top of the league but undoubtedly bears a relatively heavy burden.

On the face of it it cannot be said that a great deal has been achieved by way of harmonization. The Commission has sought to stimulate the interest of the member states in comparative social security standards but its ability to secure concrete results has been limited. While countries could not refuse to collaborate in studies of particular problems, they retained the power to accept or reject results. Member states are prone to guard their independence jealously and the achievement of harmonization is likely to be a difficult and long drawn out process.

It is perhaps worth mentioning at this point that in this sphere, and indeed in others, it would be a mistake to see progress to harmonization as depending merely upon Council directives on common or minimum standards. With increasing integration market forces may bring about greater uniformity. Then again, closer contact of the kind provided by Community institutions, as well as the publicity given to the Commission studies of relative standards, may stimulate the spirit of emulation.

Some theoretical consideration has been given to the subject of the necessity for harmonization of social costs of production. By and large the conclusion seems to be that the matter is something of a red herring. Balassa's conclusions are that, except for special cases,

... the harmonization of entrepreneur-financed social programs is not necessary for the proper functioning of a union, and measures of harmonization, if undertaken, are likely to cause distortions in the pattern of production and trade and will give rise to undesirable factor movements, no matter whether the social charges are of general or special incidence. (Balassa, 1962, p. 224)

Although the matter is of some complexity the following points are worth making.

Economic analysis would not suggest that wages should be harmonized within an economic union. Is there then a case for harmonizing the costs of social benefits borne by entrepreneurs? The general answer seems to be in the negative. This view, which appears to have commended itself to the authors of the Ohlin Report (International Labour Office, 1956), is based on the argument that social payments borne by entrepreneurs are ultimately shifted to wage earners. Wages in countries where social charges have risen most have increased less than wages in countries where social charges have risen least. Another way of putting it is to say that where entrepreneurs have had to pay high payroll taxes (to finance social security) they have been constrained to offer lower wages and vice versa. There is indeed some empirical evidence which points in this direction.

Theoretically speaking, we can ask how the shifting can occur. The process depends on the assumptions made. Let us assume that there is perfect price and wage flexibility and that wage earners regard social benefits as part of their earnings. If social benefits rise then both the supply and demand schedules for labour would shift in such a way that the wage rate would fall by an amount which reflected the rise in social benefits – employment would remain unchanged. Suppose, however, that there is a downward rigidity of wages and prices. The course of events would be different but it could be argued that the shifting would substantially and progressively occur. As productivity increased, entrepreneurs would concede wage increases which were less than they would have been in the absence of the rise in social benefits.

A few general conclusions can be drawn. Firstly, let us consider the case of social security charges borne uniformly by all industries. If the social charges imposed in the past have been absorbed into the cost structure of individual member states (in the way we discussed above) then it should be pointed out that harmonization of social charges will cause difficulties. Thus if a member state had experienced a relatively small rise in social charges then wages would have tended to rise all the more as a result. On the other hand, in some member states the reverse situation may have applied. Other things being equal, the latter states would have a cost structure in which social security costs constituted a larger percentage than in the former state. If harmonization took place on the basis of the latter state-security level (or an average of the two), the price of exports of the former state would rise and deflation or realignment of exchange rates would have to occur. Secondly, let us relax the assumption of a uniform level of social security charges. Suppose the incidence in a member state varied. Would this lead to distortions? The answer appears to be in the negative. So long as the social security burden can be shifted by entrepreneurs to wage earners then all that would happen would be that the composition of labour costs (the proportionate importance of social security charges and wages) would differ from industry to industry. Similar reasoning leads to the conclusion that no difficulties arise if there are inter-country differences in the social security charges levied on par-ticular industries. Thirdly, it can also be argued that harmonization is not necessary between member states in order to prevent undesirable movements of capital and labour. Indeed, Balassa argues that due to the influence of price and wage rigidities harmonization could lead to perverse movements of capital and labour.

With regard to the question of equal pay for equal work it should be noted that the French secured what they no doubt regarded as a success. Article 119 of the Rome Treaty required that during the first stage each member state would introduce the equal pay for equal work system. In practice the implemen-tation of this Article was at first left to member states and not surprisingly some dragged their feet. As a result the implementa-tion fell behind the timetable prescribed by the Treaty.

The recent evidence does not suggest that the aims of Article 119 have yet been achieved. An article by David Howard in the *Observer* (21 October 1972) indicated that although there had been a narrowing in the differential between male and female pay, a significant gap still existed. Equally significant is the fact that when in 1973 the Commission published its European Social Action Programme it gave priority to the need for rapid action to deal with the continuing problem of unequal pay for equal work.

The reason why the French pressed the equal pay for equal work point is obvious enough. In industries where the wages of women were raised above the level they normally would have been in the absence of the law governing equal pay, French industry would be at a competitive disadvantage in relation to member states which did not have such a law. The general espousal of equal pay under the Treaty therefore amounted to agreeing to the proposition that equalization would remedy distortions which would otherwise be caused by different legal provisions. It should, however, be pointed out that equal pay is a social and not an economic principle. Even if equal productivity is forthcoming this does not justify equal pay. According to conventional wage theory the productivity of workers relates only to the demand side of the labour market. An entrepreneur will be prepared to take on a different quantity of labour at each wage rate, the actual amount being determined by the rule that the marginal revenue product of labour should be equal to the wage rate. Given equal productivity of male and female operatives an entrepreneur would be indifferent as between the two. However, on the supply side at each and every wage rate the amount of female labour offering itself might be significantly different from the amount of male labour on offer. The absolute equalization of wages paid to males and females could therefore give rise to the unemployment of female labour. This loss would have to be set against the elimination of distortions discussed above.

The fourth strand of Community social policy is connected with the European Social Fund. It is necessary to indicate here that this section will begin by dealing with the function of the Fund in the period between 1958 and 1971. In 1971 the Fund began to operate under new rules and we shall discuss these later. The role of the Fund in the period 1958 to 1971 was similar to that played by Readaption Policy under the Paris Treaty. The Fund's main objective was the establishment of a high degree of geographical and occupational mobility among workers within the Community. The broad lines within which the Fund operated are laid down in Articles 123 to 128 of the Treaty. The main form of its operations was that it reimbursed governments with 50 per cent of any expenditure which they incurred in retraining or resettling unemployed or under-employed labour, or in supporting the wages of labour which had temporarily been laid off during the conversion of an enterprise to other lines of production. In a sense, therefore, although we have chosen to treat the Fund under social policy, it has in fact provided a method of dealing with the regional unemployment problem – a point made earlier in the section on regional policy. The retraining grants were only repaid when retraining was the only way of bringing workers back into employment and when the worker had been employed for at least six months in his new occupation. Re-settlement allowances were paid only when the workers concerned had been obliged to change their place of residence, and again only six months after employment in a new position. Reconversion support (to maintain gross wages at 90 per cent of the former level) was only given to schemes which had been submitted to the Commission by the state concerned and had been given the Commission's approval prior to introduction. To qualify for assistance a reconversion did not have to have arisen because of the effect of the new forces unleashed by the Common Market.

The initiative for using the Fund lay with member states. The Fund did not have a budget limit: it was supplied by the member states in whatever amount was required to pay the requests for 50 per cent assistance. Under the Rome Treaty a scale of contributions was fixed which deviated from the contributions to the general Community budget most noticeably in respect of Italy. The latter paid only 20 per cent to the Social Fund whereas its contribution to the Community budget was 28 per cent. It is therefore apparent that the intention of the Fund was to help Italy, and in practice this appears to have been its effect.

Between the beginning of 1958 and the end of 1971 the Fund contributed about 210 million units of account to the retraining and resettlement of 1,436,000 workers, 733,000 of whom received free vocational training and 703,000 resettlement grants. The national governments contributed the equivalent of another 210 million units of account – this was of course only a small part of their total expenditure on retraining and resettlement.

It became increasingly apparent with time that the Fund's sphere of operations was somewhat narrow – it needed to be redefined in the light of the problems which were beginning to confront the Community. In 1965 the Commission submitted proposals to increase the effectiveness of the Fund. The Commission proposed that the Fund should be used to help the vocational training not only of unemployed or under-employed workers but also of employed workers whose jobs were threatened because they lacked qualifications or because they were no longer adequately equipped for modern production techniques. The Fund would also help to maintain the wages of workers who had lost their jobs through the closing of their firms in regions suffering from or threatened with unemployment and who were waiting to be re-employed by new enterprises setting up in the region. Also the Fund would participate in the building of training centres in those regions which were not particularly well equipped in this respect. Finally, it would help to provide low-cost housing for migrant workers and their families and also to assist with social services in respect of such workers.

The 1965 proposals did not lead to any concrete action, but at the Hague summit meeting of December 1969 one of the points of agreement was that the Six would consider the reform of the European Social Fund. By 1969 it was evident that the Fund was in need of fundamental remodelling. Although it had considerable achievements to its credit its activities had lacked a unity of purpose. This was inevitable since the initiative lay with member states to introduce programmes and to call for assistance from the Fund. Money had been spent on a host of unrelated activities and the Fund was a relatively passive partner. It had also been backward-looking since it had been engaged on reimbursing programmes which had been initiated several years previously. What was in fact needed was a new constitution which would enable funds to be channelled into well-defined and selected areas which would fit in with Community policies and would enable them to be achieved. For example, the Mansholt Plan would lead to labour leaving the land. It needed to be retrained and the Fund could be directed specifically in this direction. This implied that the Council (on a proposal from the Commission) should be able to open up areas for financial assistance. This would mean that there would be a more centralized and purposeful use of funds as contrasted with the previous fragmented and decentralized system.

In 1970 the Council of Ministers agreed on the reform of the Fund's operations. It was also agreed that from 1971 the Fund would not be fed by the percentage key contributions from member states referred to above but would be a charge on the Community Budget, the nature of whose own resources were discussed above in the section on agriculture in chapter 6. In 1971 the Council adopted a number of Decisions formally embodying the new mode of operation of the Fund. Article 125 of the Rome Treaty, which laid down the objectives for which Fund aid could be advanced, was abolished and new rules were substituted. Two main areas of activity are envisaged. Firstly, the Fund can be used to take action when the employment situation (a) was endangered or affected by, for example, Community policies; (b) called for specific joint action to improve the balance between supply and demand for manpower. Intervention here would be designed to deal with specific problems and would be sanctioned by the Council who would adopt the necessary formal Decisions. Evidently the aim is to try and steer the Fund activity into specific areas which will contribute to the solution of clearly defined Community problems. For example, the Council could decide that the Fund should be used to aid in the structural adaptation of agriculture – this could be done, as we have noted, by providing retraining facilities for displaced farm workers. Secondly, the Fund can also take action in respect of unemployment difficulties not arising from measures taken by the Council but merely from the operation of the Common Market. For example, structural unemployment may arise for reasons unconnected with EEC policy and the solution of such a problem would be a proper object of the Fund. It is proposed that in the early years the latter type of objective should enjoy at least 50 per cent of the credits available but in the long run the former objective would predominate.

New bearings in social policy

The Paris Summit of 1972 was significant for its concern with what may be termed the 'image' of the Community. The Summit noted that economic expansion was not an end in itself: social considerations were also important. Disparities in living conditions should be reduced and this should be achieved with the participation of all the social partners. The quality of life as well as the standard of living should be improved, particular attention being given to intangible values and to the protection of the environment. All this has been described as giving the Community a human face – to replace the faceless economic machine centred in the Berlaymont Building in Brussels. The Summit called for an action programme and the Commission subsequently obliged by publishing in 1973 its 'Social Action Programme'. This document contains a long list of areas where action is needed, some being matters of priority; we shall not attempt to list them here but will merely seek to convey a general impression of what the Programme is about. A list of priority actions are specified relating to aid from the Social Fund for migrant workers, assistance for handicapped workers, equal pay for equal work, the general application of the principle of the forty-hour week and four weeks' annual paid holiday, the setting up of a European Foundation for the improvement of the environment and living and working conditions, the harmonization of laws on mass dismissals, the establishment of a European Centre for Vocational Training, and the protection of workers' interests in the case of mergers. These are just the pressing priorities – they do not exhaust the programme but they illustrate the philosophy of the Commission's thinking in the social field. If implemented this policy would represent a considerable intensification of Community action in the social sphere going well beyond the approach adopted in earlier years.

Postcript (December 1974)

The Paris Summit (December 1974) had one concrete consequence for regional policy. Heads of State decided to set up a Regional Development Fund from 1 January 1975. The fund would be endowed with 300 million units of account for 1975, and 500 million for each of the years 1976 and 1977 – 1,300 million units of account in total. The division of the funds would be as follows: Belgium 1.5 per cent; Denmark 1.3 per cent; France 15 per cent; Ireland 6 per cent; Italy 40 per cent; Luxembourg 0.1 per cent; Netherlands 1.7 per cent; Germany 6.4 per cent; UK 28 per cent. A further six million units of account will be given to Ireland by reducing the shares of the other member states except Italy.

8 Macro-Economic, Medium-Term and Industrial Policy

Macro-economic policy

Macro-economic policy within the E E C has operated in two distinct phases. Between 1958 and 1969 the policy was governed by the principles laid down by the Rome Treaty. The essence of policy during this phase was that the economies were increasingly interdependent and the fact that one economy was influenced by what happened in another gave rise to the need for co-ordination and for general rules governing the conduct of national monetary (including exchange rate) and budgetary policies. The second phase opened in 1969 when the Hague Summit adopted the goal of economic and monetary union. In effect the Six (and as we have seen, the goal was adopted by the three new members at the Paris Summit of 1972) decided to replace co-ordination of national policies with integration. This involved the irrevocable locking of exchange rates (with the possibility of a common currency) and the centralizing of policymaking within the ambit of Community institutional machinery. We shall discuss each of these phases in turn.

The Rome Treaty – interdependence and co-ordination

The need for a macro-economic policy at the Community level sprang basically from the fact that economic integration implied that each national economy became increasingly dependent on the others. This increased interdependence and sensitivity required that there should be some co-ordination and rules governing the way in which member states controlled their levels of activity, and in particular the way in which they dealt with balance-of-payments problems.

The origins of the increased interdependence are not difficult to demonstrate. If an economy inflates its spending then some of it spills over on to the other member states. The spill-over takes the form of imports from the member states. The other member states therefore become more prosperous and in turn spend money on goods produced by the state which originally inflated. Such an inter-action is likely where there are no tariffs and other barriers inhibiting the flow of spending between states. When, on the other hand, there is substantial tariff protection, an increase in internally generated demand may merely drive up the internal price level, since imported supplies may be rendered uncompetitive by the tariff and will therefore not enter to absorb the extra demand. (There is of course a limit to this argument. When the internal price level has risen sufficiently to render imports, with duty added, competitive, the spill-over via imports will occur.)

In the absence of tariff protection the effect which an inflation of demand in one country has on the economies of other member states will of course have a limit. Such an inflation will, as we have already seen, increase imports and will probably reduce the quantity of goods available for export. Other things being equal, a balance-of-payments problem will force the government to bring the inflation under control. A deflation of internal demand will have a contrary effect on the economies of other member states. The deflating state will import less and the other states will be less prosperous. The latter will then import less from the deflating state.

The increased interdependence was made manifest in other ways. Anti-slump policies became less effective and more costly. For example, if a government embarked on a public works policy to boost domestic employment, some of the spending would find its way abroad and would therefore create employment elsewhere. Therefore, where an economy was open to trade, more would have to be spent to achieve a given increase in employment than would be the case in an economy closed to trade. The greater cost could be measured in two ways. One was the cost of the public works programme. The other was the foreign exchange cost arising from imports.

Control of the economy was also affected in other ways. For example, a rise in interest rates designed to check spending in times of boom could be frustrated by virtue of the fact that borrowers could resort to the capital and credit markets of other member states in order to obtain finance at cheaper rates. If monetary policy consisted of making credit less easily available then again it could be frustrated by access to finance from abroad. Exchange rates were an obviously sensitive area. A unilateral change, for example a devaluation, could disturb the balance between close trading partners. Also, when capital was free to move between states, uncertainty about the future level of exchange rates could lead to massive speculative movements. These could be very upsetting as was the case between France and Germany in 1968 and 1969.

The Rome Treaty rules

The rules for dealing with cyclical and balance-of-payments problems are contained in Articles 103 to 109. Article 103 is the only one relating to cyclical policy. It states that member states shall regard as a matter of common concern their short-term economic policies and shall consult with each other and the Commission on measures to be taken in response to current circumstances. Article 104 enjoins each member state to walk the all too familiar tight-rope: they shall pursue the economic policies necessary to maintain equilibrium of the balance of payments and confidence in the currency whilst simultaneously ensuring high employment and stability of prices. In order to achieve all this, Article 105 requires the member states to co-ordinate their economic policies. This Article specifically calls for co-ordination in monetary matters as well as collaboration between budgetary authorities and central banks. Article 106 need not detain us – it is designed to deal with the problem of exchange control inhibiting the integration of commodity and capital markets. Article 107 requires each member state to treat its policy with regard to exchange rates as a matter of common interest. This Article also provides remedies against changes in exchange rates which are incompatible with the Rome Treaty. Article 108 states that where a country is already experiencing, or is threatened by, balance-of-payments difficulties, the Commission shall investigate the measures which the state has taken or intends to take and shall make recommendations. This Article also provides for mutual financial assistance, either by means of a concerted approach to international institutions (this obviously refers to the IMF), or directly by the Community. Article 109 was discussed earlier in connection with the free movement of capital. It enables a member state to take immediate protective measures if a sudden balance-of-payments crisis arises. However, any state taking such emergency action has to reckon with the fact that the Council may subsequently, after the Commission has given its opinion and the Monetary Committee has been consulted, suspend such protective measures.

Co-ordination policy

It is apparent that Articles 103 and 105 both called for close collaboration and co-ordination in those fields which influence national levels of activity and therefore trade between member states. In order to enable this co-ordination to occur the Community created a number of committees. One of the most important was the Monetary Committee, consisting of two members from each state and two from the Commission. The Committee was expressly called for by the Rome Treaty and came into existence in 1958.

It meets in Brussels ten or twelve times a year. Sessions are devoted to a general examination of the overall economic and monetary situation and also to a general study of the situation in one member state, the formula being that of a 'cross-examination' by the representatives of another member country and of the Commission. The Committee has formulated frequent opinions, which are confidential, to the Commission and the Council. In 1964 the Council formally extended the functions of the Committee to include the co-ordination of the positions of the member states in the framework of international monetary bodies, where the Community has in recent years been in a strong position resulting from its sound monetary situation. (Palmer et al., 1968, pp. 223–4)

In 1960 the Council of Ministers brought into existence the Committee on Short-Term Economic Trends – again this was drawn from member states and the Commission. The governors of the five central banks (Luxembourg did not have a separate central bank) met regularly, not only at the monthly meetings at the

Bank of International Settelements but also, since April 1964, in the Community's own Committee of Central Bank Governors. This Committee, apart from concerning itself with internal Common Market affairs, also played an important and influential external role, as for example in the case of policy formulation concerning the size of credits to be granted to the U K and the acceptable degree of devaluation by the latter in November 1967. The year 1964 also saw the creation of the Medium-Term Economic Policy Committee – more will be said about this in the next section. In 1965 the Budgetary Committee was established which brought together senior officials of national ministries of economic affairs in an attempt to co-ordinate national budgets.

The Commission, of course, exercised a watching brief over the course of events within the national economies and encouraged policies which took account of the interdependence of the various economies. Apart from bringing its views to bear in the various committees, quarterly reports were produced on the situation and outlook for the economies of each member state and the Community as a whole. Although these reports were prepared in collaboration with national civil services, they reflected the judgement of the Commission. Also, at the January session of the European Parliament it was traditional for the member of the Commission responsible for economic and financial affairs to present the Commission's assessment of the economic situation and the prospects to come.

The various committees just mentioned and the Commission exercised an important influence via the Recommendations adopted by the Council of Ministers. For example, in 1964 when the Community generally was facing a strong inflationary threat, proposals concerning national economic policy were submitted by the Commission to the Short-Term and Monetary Committees and were adopted by the Council. The Recommendation included a limit to the annual growth of public expenditure by 5 per cent, a requirement to finance any unavoidable spending above this ceiling by taxation, a call for the maintenance and tightening up of existing credit policy and for the introduction of a productivity-based incomes policy.

The Hague Summit – economic and monetary union

By the end of the 1960s it became obvious that the period of experimentation with the co-ordination of independent member state economic and monetary systems had not yielded satisfactory results and certainly did not provide a firm foundation for future developments. The events of 1968 and 1969 brought this to a head.

The need for action was underlined by the Commission which in February 1969 addressed to the Council of Ministers a memorandum – *The Co-ordination of Economic Policy and Monetary Policy within the Community*. This called for the strengthening of the co-ordination of (a) short-term and (b) medium-term economic policies and the institution of (c) short-term and (d) medium-term monetary-aid schemes. This proposal was associated with the name of M. Raymond Barre and is conveniently referred to as the first Barre Plan. The next important event was the Hague Summit of December 1969, when the Heads of State agreed in principle to the creation of an economic and monetary union and that work should begin on the details of such a union. (It was also agreed that the short-term monetary aid scheme should be implemented and that discussions should take place concerning a European Reserve Fund.)

The Hague Summit agreements appear to represent a new plane of discussion. Co-ordination, which had characterized previous policy, was replaced by the much more thorough-going concept of economic and monetary union. At this point it is necessary to pause a while and consider the implications of all this. Just what does a state of economic and monetary union imply? How long would it take to achieve such a state? Just how would the Six get there and in particular what institutional changes would be needed? (Institutional changes could well be political as well as economic – that is to say there would, for example, be a need for democratic control.) Obviously in 1969 these questions were still to be decided and views could differ. However, it is not difficult to sketch out in the most general terms how the Six *could* evolve – given the political will. The margins of fluctuation of exchange rates could be narrowed and eventually eliminated, and irrevocable rates of exchange established. Given the latter and free convertibility the Community would in effect have a common currency, since any one member state currency could always be freely guaranteed to exchange at a known rate into each of the other currencies. The way would be paved for a common currency which psychologically would be more attractive to 'Europeans'. Such a currency could be placed under the control of a Community Central Banking system. Community control could be exercised over the supply, price and availability of money. The shift towards irrevocable exchange rates would highlight the need for greater control over budgetary policy. Taxes could be harmonized and budgets subject to closer and closer co-ordination. Capital could be allowed to move freely. There would in due course be no national reserves of gold, foreign currencies, etc. but a Community Reserve Fund. The latter could also provide the means for intervention on the foreign-currency market. At the end of the process there would have to be some central agency for controlling budgetary and monetary policy in order to provide for full employment and growth without inflation in the Community as a whole. Such control would also have to be exercised in the light of the state of the Community Balance of Payments and Reserves and decisions would have to be made about the Community parity.

We can now return from the clouds to reality. In January 1970 the Council of Finance and Economics Ministers established machinery for prior consultation on short-term policy measures. It will be remembered that this had been called for in the first Barre Plan. (M. Barre had called for a system of compulsory consultation before the taking of any national decision, relating to the trend of prices, incomes and employment, overall budgetary policy and tax policy, which affected the economies of other member states.) More forward-looking was the decision in the same month to formally authorize the Central Banks to establish the short-term monetary aid scheme. This provided *unconditional* short-term credits of $1000 million made up of the following contributions – $300 million each from France and West Germany, $200 million from Italy, $100 million from Belgium-

Luxembourg, and $100 million from the Netherlands. In addition the scheme also permitted a further $1000 million of *conditional* short-term aid (three to six months) made up of quotas as above.

Meanwhile the 'great debate' on monetary integration and economic union had begun and it soon became evident that pronounced differences of view existed. Two schools, curiously called the economists and the monetarists, emerged. In so far as countries can be said to belong to schools of thought it can be said that the Germans and Dutch were economists whilst the French, Luxembourgers, Belgians (and the Commission) were monetarists. The champion of the economist school was Dr Schiller, the West German Economics and Finance Minister. The Schiller *Plan for Monetary, Economic and Financial Co-operation* envisaged a progression through four stages. Stage one would be mainly concerned with setting up a firm base for co-ordination of economic policies. Counter-cyclical weapons of control should be developed in each member state as required. The second stage would be concerned with securing a more evenly balanced economic development between the various states. This would be achieved by central recommendations on budgetary policy and more co-operation through the various monetary and banking committees. A system of medium-term monetary aid would be set up. The third stage would witness the introduction of a supra-national element with majority decisions at Community level in such matters as national budgets and so forth. A federal reserve system on the US model would be introduced. The margin of exchange-rate fluctuation around basic parities would be reduced. At this stage the basic parity could still be modified, but an intensified degree of Community control would be applied in this area. A European Reserve Fund would be set up and a part of national reserves would be transferred to it. In the fourth and final stage power over economic, financial and monetary matters would be centralized under a system of supra-national control. Exchange rates would be totally fixed and irrevocable. A single unit of European currency would make its entry. The existing Committee of Central Bank Governors would become a European Central Council of Banks.

Economists will recognize this as being a sensible way of proceeding to the goal of economic and monetary union. In particular until a very effective mechanism for co-ordinating the macro-economic policies of member states is established any move to adopt irrevocable fixed exchange rates is exceedingly dangerous. Different national macro-economic policies can lead to differential rates of inflation, and exchange rates may begin by being right but end up being wrong. If a country inflates faster than its competitors, but is precluded from devaluing, then it is likely to experience an adverse balance of payments and the only (or most likely) way to deal with this would be to deflate. (The possible early adoption of irrevocable, fixed exchange rates was at one stage regarded by many U K economists as being one of the most serious arguments against joining the E E C. Such critics had in mind the propensity of the U K to inflate relatively rapidly.)

The monetarist school was really personified by M. Barre, who produced what is now called the second Barre Plan. It would be tedious to list all the various aspects of this proposal. Like the Schiller Plan it envisaged a phased progression towards the ultimate goal. But it contrasted with the Schiller Plan in two respects. The first related to the role of exchange rates. Peter Coffey and John Presley in their study of this topic put the matter thus:

the idea of allowing fluctuating exchange rates is categorically rejected as a matter of principle. . . . Whilst changes in exchange rates might be considered in cases of exceptional necessity, it would be preferable to *irrevocably* fix the exchange rates as soon as possible. A satisfactory move would be the immediate reduction of the margin of parity between the national currencies from 1·5 per cent to 1·0 per cent. The demand for fixed exchange rates could hardly have been stated in a more emphatic fashion! (Coffey and Presley, 1970, p. 12)

Secondly, Barre also laid considerable stress on the role of the Community in the international monetary sphere.

The response of the Council of Ministers to this diversity of view was to set up a Group to examine the problems involved. This Group was led by Pierre Werner, the Prime Minister of Luxembourg. The Werner Group presented an interim report in June 1970 and a second and final report in October of that year. The Group proposed the achievement by 1980 of an economic and monetary union. In particular the nature of the final union was delineated. Community currencies would be freely convertible against each other and their parities irrevocably fixed. It would be preferable if they could be replaced by a Community currency. Monetary and credit policy would be centralized. There would be a Community monetary policy *vis-à-vis* the rest of the world. Member states would unify their policies on capital markets. The main components of budget policy would be decided at Community level. The Group also recognized that significant institutional changes would be needed. There would have to be a central decision-making centre which would influence such matters as national budgets, and the parity of the single currency (or the interlocked Community currencies). There would also need to be a Community central banking system to determine monetary conditions over the Community as a whole.

In explaining how the Community would achieve the union the Group was only really specific about the first stage – 1971 to 1973 inclusive. Its proposals for this stage seem to have involved an element of compromise between the monetarist and economist schools. The Group did not follow the monetarists who were anxious to lock the exchange rates at the outset. Rather (thanks to the Central Bank Governors) it proposed a compromise scheme in the shape of a reduction of the margin of fluctuation around the central parities when one Community currency was exchanged for another. This band of fluctuation was to be narrower than that operating in respect of exchanges of Community currencies for the dollar. This was the famous snake in the tunnel mechanism. The snake was the narrower band of fluctuation allowed in respect of intra-Community currency exchanges whilst the tunnel was the wider band allowed in respect of exchanges against the dollar. Emphasis was also placed on the need to achieve greater harmonization of national economic policies – a central feature of the economist position.

The Council decided on the first stage of the process of transition which was to run from 1 January 1970 to 31 December 1973. The main features of the agreement (which were in line with the Werner blueprint) were the narrowing of the exchange-rate margins of the Six currencies, the co-ordination and supervision of national budgets at Council level, and the setting up of a $2000 million medium-term aid fund for member states suffering from fundamental balance-of-payments difficulties. Subsequently in September 1972 the Council decided to create a Monetary Co-operation Fund. This was planned to operate as from April 1973 and did in fact do so. Its role was to take over the running of the narrow exchange rate margin system and to manage the short-term credit arrangements.

Economic and Monetary Union – motives and problems

Having now delineated the approach to E M U adopted by the Community, we can no longer delay discussing the motives which lie behind it. Clearly in the early days of the scheme a good deal of support for it came from the French. They had, and still have, a vested interest in the C A P and as we indicated earlier this was based on the assumption that exchange rates could be held. In fact in 1969 monetary stability was disturbed (by the French de-valuation and German revaluation) and the C A P system was threatened with disintegration. In the minds of the French a mone-tary union based on a fixed and unchanging exchange rate system had therefore much to commend it. A second factor which led some to espouse E M U was the prospect that it would give a fillip to political unity. It is, however, worth considering whether econ-omic unity should lead the way – should not political unity be achieved first? Other arguments in favour of E M U have been advanced, such as the stimulus given to trade when exchange rate fluctuations are eliminated. The development of international companies is also said to be facilitated by the removal of exchange rate risks. (Whilst freer trade may be beneficial, the advantages derived by the general public from international companies are less immediately obvious.) It can also be argued that the French saw E M U as a means of creating a monetary entity which would rival the dollar.

How far has the Community moved towards E M U? The answer is that progress has been very limited. In the field of ex-change rate margins the policy has met with setbacks. Originally, it was intended that the margin of fluctuation would be 0·75 per cent on either side of the par value with the dollar. This gave a band of fluctuation of 1·5 per cent – i.e. the difference between the upper and lower limits of possible fluctuations against the dollar. It also gave a maximum cross-rate band of 3 per cent since one Community currency might move from the bottom to the top limit whilst another might simultaneously move from the top to the bottom. By contrast the Central Bank Governors suggested that the maximum cross-rate fluctuation as between Community currencies was to be kept to 2·4 per cent. But this system was never inaugurated because the dollar problem of 1971 obtruded. However, in 1972 the snake in the tunnel system was introduced but the margins of fluctuation were considerably increased – the snake had grown fatter and the tunnel wider. Then in 1973 the Community made another retreat when the joint float was introduced – prior to this the tunnel had been straight but now it floated up and down. Added to this was the non-adherence of Italy, the U K and the Irish Republic. In early 1974 the French left the scheme.

Another objective of the first stage was the co-ordination of national economic policies. Perhaps the best we can do here is to quote from John Presley who has recently been reviewing Community progress in this field.

The Council of Ministers does meet three times each year to examine the economic climate in the Community, and it does put forward very general policy objective guidelines; but there is no detailed attempt to formulate economic policy, as the Werner Report envisaged, to achieve these objectives. Co-ordination Committees have been set up, their main function being to monitor the national policies, and to examine them in relation to the common guidelines laid down by the Council. Even the European Commission however admits that little progress has been made in co-ordination: 'few concrete measures have been adopted beyond recommendations of a very general nature'. (Presley, 1974, p. 153)

Why, we may ask, is the process of achieving E M U likely to be difficult ? One factor is differential rates of inflation in the member states. If, as is quite possible, one member state finds its price level getting out of line as it rises faster than those of its Community partners a balance of trade problem arises. One obvious remedy is devaluation. The need to devalue is bound to be a possibility until (if ever) national policies are harmonized so as to eliminate differences in national price level movements or until national policies are swept away and replaced by one monetary and budgetary policy for the whole Community. (We may, however, doubt whether such centralization will be sufficient if it ignores the problem of national wage movements in relation to those of national productivity.)

A second difficulty relates to foreign trade structures. Here again the possibility arises that a member state might need to break away from any agreement to hold exchange rates more or less fixed. Thus one member state may have its trade structure biased towards the rest of the Community and therefore a major factor in determining the appropriate exchange rate will be its rate of inflation as compared with the rest of the Community. But another member state may have a trade structure biased towards the rest of the world and it may therefore be subjected to differing considerations in determining its exchange rate.

There seems little doubt that E M U has been the victim of an extremely unsettled international monetary system. For example, German revaluations have been provoked by speculative flights into the mark. A reform of the international system, followed by a period of relative calm, seems an indispensable condition if the tender plant of E M U is to be brought to fruition. In this respect the prospects at the beginning of 1974 are not rosy. Reform is still being discussed and the oil crisis only adds another strain to the system.

But even if there was a calm in world monetary affairs we may question the political feasibility of the E M U proposal as an ultimate state of affairs. Here we may raise a number of queries. Did the Heads of State and Prime Ministers who met at the Hague in 1969 really appreciate the full significance of what they had decided to do? Are the member states really willing to give up sovereignty on the scale required if the Werner Plan is to be accomplished? In particular, is France, so obviously anxious to follow its own policies on crucial matters such as oil supplies, willing to see the control of its national economy handed over to central decision-making institutions?

Medium-term policy

The origins of this policy lie in the Action Programme for the Second Stage which the Commission produced in 1962. This document was the Commission's chart for progress following the successful completion of the first stage of the transition period. This memorandum, which immediately achieved something of the status of a *cause célèbre* by being the occasion of a heated debate in the European Parliament, seemed to some to exhibit a kind of economic schizophrenia. Not only did it repeat what was already known to be the Community's philosophy in respect of competition policy, but it introduced – under the name of programming – what some took to be contrary proposals which, if they did not constitute central planning, at least appeared to contain a threat to the free-market system. The most sensitive critics were the West Germans of the Neo-Liberal school. Dr Ludwig Erhard also found the proposals at variance with his concept of the social-market economy and strongly with his concept of the social-market economy and strongly criticized the Commission's proposals in the European Parliament.

The word 'programming' is conceptually capable of being defined in a number of ways. It can be a device for co-ordinating the various economic policies of governments. Given that governments tend to intervene in the workings of the economy, programming can give coherence and direction to such interventions in the light of forecasts of development. Equally well, programming can be a technique for influencing the decisions of the private sector. Here there is a spectrum of possibilities. Firstly, the government can produce long-term projections which constitute non-binding lines of guidance. Secondly, a distinction can be made between mere projections and official targets. The latter are likely to be more influential for two reasons. One is that the government is in some sense committed to a target and can therefore use such instruments as it commands to enable that target to be reached. The second is that the private sector will assume that the target is feasible because it is part of an overall plan in which the resources required for the target growth in the industry in question are consistent with other demands upon resources. Thirdly, the government may seek to bring its influence to bear in order to guarantee the realization of targets. This can be done, as was the case in French indicative planning, by involving industry in the formulation of targets. It can be argued that being involved in drawing up the plan tends to generate a willingness to co-operate in making its fulfilment possible. Also, participation by industry in formulating targets engenders the view that the drawing up of a programme is an exercise in coherence; that is to say, the growth targets of individual industries are consistent one with another. This inculcates the idea that if everyone plays his agreed role the plan will succeed. This was the philosophy behind French planning. However, it was buttressed by another important factor, namely that the government disposed of a whole range of inducements such as tax abatements, export subsidies, privileged access to credit, specially low interest rates, investment grants for regional development and subsidies for research. These could and were used to induce action consistent with the plan. Finally, programming or planning can of course take the Soviet pattern. Here mutually consistent targets are drawn up in physical terms and the state disposes of the power to direct resources in order to fulfil the plan. Needless to say, such a system precludes private ownership as the means of production and the profit motive in the normally accepted Western sense.

On the face of it the furore, particularly in West German circles, was misplaced. Planning at the Community level, in the sense of influencing the private sector on the French model (the Soviet system was clearly not even a starter), was impossible in that the Treaty of Rome did not provide the Community organs with the necessary powers. In practice the Commission's objective in proposing the introduction of a Community programme was really the co-ordination of the policies of authorities, as opposed to directing the production and investment decisions of the private sector. The Commission's adoption of programming was based on a number of factors. One was that the Rome Treaty required the Community authorities to ensure the co-ordination of the economic policies of the member states in the field of cyclical, monetary and balance-of-payments policy. The other was the Treaty's call for common policies in agriculture, transport and energy. Clearly these have to be guided by a general view of the progressive development of the Community economy as a whole. (It is, however, only fair to point out that West German reactions were not without some justification. The statements in the Action Programme on the nature and objectives of Community programming were somewhat obscure and the phraseology left open the possibility that some kind of influence on particular industries, perhaps by industrial targets, would be operative.) However, there were other forces at work which pointed to the need for a Community programming system. At the national level forces were operating which were rendering French national planning less effective whilst internal developments in West Germany were rendering opinion there more favourable to the idea of some form of programming both at national and Community level.

French support for the Community programme derived in considerable measure from the fact that the unfolding of the Common Market was making national planning increasingly impossible. The increased openness of the French system meant that it was more difficult to forecast the future development of the economy in aggregate or by sectors and industries. Equally, it was more difficult to control the economy since what happened to French industry depended on events in other member states. Difficulties caused by the free movement of goods were complemented by the free movement of factors such as capital. Then again, under the Common Agricultural Policy control of French agriculture ceased to be a national prerogative. Finally, many of the state aids which the Government employed to induce compliance with the plan were found to conflict with the Rome Treaty.

The medium-term policy would not, however, have come to fruition if there had not been a change of heart on the part of West Germany. A number of factors led to the change of direction. One of the most important was the rapid growth of public investment and public spending generally. This required the drawing up of medium- or longer-term programmes of public finance. These in turn had to be related to forecasts of the growth of other sectors of the economy. In July 1963 the Commission addressed a Recommendation to the Council of Ministers on medium-term policy and in April 1964 the Council of Ministers decided to form a Medium-Term Policy Committee. This consisted of two members (and two alternates) from each member state together with representatives from the Commission. Its task was to prepare a preliminary draft programme of medium-term economic policy. This in turn required the production of projections of economic growth. The latter function was placed in the hands of a separate Groupe d'Étude des Perspectives Économiques à Moyen Terme. This group was made up of independent experts working for the Commission. Thus, those producing the forecasts were to be separate from those erecting the policy programme on the basis of them. The resulting programme, which would deal with the economic policies necessary to keep economies on the course mapped out for them, would then be submitted to the Council of Ministers and by agreeing to it the member states would be expressing an intention to act in accordance with it. The first programme passed through all these stages and was finally adopted by the Council in February 1967.

The projections for the whole Community were that Gross Domestic Product would grow at 4·3 per cent per annum between 1966 and 1970. This compared with a growth of 4·9 per cent in the previous five years. In order to achieve this target, productive investment would have to increase at 6·1 per cent per annum and public investment at 8·5 per cent. In order for the latter to be achieved private consumption would have to be constrained; a growth rate of 4·1 per cent was proposed. The plans have been revised at two-yearly intervals – in 1969 and 1971. The latter runs from 1971 to 1975.

Industrial policy

Industrial policy is perhaps the least developed area of Community activity. There is no call for a common industrial policy in the Rome Treaty. There are, however, several provisions scattered through the Treaty which relate to industrial policy and the Commission has relied on them as a base for a number of policy proposals. The word proposal is very relevant here because in this field of policy the ratio of draft directives to those actually adopted is, to say the least, extremely high. Some aspects of what is called industrial policy have already been discussed and will not be dealt with again here. These relate to such matters as the opening up to the Community of wide competition in public works contracting and public procurement generally, the harmonization of technical and official standards and the encouragement to joint activity (R & D and specialization) particularly in the case of small and medium-sized enterprises.

Much of what remains in the industrial policy field is concerned with industrial structure and R & D. These two are not unconnected since there is obviously a relationship between the size of firms and their R & D activity.

In the early days of the Community great stress was laid upon the need to create larger firms. Data was assembled to prove that in a number of important industries the size of firm in the Community was significantly smaller than in the US. This, it was argued, put the Community at a disadvantage since there are economies of large-scale production and distribution which might only be fully reaped by large firms, and in addition R & D was an activity characteristic of large enterprises and beyond the means of small ones. Although this view was evident within the Community it would be dangerous to say it was the Community view (if such a thing can in any case be said to exist). The idea that bigger firms were desirable was most strongly held by sections of industry. For example, the Community's federation of national industrial associations, the UNICE, was strongly in favour of it and so was the Patronat Française. The French Government was particularly favourable to the greater size thesis. A prime aim of the Fifth Plan was to reduce the number of independent enterprises by creating larger groups. In some cases it was envisaged that only one or two firms should constitute the industry. The Commission on the other hand seemed in the earlier days to take a more cautious view. Clearly the larger market provided the possibility of greater size without the problems of concentration which would arise at the national level. Cross-frontier mergers would also help to cement the Community together and international companies with subsidiaries in several member states were extremely adept at providing mobility of capital (and know-how) which the Rome Treaty obviously sought to achieve. But the Commission's original stance was guarded – the aim of the policy was not simply the pursuit of larger firms but the introduction of greater neutrality in respect of those factors which determined firm size. It aimed to eliminate those factors which artificially encouraged or impeded concentration.

The Commission focused particular attention on the fields of taxation and company law as ones in which conditions of neutrality should be brought about. In the fiscal field the most obvious distortion was the artificial stimulus to vertical concentration presented by the multi-stage or 'cascade' type of turnover taxes. Originally these existed in all the member states of the EEC except France, being particularly prominent in Germany. As we have seen, the 'cascade' system involves imposing a turnover tax upon raw materials, semi-finished products, or bought-in component parts every time they are sold by one firm to another. The result is that the taxes imposed in the earlier stages of manufacturing a product that passes through several stages are compounded in the final selling price of the product, which is thus higher than it would be but for the multiple incidence of tax. Under these circumstances, it is not surprising that industries in Germany should have chosen to avoid this multiple incidence wherever possible by vertical integration. In a completely vertically integrated concern that extends right back to the sources of raw materials, taxes are imposed only once at the final stage of production. The implications for the economy as a whole of this artificial inducement to vertical concentration are that the real economic advantages of specialization are less likely to be achieved, since the firm is encouraged to spread its activities for purely fiscal reasons, and vertical integration may in some circumstances make it possible for a vertically integrated concern to embarrass its non-integrated competitors, even if they are more efficient, by denying them raw materials, components or markets. The Commission always held, therefore, that the solution to this problem lay in the adoption of the value-added system which had been operational in France. This form of tax neither encouraged nor discouraged vertical concentration and this is one reason why the Community adopted the V A T.

The other area where the EEC Commission sought to bring about greater neutrality was in respect of company law, although it should be noted that in practice it is very difficult to separate the legal and the fiscal factors in operation here. The Commission recognized that where greater business units were required one way of bringing them about was by merger. These mergers might take place within frontiers or might be cross-border in character. The Commission detected in particular significant legal (and fiscal) impediments to the cross-frontier variety and a priority was given to dealing with this aspect of the merger problem. (The Commission was also aware that despite the existence of the Common Market there had been few genuine cross-border mergers.)

The nature of these inhibiting factors is best appreciated by considering what happened when two companies located in different member states chose to merge. Suppose a Belgian and a German company decided to amalgamate and form a single company in Germany. Immediately, they faced the problem that, under Belgian law, before the company could move out of Belgium it had to have the unanimous consent of the shareholders. Where there were a lot of small shareholders, chances of unanimity were small. Some patriot was going to object. Moreover, under Belgian, German, French and Dutch law a domestic company could not be absorbed by a foreign one in one simple move. For the above merger to occur, there had to be a legal liquidation in one country and a legal reconstruction in the other. Lawyers and registration fees naturally arose in the process. When a company was liquidated some countries imposed a liquidation tax on the difference between the book value and the actual value of the company's assets. In addition, in most countries capital gains arising at the time of liquidation were subject to taxation. If the tax liability was substantial, it might make the cost of an amalgamation prohibitive. Within each of the member states of the EEC, therefore, the fiscal authorities made certain concessions to companies in these circumstances, perhaps by levying the tax at a reduced rate or by permitting the payment to be phased over a number of years. But this understanding attitude on the part of the authorities usually

vanished when cross-frontier amalgamations were under consideration. In particular, the possibility of phasing the tax payment over a number of years became unattractive to the official
mind when the company on which the tax was levied was due to
disappear from the national scene. Thus economically desirable
mergers might be impeded.

Further obstacles could also arise. If an amalgamation took
the form of a parent in one country and a subsidiary in the other,
the possibility of double taxation of dividends was a real one.
Even in respect of national mergers, the fiscal systems of the Six
only went part of the way toward eliminating this double taxation.
In Germany, the Netherlands and Luxembourg, only when the
degree of participation of the parent in the subsidiary was at least
25 per cent did companies enjoy the *schachtelprivileg* under
which they were regarded by the fiscal authorities as part of a
self-contained group, and double taxation of the subsidiaries'
dividends was thus avoided.

To deal with these problems as they affected cross-border
mergers two developments were called for. Firstly, legal impediments should be swept away. There were two possible approaches to this problem. The first was to harmonize company
law in the member states. The provisions for bringing about the
Freedom of Establishment (Articles 52 to 58) applied to companies and provided for certain forms of harmonization of the
law relating to them and Article 220 explicitly called for negotiations between member states with a view to facilitating cross-
frontier mergers. The Commission has in fact produced a number
of draft directives but so far the majority of these have not been
adopted. Perhaps recognizing the difficulties of harmonization
the Commission has also been pursuing for a number of years the
idea of establishing side by side with national law a system of
Community company law which would enable a European
Company or *Societas Europea* to be formed. To draft the statute
the Commission engaged the services of Dutchman Professor
Pieter Sanders. As a result of the labours of Professor Sanders
and his group a draft statute was produced in 1970 and was
adopted by the Commission. The intention is that the European
Company system would facilitate cross-frontier mergers by

cutting across the legal and fiscal difficulties which stand in the way of such mergers under the separate national systems of law and taxation. The 1972 Paris Summit agreed on the rapid adoption of the European Company Statute. However, by the beginning of 1974 the Statute had not been adopted; partly this was due to enlargement, which brought with it a different system of law, particularly that of the U K.

The second development required that the fiscal factors which discriminated against cross-border mergers should be eliminated. If liquidation taxes were eliminated on domestic mergers, they should be dropped in respect of the cross-border variety also. Capital gains taxes on liquidation should be as liberally applied to cross-border mergers as they were to internal amalgamations. In some cases means of eliminating double taxation were needed. Again the Commission has produced draft directives to deal with such problems. For example, in 1969 two draft directives were sent to the Council concerning double taxation and the treatment of hidden reserves arising during merger operations – neither has yet been adopted.

Recently the Commission has adopted a more positive approach to the restructuring of Community industry through cross-border amalgamation and co-operation. Indeed the neutrality element evident in earlier approaches seems to have receded. This became clear in 1970 when the Commission produced its memorandum 'Industrial Policy in the Community'. For example, the Commission proposed that it should actively intervene by operating a 'marriage bureau' to bring together prospective partners to a merger. The bureau did in fact begin to operate in May 1973. The Commission has also been urging the general adoption of the French concept of *groupement d'intérêt économique*. This is an organization which lies half-way between association and merger. It is simple, flexible and possesses a legal personality. The system has existed in France since 1967 and, were all the member state laws to encompass such an arrangement, then it could be a vehicle of cross-border collaboration. Equally the Commission has suggested that trans-national collaboration could arise through the agency of the joint undertaking – a device restricted to uses under the Euratom Treaty.

According to Prag and Nicholson (1973, p. 256) the legal features would include

full rights and powers normally granted to corporate bodies in each country; financial contributions from the Community; tax concessions, low-interest loans and other privileges linked with the public interest. Joint undertakings would be established only for two well-defined types of operation: the complete or partial pooling of public services, e.g. transport, telecommunications, personal and public health, the environment; and the linking of companies or bodies belonging to at least two Community countries and designed to perform a major service to Europe either in technological development or in the supply of raw materials.

The Commission has also proposed that the European Investment Bank should play a direct role in promoting cross-frontier mergers.

Before we leave the subject of facilitating cross-frontier mergers it seems appropriate that the reader's attention should be drawn to the possibility that there might be a clash between the new interpretation of Article 86 following the *Continental Can* case and the proposed draft regulation on mergers on the one hand and the encouragement to mergers under the industrial policy on the other.

Another main area of industrial policy is research and development. In 1967 the Council of Ministers designated seven sectors which were suitable for technological collaboration – these were computers, telecommunications, the environment (noise and pollution control), new methods of transport, meteorology, oceanography and metallurgy. But political problems prevented the matter being proceeded with until late 1971 when the Six plus the U K and twelve other European states embarked on seven joint projects in the fields listed above. The Paris Summit called for a common policy in the field of science and technology. The Commission has in fact proposed, both in the 1970 Memorandum and since in a host of measures (space does not permit them all to be detailed here) that the Community should co-ordinate R & D in the member states. The Community should grant subsidies (repayable in the case of success) in the form of industrial development contracts. These would be designed to encourage co-operation and might, for example, be aimed at the development of new industrial processes. It has also been suggested that national procurement policies be co-ordinated so as to encourage and maintain European firms which might otherwise succumb to American and other outside competition. The Commission also proposed a European Research and Development Committee, consisting of prominent persons in the world of research, who would assist in the preparation of research programmes etc. A European Science Foundation would be established with adequate resources to carry out pure research, which would complement that already being undertaken in existing research institutions. Some progress has been made – for example, the European Research and Development Committee held its first meeting in April 1973.

9 The Community and the World

The subject of the Community's relations with the rest of the world can best be treated under four heads. The first two are forms of association. The Rome Treaty made special provision for the association of the then dependent territories of member states. Technically speaking this is covered by the Part Four Association provisions laid down in Articles 131 to 136. But the possibility of association was not limited to dependent or erstwhile dependent territories. Article 238 allows the Community to conclude agreements, creating an association, with any third country (or with a union of states or an international organization). The third form of relationship is full membership – this is limited to *European* states. It will be discussed at length primarily in the light of UK accession. Fourthly, the Rome Treaty calls for a common commercial policy. This in particular provides an opportunity to discuss the activities of the Community in the General Agreement on Tariffs and Trade (GATT) and the United Nations Conference on Trade and Development (UNCTAD).

Part Four Association

During the negotiations leading up to the Rome Treaty the French vigorously pressed the idea of associating overseas territories. The Spaak Report made no mention of them and it was only at the Venice meeting of Foreign Ministers in May 1956 that France, by making association a condition of going ahead with the scheme for a Common Market, got the subject on the agenda. The French had good reasons for taking this line. Firstly, they regarded the overseas territories as an extension of France, but a customs union of the Six would definitely discriminate against them. Secondly, France bore a considerable burden both in the form of aid and relatively high prices for colonial raw materials. She felt that the Six should be placed on a more equal footing by taking on part of the financial responsibility. This was further emphasized by the fact that countries such as Germany were investing in commercial enterprises in the French dependencies and therefore derived much advantage from French expenditure on the necessary infrastructures. The overseas dependencies were listed in Annex IV and included French West Africa, French Equatorial Africa, the French Trustee territory in the Cameroons, Madagascar, a range of other French overseas settlements and Togoland, the Belgian Congo and Ruanda Urundi, the Italian Trustee territory of Somalia and Netherlands New Guinea. The Netherlands Antilles was added in 1964.

The original basis of association was concluded for five years. Essentially it had a double character. The Community undertook to reduce its tariffs on goods coming from the dependencies in line with internal tariff disarmament. This was a vital concession in so far as the primary products supplied by non-associated states faced the Community's common external tariff. The dependent territories were required to reciprocate but could, however, retain protection needed for their development, industrialization or revenue, provided they extended to all member states the preferences they had previously extended to the mother country. The Treaty also brought into existence the European Development Fund (EDF) which was to channel aid to the associated territories. Such EDF aid is a distinctive feature of Association under Part Four. The Six agreed that over the first five years they would make available $581·25 million. France and West Germany subscribed $200 million, Italy $40 million, Belgium and the Netherlands $70 million each and Luxembourg $1·25 million. French territories obtained no less than $511·25 million of this aid. It should perhaps be added that owing to administrative and technical difficulties there was a considerable delay in disbursing this money.

By 1960, many of the overseas territories had become independent and a new basis of association was required. Therefore in 1961 and 1962 negotiations took place which led to the first Yaoundé Convention. This was signed on 20 July 1963 and came into effect, for a further period of five years, on 1 June 1964. It covered eighteen associated states, namely, Burundi, Cameroon, the Central African Republic, Chad, Congo (Kinshasa), Congo (Brazzaville), Dahomey, Gabon, Upper Volta, the Ivory Coast, Madagascar, Mali, Mauritania, Niger, Rwanda, Senegal, Somalia and Togo. The Convention also extended to Surinam, the Netherlands Antilles and French overseas territories and departments. Because of the criticism of non-associated primary producing countries the preference accorded to associated states was reduced by lowering the common external tariff on some tropical products. As a concession, the aid from the EDF was stepped up to $730 million ($620 million of grants and $46 million of soft loans, and a further $64 million was to be made available as loans at normal terms). The sum of $70 million was also made available in the form of grants and loans to the overseas dependent territories of the Six. As in the first association arrangement, firms of the member states enjoyed the right of free establishment in the associates and free movement of capital was provided for. However, unlike the first arrangement, the Yaoundé Convention also created an institutional framework including a Council of Ministers.

Inevitably, the preferences granted to the associated states have given rise to criticism. The Latin American states have persistently called upon the EEC to abolish the preferential system. Raoul Prebisch, when Secretary General of UNCTAD, launched vigorous attacks on the system and as a result the EEC showed itself prepared to make concessions at the second UNCTAD at New Delhi in 1968. However, it ought to be added that the preferences enjoyed by virtue of association have not enabled the associates to expand their exports to the Six more rapidly than the developing world as a whole. Indeed, between 1958 and 1967, whereas the exports of the associates increased by 47 per cent, the figure for the developing world as a whole increased by 68 per cent. In 1969 the Yaoundé Convention was renewed and the present arrangement governs the aid and trade relationships between the eighteen and the Six until 31 January 1975. Two aspects of Yaoundé II are worth noting. Aid was again stepped up. A sum of $748 million in the form of grants and $80 million in the form of soft loans was provided for. Additionally $90 million of loans at normal terms were to be available ($82 million in the form of grants and loans were to be available for overseas territories). Also, following undertakings at the second UNCTAD, it was agreed that the common external tariff towards third countries generally on tropical products should be reduced. As a consolation the associates were to benefit from a reduction in the defences for Community agricultural producers under the Common Agricultural Policy. Currently (1974) negotiations are under way for a third convention to replace Yaoundé II which expires in 1975.

Association under Article 238

So far the discussion has been about the association provisions designed originally for the Community's colonial dependencies. In addition, as we have indicated, Article 238 provides for association with third countries generally. The first two countries to take advantage of this provision were Greece and Turkey. The Greek Treaty of Association began operation on 1 November 1962. Under it a customs union was to be founded between the Six and Greece over a period of twelve years. This involved Greece in accepting the common external tariff. The cuts in tariffs on intra-Community trade were extended to Community imports of Greek goods. On the other hand, Greece had twelve years to remove her tariffs on Community goods. Moreover, in respect of industrial goods, which constituted about a third of the Greek imports, Greece was allowed twenty-two years to eliminate tariffs. This was specifically designed to enable Greek industry to develop to a state where it would face Community industry on equal terms. The association agreement also provided for $125 million of loans from the European Investment Bank (EIB) over the first five years. Apparently, up to the end of 1966 only $63 million had been lent and this led to some dissatisfaction on the part of the Greeks. Provision was also made for the gradual harmonization of Greek agricultural, economic and trade policies with those of the Community. The Treaty also envisaged the eventual prospect of full membership of the Community. However, following the *coup d'état* in 1967 the Greek association agreement has been frozen. The Turkish association began operating on 1 December 1964. Under the Treaty a five-year (extendable to nine or more years) preparatory period was provided for which was aimed at strengthening the Turkish economy. Imports into the Community of four Turkish crops (tobacco, dried figs, raisins and hazelnuts), which provided about 40 per cent of Turkish export earnings, were to benefit from tariff-free quotas which were subsequently increased. Also during the five-year preparatory period the E I B was to lend $67 million for Turkish development. The preparatory period was to be followed by a twelve-year transition period during which a customs union would be established between the Six and Turkey. Over this period Turkish economic policy was to be harmonized with that of the Community and as in the case of Greek association the possibility of eventual full membership was held out. By and large the Turks seem to have found their arrangement satisfactory.

Other states have been attracted by the possibilities of association. When the first Yaoundé Convention was signed a statement was issued indicating the willingness of the Community to give favourable consideration to requests for association from countries in similar economic situations to those already associated. This point was taken up by Nigeria. As a result an Association Treaty was signed in Lagos in June 1966. Under it Nigerian goods were to be accorded the same terms of entry into the Community market as were granted to the eighteen Yaoundé Convention states except for certain goods in respect of which import quotas were agreed. In return Nigeria undertook to grant duty-free entry to Community goods. However, she undertook to avoid discrimination against non-Community countries by changing her customs duties to fiscal duties and charging these on Community goods. In respect of imports of twenty-six products a small customs duty was to be levied but this was not to apply to Community goods. The entry into force of the association could only occur after ratification by all the contracting parties. This process was delayed by political factors and at the end of May

1969 the Treaty was due to expire simultaneously with the Yaoundé Convention.

In 1968 the Community negotiated the Arusha Agreement with Kenya, Tanzania and Uganda. However, this expired in 1969 before being ratified. The association was renegotiated in 1969 and runs until 1975. The agreement is based on a free-trade area between the two sides, but the Community has set limits on its imports of coffee, cloves and canned pineapples. Produce subject to the Common Agricultural Policy is governed by other arrangements. The Arusha associates have undertaken to remove tariffs and quotas on imports from the Community – except where balance of payments, industrialization and government revenue considerations dictate otherwise – and have given the Community a 2 to 9 per cent preference on about sixty products. This agreement is currently (1974) the subject of renewal negotiations. In 1969 association agreements were signed with Morocco and Tunisia. A similar arrangement with Algeria was vetoed by the Dutch following the declaration of war by Algeria on Israel in 1967 but more recently negotiations have been re-opened. In 1970 the Community also concluded an association agreement with Malta whereby the latter will over ten years form a customs union with the Six. In 1972 the Community also concluded a ten-year association agreement with Cyprus. The Community has at various times reached forms of trade agreement with Lebanon, Israel, Iran, Spain, Egypt, Uruguay, Argentina and Yugoslavia. Other countries are currently waiting in the wings.

Membership

Article 237 of the Rome Treaty declares that any European state may apply to become a member. Unanimous agreement is required within the Council of Ministers before a state can be admitted – this explains the ability of the French to veto British membership.

Until quite late in the 1950s various British Ministers went on record as saying that the UK could never become a full member of the Community. As we have seen, a number of factors were adduced in support of this view. The first was the effect upon the Commonwealth. Commonwealth preference would have to give way to the common external tariff. This would harm Commonwealth members at a time when the idea of a multi-lingual, multi-racial Commonwealth was still on the lips of most politicians and was still regarded as an important vehicle of British influence. Also, the elimination of Commonwealth countries' preferences in the British market was almost certainly likely to lead to a loss of British preferences in Commonwealth markets. There were also some specific problems. One was that New Zealand relied heavily on the UK as an outlet for her butter production. The other was the British import of sugar from low-income Commonwealth countries under the Commonwealth Sugar Agreement. Secondly, there was the British agricultural system. It was supported in a radically different way from that adopted on the Continent. The level of farm incomes and the participation of farmers in price determination were at stake. Also, as we shall see later, the adoption of a Community system was bound to raise prices and the food import bill. Thirdly, the formation of the EFTA raised the problem that British membership of the Community would require that adequate arrangements be made for our EFTA partners. Then finally there was the critical point of supra-nationalism. The need to give up sovereignty was not welcomed then and it has remained a subject upon which British politicians still tend to be wary.

However, it was apparent by 1960 that the Conservative Government was beginning to change its tune and in the House of Commons on 31 July 1961 Mr Macmillan, the Prime Minister, formally announced that the UK had decided to apply for full membership. A letter to this effect was sent on 9 August 1961. The Irish Republic despatched its request before the UK – on the day of the House of Commons announcement. Denmark's application was despatched the day after the UK's. Norway, however, waited until 1962 before applying. Subsequently Austria, Sweden and Switzerland made separate applications for association. Portugal also applied, though no clear indication was given of the arrangement sought. The Council of Ministers decided to accept the British application of 26 September 1961 and on 10 October of the same year the UK, through Mr Edward Heath, made a comprehensive statement of its position at a

Ministerial Conference in Paris. The negotiations which subsequently followed dragged on until 14 January 1963 when General de Gaulle at a Paris Press Conference declared that Britain was not ripe for membership and it was left to M. Maurice Couve de Murville to deliver a *coup de grâce* on 29 January at Brussels by securing the indefinite adjournment of negotiations.

The issues involved in the negotiations were extremely complex. Basically the origin of the problem was quite simple. Britain did not approach with a view to signing the Rome Treaty as it stood. Rather, because of her commitment to the Commonwealth and the EFTA, as well as her different farming system, she sought modifications and accommodations on most fronts.

In the short space available the issues involved can be sketched only in outline. On the agricultural front Mr Heath admitted that the UK would have to move over to the EEC system. One of the main areas of conflict here was the speed of transition. The UK thought in terms of a transition period of up to twelve to fifteen years, but the Six were adamant that the Common Agricultural Policy would have to be applied in its entirety by the end of the Treaty transition period. On the question of a need for an annual farm price review the UK obtained a tolerably satisfactory solution.

The major problems of the Commonwealth sprang from the protection which the Community was destined to place around itself when the common external tariff and the common agricultural policy were fully operational. The UK accepted that the common external tariff was a *fait accompli* but called for a 20 per cent cut. The UK also called for nil duties on twenty-six industrial products. Progress on this issue was slow. By the time of the suspension of negotiations only ten products had been dealt with, some on the basis of nil solutions but others by virtue of the UK withdrawing its request and accepting a form of transitional provision. On the subject of industrial goods produced by Canada, Australia and New Zealand, the UK recognized that the common external tariff would have to be applied and an agreement was reached on its application stages and full operation by 1970. The Community did, however, declare its willingness in 1966 and 1969 to examine the possibility of developing trade with these countries. In the case of processed foodstuffs, Britain produced a list of eighty products which were regarded as being entitled to nil duty or preferential measures. In practice in the case of half it was decided to apply the common external tariff at the same rate as industrial goods, but in the case of the other half a more gradual alignment was agreed.

One of the most acute Commonwealth problems arose in connection with temperate foodstuffs. Britain proposed that once she was within the Community the latter should provide comparable outlets to those which temperate food producers had enjoyed previously. The Six, however, were adamant that they could offer no permanent or indeed long-term guarantee to Commonwealth producers. They were prepared to negotiate specific and limited agreements but permanent solutions would have to be sought in the framework of world-wide agreements. New Zealand was considered as meriting exceptional treatment as regards butter but no solution in terms of guarantees was achieved.

In the case of India, Pakistan, Ceylon and Hong Kong the general solution was twofold. Firstly, there was to be a very gradual application of the common external tariff but with special treatment in certain cases. Thus, in the case of tea there was to be a nil duty and in other cases there was to be an indefinite suspension of duties. Secondly, the Community would negotiate comprehensive trade agreements with India and Pakistan in order to guarantee or indeed increase their foreign currency earnings. For cotton goods special agreements would be made to ensure that exports to the enlarged Community were not harmed.

In the case of other less developed countries in Africa and the West Indies, the UK hoped that they would be able to take advantage of the association provisions. Nigeria, Ghana and Tanganyika, however, disliked the political overtones and declined this offer. The Commission countered by offering either participation in a new Yaoundé Convention (an arrangement which acknowledged independence of what were formerly colonial dependencies) or specific trade agreements.

The solution to the EFTA problem lay in the participants becoming either full or associate members. Three took one course and three the other, whilst Portugal's intentions were unclear. At the time when the UK negotiations were suspended the negotiations with Norway and Denmark were advanced. Formal talks on the Irish application had hardly begun. In the case of the three applicants for association the first round of talks to ascertain the problems to be dealt with had taken place between the EEC Commission and a delegation from the country concerned, and on this basis the Commission had reported to the Council. But no formal negotiations had been opened.

As already indicated, negotiations were abruptly terminated by General de Gaulle. Britain was an independent maritime power not yet sufficiently European to be admitted. This was a half-truth. The fact that she had applied indicated a new European emphasis in foreign policy. The fact that she did not merely accept the Treaty but sought to negotiate so many modifications in the interests of the Commonwealth was a reflection of the fact that her imperial past, although no longer a dominating interest, still exercised a significant constraint on policy. There can be no doubt that the arduous negotiations arising out of the need to seek special treatment on products as divergent as kangaroo meat and cricket bats played into the hands of the French. But the real root of French opposition was undoubtedly political. Firstly, Britain would be an American 'trojan horse'. Secondly, in a Community of ten, French influence would be watered down.

Having laid the blame largely at the door of the French, it is fair to ask whether the negotiations could have succeeded. The general impression of the delegations, except the French, was that there was a good chance of reaching a successful conclusion if the negotiations had continued. Professor Hallstein, President of the Commission at the time, was more guarded. Speaking before the European Parliament in 1963 he observed

it is not possible to say of the negotiations at the moment when they were interrupted that they had in practice failed, or to say that it had been proved that they could succeed. (quoted in Palmer *et al.*, 1968, p. 243)

The change of government in the UK did not, however, change the course of British policy, since the Labour Party itself became convinced of the need for the UK to join the Community. On 10 November 1966 the Prime Minister, Harold Wilson, announced to the House of Commons plans for a high-level approach to the Six with the intention of becoming a full member of the Community. This was followed between January and March 1967 by visits to the capitals of the Six. Having judged the prospects to be satisfactory, the Prime Minister announced to the House of Commons on 2 May that the UK would submit its second application. This was made on 11 May and was followed by applications from Ireland, Denmark and Norway.

The British approach on this occasion was radically different from that of the 1961–3 period. No attempt was going to be made to secure a multitude of accommodations and concessions. The areas for negotiation were reduced to these: the Common Agricultural Policy was bound to have a substantial repercussion on the balance-of-payments and cost of living; the basis of the policy was accepted but an adequate transition period was required; also a more equitable sharing of the financial burdens of the policy would be necessary; a comprehensive annual review of the agricultural industry should be held, broadly similar to that introduced within the Community but with agricultural producers' organizations formally participating in the review procedure. There were some Commonwealth interests which needed safeguarding and in particular New Zealand and the sugar producers. The problem of capital movements would also require attention. The UK stance also differed in that on this occasion it claimed that it would bring with it a dowry in the form of its considerable achievements and potential in the field of science and technology. The latter led to suggestions about a new Community – the European Technological Community. The British bid was also sweetened, although somewhat weakly, by references to Britain's awareness of the possibility of progress towards political unity.

The application for membership was examined by the Council of Ministers on 10 July 1967 and the Council decided to obtain the opinion of the Commission. The Commission presented its conclusions in September. It noted that views differed as to the priorities that were given to solving the Community's own internal problems as opposed to solving the problems inherent in an extension of the Community. It recommended that an attempt be made to deal with both simultaneously and that negotiations should be opened. The Commission did, however, note the urgent need to solve the British balance-of-payments problem and to adjust the role of sterling so that it could be fitted into a Community monetary system. The reference to the problem caused by sterling was an entirely new and indeed ominous feature of the UK–EEC dialogue. As one observer has remarked of the previous negotiations

In those long weeks ... in Brussels in 1962, everything else was gone into – every detail of Commonwealth trade from carpets to kangaroo tails – but never a word about sterling. (Strange, 1967, p. 5)

In October and November the question of negotiations was discussed by the Council of Ministers without result. In November the Prime Minister re-emphasized the UK's technical dowry, proposing a seven-point plan for European technology. These covered bilateral projects with other European partners, multilateral discussions on improving Europe's technological capability, the establishment of a European Technological Institute as well as offers to co-operate in the field of European business mergers, company law, and patents. However, later that month General de Gaulle delivered another of his famous press conferences which effectively closed the door to entry. The General took the view that full membership for Britain would lead to the destruction of the Community. Some form of association would, however, be acceptable. Great play was made of the British balance-of-payments deficit which was said to indicate a permanent state of disequilibrium. The restrictions on the export of capital by the UK were contrasted with free movement within the Six. Then there was the sterling system with its large and vulnerable liabilities. At the Ministerial meeting on 19 December 1967, the Five expressed themselves in favour of commencing negotiations but France took the view that enlargement would profoundly modify the nature and ways of administering the Community. In addition, the UK economy had to be restored to health before its application could be considered. No vote was taken. The Community once more agreed to disagree and the application remained on the agenda.

Subsequently, various member states put forward proposals to bring the UK closer to the Community and prepare her for membership. The Commission lent a hand by proposing a preferential trade arrangement with the states seeking membership, together with closer consultation and collaboration on scientific and technological matters. No progress was made. However, the events of May 1968 and the resignation of General de Gaulle in 1969 brought the subject of British membership back into the foreground. This was followed by the accession to power of President Pompidou and at the Hague Summit of December 1969 the Six agreed to open negotiations with the applicant countries 'in the most positive spirit'. The Six were therefore agreeing to take up the British application which had lain on the table since the Labour Government's previous bid. Britain was accompanied by three other applicants – the Irish Republic, Denmark and Norway.

Negotiations and terms

In June 1970 Anthony Barber was charged with the conduct of the British negotiations but following the tragic death of Iain Macleod and the translation of Mr Barber to the role of Chancellor of the Exchequer the negotiating role was passed to Geoffrey Rippon. The negotiations were conducted relatively expeditiously as compared with 1961–3. Mr Barber made his opening statement at a meeting between the Six and the UK at Luxembourg on 30 June 1970 and the Six replied. A series of ministerial meetings then took place at roughly six-weekly intervals in the second half of 1970 and the first half of 1971. (There were of course more frequent meetings between the Permanent Representatives of the six states and a British team led by Sir Con O'Neill, and there was continuous study of the problems arising by all the parties involved, including the Commission.) Although considerable progress was made, it became apparent by the beginning of 1971 that some political impetus was needed if certain particularly knotty problems were to be solved, and that in practice it was necessary that Britain and

France should come to a clear understanding. The Heath–Pompidou meeting of 20 and 21 May 1971 served this purpose. The discussions were centred on the difficult problems of EEC membership which still remained to be solved, in particular those concerning New Zealand, sugar, the role of sterling and the UK contribution to the Community budget. The available evidence suggests that the two leaders achieved at least a close identity of view, and political commentators noted the relatively rapid pace of the negotiations after the summit. The final ministerial round was completed in Luxembourg on 23 June – the entry talks had been completed successfully. The terms were embodied in a White Paper *The United Kingdom and the European Communities* (Cmnd 4715) which was presented to Parliament in July 1971. Parliament had a 'take note' debate in July during which the terms were considered. Then in October both Houses debated the issue again with the intention that a final vote for or against entry should be taken. This vote occurred on 28 October. The House of Commons voted 356 to 244 in favour. The House of Lords majority was even greater – 451 to 58. The problem of getting the subsequent enabling legislation through both Houses still remained but was eventually surmounted.

With respect to the actual conduct of the negotiations the British attitude was again to reduce the number of issues to manageable proportions. Membership of Euratom and the ECSC would not pose major problems and the UK would seek only a short transitional period. The EEC would, however, throw up more difficult problems. These related to agricultural policy, the UK contribution to the Community budget, Commonwealth sugar exports, New Zealand dairy exports, and certain other Commonwealth issues. There was also a new problem – fisheries policy. Undoubtedly, of all these the major obstacles were bound to be encountered in negotiating an acceptable UK contribution to the budget. The length of the transitional period before the barriers to free movement of industrial and agricultural goods were removed was also capable of causing some difficulty, as was the role of sterling.

It is not intended in this account to list in detail all the terms of the final settlement. The reader can find these laid out in the

1971 White Paper. This account will only be concerned with major issues.

One of the early matters to be settled was the length of the transitional period. The U K originally asked for three years for industry and six for agriculture. A solution was finally hammered out. The U K and the Six compromised on a transition period of five years' duration for both agricultural and industrial goods. On the assumption that the U K joined on 1 January 1973 (which she did) industrial tariffs on trade between the Six and Britain would be removed in five stages, consisting of five cuts of 20 per cent, one in each of the five years 1973 to 1977. The U K would also adopt the common external tariff in four movements, one in each of the four years 1974 to 1977. In the case of agriculture the U K would in the first year of membership introduce the Community system of support. Threshold and intervention prices would be set; at first these would be lower than those in the Community, but they would be gradually increased to Community levels in six steps over the five-year period.

From a negotiating point of view as long a transition period as possible was desirable in the case of agriculture, since this would put back the day when the full weight of the Community agricultural policy would be felt. Weight in this sense relates not only to the effect on the price of food but also to the contribution which the U K would have to make to the Community budget (which of course includes farm finance).

The U K proposal on the budget was that its initial contribution to it should be 3 per cent, rising to 15 per cent by the end of the transition period. This was a highly provocative proposal since the Commission envisaged two possibilities which both involved a much more onerous régime. One envisaged an initial contribution level of 21·5 per cent and the second involved a progressive rise in contributions from between 10 and 15 per cent in the first year to 20 to 25 per cent in the final year of the transition period. There was also the question of what would happen thereafter. The Six had agreed on a system whereby the budget would be fed by 90 per cent of the proceeds of the levies and customs duties plus the proceeds of a 1 per cent rate of the value added tax.

In the event the negotiated settlement involved the UK in paying the following percentage costs of the budget – 1973 8·64, 1974 10·85, 1975 13·34, 1976 16·03, 1977 18·92. Possible gross contributions, possible receipts and possible net contributions were shown in the 1971 White Paper and are laid out in Table 8.

Table 8 UK contributions to and receipts from community budget, 1973–7 (£m)

Possible gross contribution	Possible receipts	Possible net contribution
120	20	100
155	40	115
195	55	140
245	75	170
300	100	200

From the UK point of view this was certainly better than the Commission had originally proposed, but worse than it had initially hoped for. In 1978 and 1979 the UK would normally have been subject to the Community budgetary system. It was, however, agreed that in 1978 the UK contribution should not increase above the 1977 level by more than two fifths of the difference between the 1977 level and what the level should be under the new system. Likewise in 1979 the increased contribution over the 1978 level would be similarly determined. Then there was the question of what would happen in 1980 and beyond – in other words what would the permanent as opposed to the transitional system be? The answer is that the UK will be subject to the Community budgetary finance system and 90 per cent of levies and customs duties will be paid into the Community budget, together with the proceeds of a 1 per cent rate of the value added tax. In other words the UK accepted the Community system as it stands. The 1971 White Paper points out that the size of the commitments so arising are not susceptible to valid estimation nor is the size of any possible benefits. Because of this the White Paper goes on to say that the Community declared in the course of the negotiations that if unacceptable situations should arise 'the very survival of the Community would demand that the institutions find equitable solutions'.

New Zealand was a particularly difficult problem. Butter and cheese represented about 15 per cent of her exports and 85 per cent of her dairy export receipts came from sales to the UK. The problem was therefore one of attempting to guarantee New Zealand access to the UK market after membership. The solutions devised were as follows. In the case of butter the guaranteed quantity would be reduced over the first five years by 4 per cent per annum. Thus in the fifth year she would still be able to sell at least 80 per cent of her 1971 entitlement in the UK. She would also enjoy a guaranteed price at a level equal to the average of prices in the UK in the four years 1969 to 1972. In the third year after the UK accession the Community would look again at the position and would decide 'on suitable measures for ensuring beyond 1977 the continuation of special arrangements for New Zealand butter' (1971 White Paper). For cheese access would be reduced so that in the fifth year she would be able to market 20 per cent of her 1971 level of sales. No guarantee is held out after 1977 in the case of cheese, but substantial sales are expected to continue because New Zealand cheese does not compete directly with Community production. According to the 1971 White Paper New Zealand described the agreement as highly satisfactory. In the case of lamb no common organization exists within the Six. A common external tariff of 20 per cent has therefore been agreed. The White Paper states that the UK and New Zealand believe that an acceptable level of trade in lamb will continue to flow over such a tariff.

In the case of sugar, Mr Rippon sought what he termed 'bankable assurances'. The UK's contractual obligations under the Commonwealth Sugar Agreement, which require it to buy agreed quantities until the end of 1974, will be fulfilled. Thereafter it has been agreed that the arrangements for sugar imports from developing Commonwealth sugar producers will be made within the framework of an association or trading agreement with the enlarged Community. It has further been agreed 'that the enlarged Community will have as its firm purpose the safeguarding of the interests of the developing countries concerned whose economies depend to a considerable extent on the export of primary products and in particular of sugar' (1971 White Paper). The countries concerned expressed the view that this solution was satisfactory.

One of the important issues which seems to have concerned France in particular was the role of sterling and indeed the whole question of how in monetary terms the U K could be fitted into the Community. In the weeks before the Heath–Pompidou meeting the French built the subject up into a major negotiating issue. But more or less immediately after the meeting the French did a volte-face by agreeing without demur to the British proposals to discuss sterling's role after her entry. However, the U K agreed to stabilize the size of the sterling balances and in the longer term to run them down. But no agreement was reached about just how they would be run down or how long the process would take. Basically therefore the position is that in any detailed sense the policy has still to be shaped.

The U K also had to deal with the market-access problems of developing countries in the Commonwealth. The details of the position of various countries will not be discussed here. Basically the solution was that a variety of arrangements would be brought to bear. Independent Commonwealth countries in Africa, the Caribbean, the Indian Ocean and the Pacific could choose between the renewed Yaoundé Convention, some other form of association, or a commercial agreement. All British dependent territories (except Gibraltar and Hong Kong) would be offered association under Part Four of the Rome Treaty. Hong Kong would be included within the scope of the Community's Generalized Preference Scheme (see pp. 240–41). In the case of India, Pakistan, Ceylon, Malaysia and Singapore the Community was willing to examine with them trade problems which might arise, taking account of the Generalized Preference Scheme which would benefit them considerably. One specific problem which the Community expressed its willingness to discuss was India's sugar exports to the enlarged Community. The continued suspension of the tariff on tea would help India and Ceylon. Malta has as we have seen concluded a customs union agreement with the Six. Arrangements would be made for Cyprus and Gibraltar – for Cyprus see above.

On the matter of fisheries policy the UK indicated that the existing policy was not satisfactory. The Community agreed that the arrangements would have to be reconsidered in the light of enlargement.

The successful conclusion of negotiations for UK entry was also accompanied by successful conclusions in respect of the Irish Republic, Denmark and Norway. However, the latter did not ulimately join – a national referendum did not produce the necessary votes for membership. The Irish and Danish negotiations were not as complicated as those relating to the UK. Their terms were similar to those obtained by the British but a number of special accommodations were provided and are detailed in the Community's *Fifth General Report* (1972, pp. 49–67). A link with those EFTA states who had not become full members was provided by means of industrial free trade arrangements. Countries benefiting from these agreements are Austria, Finland, Iceland, Portugal, Sweden, Switzerland and Norway. (Austria, with the agreement of EFTA, had been seeking association with the Community for a number of years. Under the State Treaty of 1955 Article 4 precluded any form of economic union with West Germany and the best that Austria could hope for was some form of association.)

Common commercial policy and aid

Although a common commercial policy embraces a variety of subjects, clearly the most important is the level of the common external tariff. Since the tariff is the distinguishing feature of a customs union, and is the aspect of the Common Market which touches so many of the leading trading countries in the world, it is fitting that the negotiations concerning its size should be one of the final topics for consideration in this book.

The Rome Treaty confers upon the Commission the specific responsibility of conducting tariff negotiations with third countries. In 1960 the Six had to present to the GATT the common tariff which was to replace the tariffs of France, West Germany, Italy and the Benelux. The GATT rules require that the average incidence of the common tariff be no greater than the average incidence of the tariffs it replaces. In practice the common level was 8·2 per cent which was less than the 9·3 per cent of the tariffs it replaced. As a result the majority of the contracting parties to the GATT were satisfied. Furthermore, in anticipation of the Dillon Round of tariff negotiations (named after Douglas Dillon the then US Under-Secretary of State), the Community decided provisionally to reduce the new tariff by 20 per cent. As a result, national tariffs were initially aligned on the original tariff less 20 per cent, except where smaller cuts were negotiated and consolidated in the Dillon Round.

In July 1962 President Kennedy, speaking in Philadelphia, made his Declaration of Interdependence. This foreshadowed a US policy of North Atlantic free trade and partnership with a united Europe on terms of equality. The Trade Expansion Act of 1962 gave concrete expression to these aspirations. It conferred a negotiating mandate to establish full free trade in goods where the US and the EEC together accounted for 80 per cent of free world trade. Otherwise only a 50 per cent across-the-board cut could be negotiated. In practice the failure of the UK to join the EEC meant that full free trade was ruled out of the ensuing Kennedy Round. Negotiations proper opened in Geneva in May 1964 and were concluded in May 1967.

Although the participants failed to achieve all their objectives, substantial progress was made. A number of difficulties had stood in the way of a successful outcome. One was the fact that the US Congress insisted that agriculture be included in the negotiations. This was partly necessary in order to secure the successful passage of the Act, but it was also justified by the fact that US sales of agricultural products to the Community constituted $1600 million of the $5500 million total sales thereto. The agricultural negotiations were also complicated by the somewhat protectionist tendency in the Community's agricultural policy together with the fact that, partly as a result of the French withdrawal, the financial rules and the common prices for products other than grain were not agreed until quite late on.

Another problem was the issue of excluding altogether some products from the tariff-cutting and applying cuts of less than

50 per cent in the case of others. In particular, there was the problem of how to deal with the disparity problem where, for example, US tariffs were so much higher than those of the Six and a straight 50 per cent cut would be unacceptable. The main sticking point came in the case of chemicals. The Six, backed by the UK and the Swiss, were anxious to have the American Selling Price (ASP) system abolished. Under this arrangement the price upon which US import duties were applied was not the European export price but the price at which comparable goods were produced in the US. This resulted in duties of up to 170 per cent *ad valorem*. The system also applied to other products such as rubber shoes.

The outcome of the negotiations was as follows. Although many cuts of 50 per cent were agreed, and the number of products excluded from tariff-cutting altogether or subject to cuts of less than 50 per cent was greatly reduced, the average cut was only about 35 per cent. The total value of international trade affected was $40,000 million per annum, that is to say, about one quarter of free world trade. In respect of chemicals, the US accepted that should the ASP system be abolished, irrespective of whether products were subject to it, duties would be reduced by 50 per cent and down to a ceiling of 20 per cent (except in special cases). The Community for its part undertook to reduce its duties by 50 per cent (subject to exceptions). If the ASP system was not abolished,[1] the US would reduce by 50 per cent its duties in excess of 8 per cent and by 20 per cent those below that rate. The Community would then only reduce by 20 per cent duties below 25 per cent and by 30 per cent those above that figure.

In the agricultural sector the Kennedy Round fell far short of the hopes entertained by the US and the Six. The Community argued for a system of international discipline and commitments about the levels of national support for farmers. But in the event these were dropped. All that emerged was an increased minimum world price for wheat of $1·73 per bushel[2] and an agreement to

1. It has in fact not been abolished.
2. This was a concession to the US which had looked for greater access to the EEC agricultural market. By the middle of 1969 there were signs that the agreement to keep the price level above the minimum had been breached.

give 'food aid' to needy countries. This was to consist of 4·5 million tons of grain a year. The US was to finance 42 per cent of the cost, the EEC 23 per cent, Canada 11 per cent and the UK and Australia 5 per cent each.

Food aid has been governed by Food Aid Conventions – the first dates from 1967 and was followed by a second in 1971. These Conventions relate to aid in the form of gifts of cereals. (The Community has also given aid in kind in the form of skimmed milk powder and butter oil but this has been an autonomous act outside any international engagements.) Under the second Convention the Community undertook to supply 1,035,000 tons of grain annually (as under the first Convention) but in 1973, following enlargement, this was raised to 1,287,000 tons.

Before leaving the subject of trade liberalization we should note that a further round of international trade negotiations (within the framework of the GATT) opened in Tokyo in September 1973. The so-called Nixon Round, scheduled to end in 1975, is expected to be extremely complicated and will take in not merely industrial tariffs but also trade in farm products and non-tariff barriers. The Community position, finally hammered out by Council in July 1973, links trade and monetary progress – 'the policy of liberalizing world trade cannot be carried out successfully unless parallel efforts are made to set up a monetary system which shields the world economy from the shocks and imbalances which have recently occurred.'

Earlier in this book the subject of association was dealt with. During the process of that discussion it was pointed out that the Secretary General of the UNCTAD had persistently called for an end to the preferential system adopted by the EEC whereby certain states obtained more favourable access terms to the Community market, and it was indicated that at the second UNCTAD at New Delhi in 1968 the Six had indicated a general willingness to shift ground. This brings us face to face with the idea of a generalized preference system which was raised at the first UNCTAD in 1964. The general implication of this idea for the Community was that it should give a generalized preference to developing countries rather than be selective. Secondly, if developing countries were to expand their output of manufactured and semi-manufactured goods they would need outlets in the markets of developed countries. The outlets would in fact take the form of a tariff preference for developing countries in respect of these goods – that is to say, in the case of the EEC it would levy a lower rate of duty on imports from developing countries than from developed ones. At the second UNCTAD the idea of generalized preferences was formally accepted and the rich nations agreed to table offers.

Negotiations followed and a generalized preference plan was eventually worked out. For its part, in March 1971 the Six agreed that in July 1971 it would abolish import duties on developing country exports of manufactured and semi-manufactured goods and some processed agricultural products. This does not mean that the Six will import such goods in unlimited quantities. Rather the Community has undertaken to operate a straightforward but liberal system of quantitative ceilings or quotas on zero-duty imports. Under this system developing countries will know the exact limits of their privileged access to the market of the Community.

Finally something must be said about aid. Apart from the activities of the EDF and EIB, and Food Aid, help for developing countries is a national responsibility. Nevertheless it is a fitting subject to conclude this assessment of the activities of the Community.[1] Total aid (official and private, in dollars) expressed as a percentage of GNP ranged in 1971 from 0·80 (Denmark) to 1·63 (Netherlands). This compared with 0·67 for the USA, 0·96 for Japan and an average of 0·82 for the sixteen Development Assistance Committee countries. Taking only official aid, the figures for the Community states in 1971 ranged from 0·17 (Italy) to 0·68 (France). This compared with 0·32 for the USA, 0·23 for Japan and an average of 0·35 for the sixteen DAC countries.

1. The enlarged Community but excluding the Irish Republic.

10 The Renegotiation Issue

By the beginning of the present decade the subject of British membership was not a matter of disagreement in principle between the main political parties. The Conservatives sought entry in 1961–3 and obtained an agreement in 1971; the Labour Party tried to enter in 1967 but was baulked; the Liberals consistently advocated entry. The matter nevertheless remained controversial for two reasons. Firstly, among expert commentators there has been a difference of assessment as to the balance of advantage and disadvantage likely to arise from entry. Secondly, since 1971 there have been differences of view between the political parties on the acceptability of the entry terms obtained by Mr Geoffrey Rippon.

Advantages and disadvantages of joining

Even when prejudices, and errors of appreciation as to what the Community was and sought to become, were eliminated from the discussion, the assessment of whether the UK ought to join was rendered extremely difficult, if not impossible, by two factors. The first was that political as well as economic repercussions were held to be relevant. The latter may be susceptible to quantification in money terms, the former are not. Only if both economic and political factors pointed in the same direction was an unqualified assessment possible. When they fell on opposite sides of the scale, as in some commentators' view they did, the assessment became, to say the least, difficult. But secondly, even in respect of the economic aspect there were difficulties of estimation. The static balance-of-payments and welfare costs arising from tariff changes, the Common Agricultural Policy and associated financial arrangements were relatively amenable to calculation, and the results tended to agree very roughly about the size of the adverse balance-of-payments effect and welfare cost. On the other hand there were said to be dynamic factors which would give rise to economic advantages. These related to the fuller reaping of economies of scale, the stimulating effect of increased competition and the stimulus to investment. These were difficult to estimate.

A number of studies were carried out which gave some indication of the static balance-of-payments and welfare effects of membership. Three sets of studies will be considered. Firstly, Professor J. H. Williamson carried out a study of the effects on trade in manufactures and the effects of the agricultural aspects of the EEC were surveyed by Tim Josling. Secondly, the trade in manufactures and the agricultural aspects were the subject of a study by Marcus Miller and John Spencer. Thirdly, there was the 1971 White Paper (*The United Kingdom and the European Communities*, Cmnd 4715). All of these were compared in an immensely useful summary study by Marcus Miller (1971). It is important to reiterate that all of them were concerned with the 'static' effects as they were expected to work themselves out by 1980. There were also the 'dynamic' effects which were the subject of tentative calculation by Professor Williamson (1971) and these will be discussed later.

It was recognized for a long time that the effect of the Common Agricultural Policy on the UK was likely to be disadvantageous from a balance-of-payments, welfare and price point of view. Let us concentrate on the first two. As members we would no longer be able to buy food at low world prices. If the UK imported food from, for example, the Commonwealth, levies would be applied and under the Community system for financing the budget 90 per cent would be handed *not* to the Chancellor of the Exchequer for the benefit of UK citizens but to the Community for financing, amongst other things, Community agricultural policy. (The UK would of course be able to draw benefits from the budget, but no study suggested that these would match UK payments.) Also payable into the budget would be 90 per cent of the proceeds of the common external tariff (again the Chancellor would relinquish these) and the proceeds of a one-percentage point of the value added tax. The effects of the

CAP could be viewed as giving rise to deterioration in the terms of trade: that is, unless something happened to improve export prices of manufactures the terms of trade were likely to worsen to the extent that the UK would have to pay more for food imports. Alternatively the CAP could be said to involve a significant piece of trade diversion. In the light of the elementary analysis presented in chapter 3 food imports would not be produced by efficient Commonwealth producers, but by relatively less efficient European farmers. But the effect on the balance of payments (and welfare) could not be discovered by merely taking account of the impact of financing the Community budget. It also required a consideration of what would happen to trade flows generally.

On the import side the removal by the UK of tariffs on EEC manufactured goods could be expected to lead to a rise in imports. On the other hand the imposition of the common external tariff on manufactures and the levies on food would have an opposite effect as regards imports from non-EEC sources. In respect of exports the removal of EEC tariffs against UK goods would lead to an increase. But the EEC would remove its import tariffs in respect of other new member exports. Also the new members would remove their import tariffs against EEC goods and the UK would lose the advantage of Commonwealth Preference. All this would be to the detriment of UK exports. How would all this (including the Community budget) affect the balance of payments? The Josling–Williamson study calculated that it would lead to an adverse movement of £266 million; the Miller–Spencer study suggested an adverse effect of £342 million; and the 1971 White Paper estimated a cost to the balance of payments of £345 million.

What about the welfare costs? The Miller study provided estimates of these in respect of each calculation of the effect on the balance of payments. The assumptions upon which these estimates were based were that the balance-of-payments deficit could be eliminated by a devaluation, the size of which depended on the relevant elasticities of demand. The welfare cost of correcting a balance-of-payments deficit could be defined as the consequent terms of trade loss on imports. According to Miller the welfare cost following the Josling–Williamson study was

£389 million; in the case of the Miller–Spencer study it was £657 million; and the estimate based on the 1971 White Paper was £560 million. If it was assumed that by the end of the 1970s the GNP would be of the order of £50,000 million, the welfare costs would amount to between ¾ per cent and just under 1½ per cent of the GNP.

As indicated earlier, Professor Williamson had studied the possible dynamic benefits in terms of scale economies, greater competition and the stimulus to investment. While being aware of the possibility of these advantageous effects, most economists recoiled from putting a value on them. However, Professor Williamson was not daunted. He believed economic growth would result from the effect of these factors and estimated that collectively they would add 0.3 per cent to the growth rate over the five years to 1978. This suggested that by 1978 the GNP would be about 1.5 per cent greater as a result. Assuming a £50,000 million GNP by 1978 it followed that the dynamic advantages could add up to £750 million. This was 1.5 per cent of GNP. There would therefore by a ½ per cent gain if a comparison was made with the Miller–Spencer calculation of the 'static' disadvantageous effects. But it must be emphasized that whilst the Miller–Spencer (and the other) studies pointed to a loss and were based on quite explicit data and assumptions, the Williamson gains had something of a rabbit-out-of-a-hat character. There was therefore room for formulating an adverse economic judgement. Even if there were political advantages (as was fairly generally maintained) it was difficult to decide whether this gave rise to an overall gain.

It must, however, be admitted that since these studies were made the static economic case seems to require some reappraisal. A considerable part of the economic case against membership turned on the effect on the price of agricultural imports into the UK once she was fully under the influence of the CAP. Cheap Commonwealth (and other) food would be replaced by dear European food. But following the vast upsurge in the price of food products on the world market in the early seventies, with world levels at and above Community levels, the analysis is now almost certainly likely to produce different results.

The balance-of-payments and welfare consequences of being in as opposed to out have changed. It seems probable that a more favourable economic impact is indicated.

Renegotiation

Within the British Labour Party there have been serious differences of opinion as to the desirability of UK membership of the European Community. But it appears that even among those who are firmly committed to membership there is an acceptance of the view that better entry terms should be sought. Arising out of the Labour Party's 'great debate' a renegotiation of the terms became a part of the party's election platform. When Labour was elected in February 1974 the Foreign Secretary, Mr James Callaghan, followed this up in April with a statement to the Council of Ministers at Luxembourg setting out the British Government's position. This was reproduced as a White Paper (*Renegotiation of the Terms of Entry into the European Economic Community*, Cmnd 5593).[1]

The Foreign Secretary made it clear that the UK would negotiate in good faith with a view to achieving an early and successful result. If the UK obtained the 'right' terms the Government would put them to the British people for approval[2] – either by a referendum or a general election. If the renegotiation did not succeed the UK would not regard the Treaty obligations as binding on it and would consult the British people on the advisability of negotiating a withdrawal.

The main points in the Foreign Secretary's statement were as follows:

(a) Economic and Monetary Union by 1980 is dangerously over-ambitious.

(b) The method of financing the Community Budget is unfair – for example, the UK percentage contribution is likely in due course to be significantly greater than the ratio of its GNP

1. Mr Callaghan also made an amplifying statement to the Council of Ministers at Luxembourg on 4 June 1974.

2. Whether the Government would commend the terms to the people was not made clear.

to the Community GNP. The ways in which Budget funds are spent (i.e. mainly on agriculture) do not fairly take account of UK interests.

(c) The CAP as currently conceived is in need of major change. It represents a threat to world trade and keeps low-cost producers out of the UK market. It has been unsatisfactory in a number of ways – for example, it has given rise to costly surpluses (cheap butter for the Russians). Emphasis should be placed on greater financial control and on the interests of consumers.

(d) There should be no harmonization of VAT which involves the taxation of necessities.

(e) The British Parliament should retain powers needed to pursue effective regional, industrial and fiscal policies.

(f) The economic interests of the Commonwealth and developing countries need to be better safeguarded. This involves continued access to the UK market, and intensified Community trade and aid policies.

How do we appraise this statement of the British position? In respect of EMU it is quite judicious. It does not oppose EMU in principle but draws attention to the danger of fixing the parities before there is convergence of such things as wage rate and productivity movements. (It could have been added that not only would there have to be a centralization of control over monetary and budgetary policies but, insofar as inflation is cost–push in character, an effective incomes policy would have to be operative, and that attitudes and experience do not yet give grounds for confidence on this score.) It can of course be argued that EMU is not really likely to occur since little if any real progress has been made – in other words why worry? However, this does not deal with the problem that the Community has pledged that it will proceed to EMU. Irrespective of how the Community reacts to the British approach, it is clear that the UK has declared EMU a vital national interest and it will not be lost on the other member states that the British are aware that the Luxembourg voting compromise is ready to hand.

The case for some change in the position of the UK in relation to payments into and receipts from the Community Budget seems reasonable and to that extent is probably negotiable. A means of spending Community funds in a way more relevant to UK needs presents itself in the shape of the proposed Regional Development Fund. The UK would therefore seem well advised (a) to press for setting up the Fund; (b) to demand an adequate financial allocation to it; (c) to require that the aid be given selectively to those really in need.

The inadequacies of the CAP cannot be denied. Moreover the process of renegotiation may very well already have been set in train. This arises from the October 1974 negotiations concerning farm price increases. The Community has agreed to carry out a thorough review or stocktaking of the CAP. There is now evidence of a greater willingness to consider that alternative schemes might be better. Particularly significant is the reported West German view that the CAP system is not well adapted to simultaneously balancing supply and demand and supporting farm incomes. We have of course already seen that the UK is not being denied access to cheap food in the world market – currently there is no cheap food available! Even Mr Callaghan had to admit this, although he questioned whether it would be a permanent state of affairs. An appraisal of this latter point requires us to forecast the future – all we can say is that currently there is in the view of the experts no sign of a new cheap food era beginning to emerge.

The issues arising in connection with the harmonization of VAT are difficult to appraise – the British position refers to 'necessities' but these are not defined. It is doubtful whether this is a crucial or urgent issue (the British Government is not opposing harmonization in principle – if it were then there would be significant implications for the customs union and difficulties would arise). Harmonization is likely to be delayed. In the immediate future some approximation of national rates may be all that will be achieved with possible, at least temporary, exceptions for articles such as food.

The British position on regional policy is misconceived. The idea of a Regional Development Fund indicates that the Community intends to help member states with their regional problems rather than the reverse. But, more important, Community

control of aids is clearly intended to assist countries such as the
U K since it will be operated in a way which prevents extravagant
and unnecessary aid-giving in the prosperous central regions of
the Community. The U K has everything to gain by such control and if the Community were to break up Britain would be
hard pressed to compete with the more prosperous economies of
France and Germany in attracting footloose investment. This
part of the statement reveals a quite fundamental weakness in
thinking. There is a tendency to assume that true sovereignty is
always best maintained by curbing powers outside Westminster.
There is a failure to recognize that the conquest of internal problems may sometimes be aided by bodies such as the European
Community Commission.

The protection of Commonwealth and developing country
interests is an unexceptionable aim. The statement, however,
does not argue that the Community has failed to address itself to
the problem but that it needs to do more. A reformed CAP will
not help developing countries to a great extent (although sugar
producers would be possible beneficiaries). The main gains would
go to producers of temperate food products who are generally
developed (Canada, New Zealand, Australia etc.) – but they are
in fact already getting extremely good prices. The developing
countries are important suppliers of raw materials but these are
accorded favourable treatment in the common external tariff.
One way in which assistance could be given to developing
countries is through a more generous application of the Generalized Tariff Preferences and the Community's programme in that
area for 1975 is noticeably more liberal. The U K Government,
in calling for a more generous aid and trade policy, will have to be
ready to foot the bill and to face the consequences – which could
be significant unemployment in hitherto protected industries.
Perhaps we can end this appraisal by quoting the Labour
Committee for Europe which in 1974 remarked:

Partly as a result of the pressures that Britain has been able to exercise
as a member of the Community, policies towards the Third World,
both in trade and in aid, are now moving in a much better direction.
The Kingston talks between the Community and the forty-four Third
World countries from Africa, the Caribbean and the Pacific, provide a

basis for agreement on measures for giving these countries better access to the European market without demanding that they give privileges in return, and for a better spread of Community aid. And we are gradually improving the Community's position through Generalized Tariff Preferences and in other ways, towards India and the other Asian countries of the Third World.

Though a great deal remains to be done, the fundamental point is this. There is not now a single Third World member of the Commonwealth that wants Britain to leave the European Community. They recognize the facts of life – the relative sizes of markets of Britain and the rest of the Community. They know that we can do more good for the Third World Commonwealth by staying inside to press their interests there, than we could possibly do for them if we were standing alone outside the Community. (Labour Committee, 1974, p. 3)

References

Balassa, B. (1962), *The Theory of Economic Integration*, Allen & Unwin.
Beever, R. C. (1969), *Trade Unions and Free Labour Movement in the E.E.C.*, PEP and Chatham House.
Coffey, P., and Presley, J. R. (1970), 'Monetary developments within the European Economic Community: 1970 – a year of achievement', *Loughborough Journal of Social Studies*, no. 10, November 1970.
Dahlberg, K. A. (1968), 'The EEC Commission and the politics of the free movement of labour', *Journal of Common Market Studies*, vol. 6, no. 3, pp. 310–33.
EEC Commission (1961), *Memorandum on the General Lines of the Common Transport Policy*, EEC.
EEC Commission (1962), *Programme for Implementation of the Common Transport Policy*, EEC.
EEC Commission (1965), 'Options de la politique tarifaire dans le transport', *Etudes Série Transport*, no. 1.
EEC Commission (1967), *First General Report on the Activities of the Communities*, EEC.
EEC Commission (1968a) 'First guidelines for a Community energy policy', *Bulletin of the European Communities Supplement*, no. 12.
EC Commission (1972), *First Report on Competition Policy*, EC.
EFTA (1966), *Building EFTA*, EFTA.
European Coal and Steel Community High Authority (1967), *Europe and Energy*, ECSC.
International Labour Office (1956), *Social Aspects of European Economic Co-operation*, ILO.
Labor Committee for Europe (1974), *The Labour Case for Europe*.
Levi Sandri, L. (1965), 'The contribution of regional action to the construction of Europe', *Third International Congress on Regional Economics*, Rome.
Lundgren, N. (1969), 'Customs unions of industrialized West European countries', in G. R. Denton (ed.), *Economic Integration in Europe*, Weidenfeld & Nicolson.

Miller, M. H. (1971), 'Estimates of the static balance-of-payments and welfare costs compared', in J. Pinder (ed.), *The Economics of Europe*, Charles Knight.

Palmer, M., Lambert, J., Forsyth, M., Morris A., and Wohlgemuth, E. (1968), *European Unity: A Survey of the European Organisations*, Allen & Unwin.

Prag, D., and Nicholson, E. D. (1973), *Businessman's Guide to the Common Market*, Pall Mall.

Presley, J. R. (1974), 'Progress Toward European Monetary Union', *Economics*, vol. X, part 3, winter 1973/74.

Saraceno, P. (1965), *The Economic Development of the Mezzogiorno*, Giuffre.

Strange, S. (1967), *The Sterling Problem and the Six*, P E P and Chatham House.

The United Kingdom and the European Communities (1971), H M S O, Cmnd 4715.

Williamson, J. H. (1971), 'Trade and economic growth', in J. Pinder (ed.), *The Economics of Europe*, Charles Knight.

Williamson, J. H., and Bottrill, A. (1971), *The Impact of Customs Unions on Trade in Manufactures*, Warwick Economic Research Papers.

Yannopoulos, G. N. (1969), 'Economic integration and labour movements', in G. R. Denton (ed.), *Economic Integration in Europe*, Weidenfeld & Nicolson.

Further Reading

K. W. Allen and M. C. MacLennan, *Regional Policies in France and Italy*, Allen & Unwin, 1971.

B. Balassa, *The Theory of Economic Integration*, Allen & Unwin, 1962.

C. Balfour, *Industrial Relations in the Common Market*, Routledge & Kegan Paul, 1972.

W. G. Barnes, *Europe and the Developing World*, PEP and Chatham House, 1967.

S. Barzanti, *The Underdeveloped Areas within the Common Market*, Princeton University Press, 1965.

B. T. Bayliss, *European Transport*, Mason, 1965.

W. R. Bohning, *The Migration of Workers in the United Kingdom and the European Community*, Oxford University Press, 1972.

M. Butterwick and C. J. Rolfe, *Food, Farming and the Common Market*, Oxford University Press, 1968.

M. Camps, *Britain and the European Community 1955-1963*, Oxford University Press, 1964.

P. Coffey and J. R. Presley, *European Monetary Integration*, Macmillan, 1971.

D. Coombes, *Politics and Bureaucracy in the European Community*, PEP and Chatham House, 1970.

N. Despicht, *Transport Policy of the European Communities*, PEP and Chatham House, 1969.

D. Dosser, *British Taxes and the Common Market*, Allen & Unwin, 1973.

D. Dosser and S. S. Han, *Taxes in the EEC and Britain: The Problems of Harmonization*, PEP and Chatham House, 1968.

S. S. Han and H. Leisner, *Britain and the Common Market: The Effect of Entry on the Pattern of Manufacturing Production*, Cambridge University Press, 1971.

T. E. Josling, 'The Reform of the Common Agricultural Policy' in D. Evans (ed.), *Britain in the EEC*, Gollancz, 1973.

F. Knox, *The Common Market and World Agriculture*, Praeger, 1972.

R. Lawson and B. Reed, *Social Security within the European Community*, PEP and Chatham House, 1974.

C. Layton, *European Advanced Technology: A Programme for Integration*, PEP and Allen & Unwin, 1969.

H. Lind and C. Flockton, *Regional Policy in Britain and the Six*, PEP and Chatham House, 1970.

G. Magnifico, *European Monetary Unification*, Macmillan, 1973.

J. Marsh and C. Ritson, *Agricultural Policy in the Common Market*, PEP and Chatham House, 1971.

R. Mayne, *Institutions of the European Community*, PEP and Chatham House, 1968.

G. McCrone, 'Regional policy in the European communities', in G. R. Denton (ed.), *Economic Integration in Europe*, Weidenfeld & Nicolson, 1969.

D. L. McLachlan and D. Swann, *Competition Policy in the European Communities*, Oxford University Press, 1967.

J. Meade, *The Theory of Customs Unions*, North-Holland Publishing Co., 1955.

P. M. Oppenheimer, 'The Problem of Monetary Union', in D. Evans (ed.), *Britain in the EEC*, Gollancz, 1973.

J. Pinder, *The Economics of Europe*, Charles Knight, 1971.

D. Prag and E. D. Nicholson, *Businessman's Guide to the Common Market*, Pall Mall, 1973.

T. Scitovsky, *Economic Theory and Western European Integration*, Allen & Unwin, 1958.

J.-J. Servan-Schreiber, *Le Défi Américain*, Denoel, 1967; translated as *The American Challenge*, Penguin Books, 1969.

A. Shonfield, *Europe: Journey to an Unknown Destination*, Penguin, 1973.

C. S. Shoup (ed.), *Fiscal Harmonization in Common Markets*, vols. 1 and 2, Columbia University Press, 1967.

S. Strange, *The Sterling Problem and the Six*, PEP and Chatham House, 1967.

D. Swann and D. S. Lees, *Antitrust Policy in Europe*, Financial Times, 1973.

D. Swann and D. L. McLachlan, *Concentration or Competition? A European Dilemma*, PEP and Chatham House, 1967.

G. Taber, *Patterns and Prospects of Common Market Trade*, Peter Owen, 1974.

D. Thompson, *Proposal for a European Company*, PEP and Chatham House, 1969.

J. Viner, *The Customs Union Issue*, Carnegie, 1950.

T. K. Warley, *Agriculture: The Cost of Joining the Common Market*, PEP and Chatham House, 1967.

T. K. Warley, 'Economic integration of European agriculture', in G. R. Denton (ed.), *Economic Integration in Europe*, Weidenfeld & Nicolson, 1969.

G. N. Yannopoulos, 'Economic integration and labour movements', in G. R. Denton (ed.), *Economic Integration in Europe*, Weidenfeld & Nicolson, 1969.

Index

Adenauer, C., 32
Advocate General, 43–4
Agriculture, *see* Common
    Agricultural Policy
Agricultural Guidance and
    Guarantee Fund, 125, 131,
    177
Aid schemes, 241
Algeria, association, 224
Allais Report, 142
Aniline Dye case, 80, 86
Annual Farm Price Review,
    118
Anti-trust problem, 79–80
Argentina, association, 224
Arusha agreement, 224
Association
    Algeria, 224
    Argentina, 224
    Austria, 225
    Egypt, 224
    Greece, 222
    Iran, 224
    Israel, 224
    Lebanon, 224
    Malta, 224
    Nigeria, 223
    overseas territories, 219–22
    Spain, 224
    Sweden, 224
    Switzerland, 225
    Turkey, 222
    Uruguay, 224
    Yaoundé Convention, 221
    Yugoslavia, 224
Atlantic Alliance, 31
Attlee, C., 20
Australia, 226
Austria, 29, 225

Balance-of-payments policy,
    109–14
Barber, A., 231
Barre plans, 200–201, 203
Beer standards, 99
Beever, R. C., 105
Belgium
    corporation tax, 113
    devaluation, 133
    grain prices, 119
    incomes, 182
    industrial integration prob-
        lems, 169
Benelux States
    customs union, 23
    and EEC, 23–4
Birkelbach Report, 171
Bonn Declaration, 30–31
Briand, A., 13
Brown, G., 29

Brussels Treaty Organization, 15, 22
Butter, 227

Callaghan, L. J., 246, 248
CAP, *see* Common Agricultural Policy
Capital
  Denmark liberalization, 111
  directives, 110–11
  free movement, 109–14
  Irish Republic, liberalization, 111
  restrictions and distortions, 111–14
  UK liberalization, 111
Cartel policy, 79–89
Cascade taxes, 89, 91
CEEC (Committee of European Economic Co-operation), 17
Ceylon, 227
Churchill, W. S., 16, 18
Coal, decline, 150–53
  coking, subsidy, 155–6
  see also Common energy policy
Coffrey, P., 203
Collusion, 81–2
Comecon, 15
Commissioners, EEC, 34
Committee of Permanent Representatives, 42–3
Common Agricultural Policy, 116–38, 242–4, 245, 247–9
  basic problems, 134–8
  devaluation, revaluation and floatation, 131–3

evolution, 119–21
farm incomes, 126, 135
farm sizes, 128
finances, 121–6
  proportions, 124
free trade area, 126
grants, 121
logic of inclusion, 116–17
prices, 134–8
reform, 133–8
surpluses, 127–30
system of price support, 117
Common commercial policy and aid, 237–41
Common energy policy, 149–65
  coal, decline, 150–53
  coal production, 161
  coking coal subsidy, 155–6
  crisis, 1973, 159–65
  harmonization, 163
  Memorandum, 156–9
  price movements, 152
  Protocol of Agreement, 153–4
  reasons for, 150–53
  security of supplies, 153
Common external tariff, 72, 226, 237
Common target price, 118
Common transport policy, 139–49
  achievements, 144–8
  basic policy, 140–44
  community quota (passport), 145–6, 147
  competition, 141–3
  discrimination, 144
  harmonization, 148

infrastructure costs, 145
licences, 143–4, 147
new developments, 148–9
tariff brackets, 146–7
Commonwealth, 228
effect upon, 224–5
Sugar Agreement, 225, 235
Community Budget, 243–4, 246–7, 248
Community Farm Accounts Survey, 127
Community Regional Development Fund, 30, 39, 126
Concentration policy (EEC), 80–89
Congress of Europe, 1948, 18
Continental Can case, 80, 83
Contract procurement, 101
COPA, 33
Copenhagen Summit, communiqué, 162–3
Coreper, 42–3
Council of Europe, 15, 18
Court of Justice, 43–4
Couve de Murville, N., 226
Customs union, 50–56
effects, 52–78
theory, 50–51
trade creation and diversion, 51–4

Darendorf, R., 115
Davignon Committee, 32
Declaration of Interdependence, 238
de Gaulle, General, 30, 31, 123, 226, 228, 230
Denmark, 228, 231

capital liberalization, 111
incomes, 182
Developing countries, 236
Dillon, D., 238
Dillon Round, 238
Direct taxes, 94
harmonization, 112
Director-General, EEC, 35
Doctors of the Common Market, Standing Committee, 115
Dominant firms, 80, 82, 83
Dubois, P., 13

ECE, 16
Economic Commission for Europe, 14
Economic and Monetary Union, 205–7, 246, 247
Economic and Social Committee, 46–7
'Ecosoc', *see* Economic and Social Committee
EFTA, *see* European Free Trade Association
Egypt, association, 224
Entry terms (1971), 242–6
Euratom, 16, 34, 46, 232
European Centre for Vocational Training, 194
European Coal and Steel Community, 16, 17, 19, 20
Agreement of Association, 24
High Authority and Commission, 34
structure, 34

European Communities Commission, 101

European Company Statute, 216

European Defence Community, 21
  Treaty (1952), 21–2

European Development Fund, 220

EEC
  anti-trust law, 86
  anti-trust problem, 79
  association, 219–24
  capital movements, 109–14
  cartel policy, 79–89
  collusion, 81–82
  Commission, role, 34, 35–40
  common energy policy, 149–65
  common commercial policy and aid, 237–41
  common external tariff, 72, 226, 237
  Community Regional Development Fund, 30, 39, 126
  concentration policy, 80–89
  contract procurement, 100
  council, 40–43
  Court of Justice, 43
  economic integration, 48
  economic and monetary union, 38–9
  and efficiency, 88
  ex officio actions, 85
  fiscal factors, 89–95
  formulation of policy, 33
  free movement of capital, 109–14

  free movement of labour, 105–9
  generalized preference system, 240
  and industrial policy, 211–18
  Luxembourg compromise, 42
  and macro-economic policy, 195–207
  and medium-term policy, 208–11
  membership, 224–31
  mergers, 83
  negotiations and terms, 231–7
  non-tariff barriers, 79–104
  notification of agreements, 84
  official and technical standards, 98
  public purchasing, 100–102
  restrictive practices, 87
  right of establishment, 114
  social policy, 184–94
  state aids, 95–8
  state monopolies, 102
  structure, 34
  Third General Report, 101
  transition period, 38
  voting procedure, 40–41, 42

Europe, East–West division, 14

European Free Trade Association (EFTA), 15, 27, 28–9, 225, 237

European Investment Bank, 173–7, 222

European Movement, 17, 22

European Parliament, 13, 21, 44–6, 171, 228
  delegates, 44–5
  power, 45–6
European Parliamentary Assembly, 18
European Political Authority, 21
European Political Commission, 31
European Political Community (EPC), 21
European Regional Development Fund, 126
European Research and Development Committee, 218
European Science Foundation, 218
European Social Fund, 125, 173, 176, 190–93
  reform, 192–3
European Technological Community, 229

Farm incomes, 126
  sizes, 128
Finland, and EFTA, 27
Fisheries policy, 232, 237
Fouchet, C., 30, 31
France
  attitude to sterling, 236
  boycott of EEC, 123
  CAP, 116
  common transport policy, 146
  corporation tax, 113
  devaluation, 131

and EDC, 22
grain prices, 120–21
incomes, 182
and medium-term policy, 210
oil crisis, 160
opposition to UK membership, 228, 230–31
and overseas territories, 219
and package deal, 41
regional policy, 167–8
supra-nationalism, 17–18, 22
value added tax, 89–90
Franco-German Treaty, 32
Free movement of capital, 109–14
Free movement of labour, 105–9
Free trade area, proposal, 25–7
  origin of goods, 48–50
Freedom of Establishment, 215
Freight charges, 139

GATT, *see* General Agreement on Tariffs and Trade
GEMA case, 88
General Agreement on Tariffs and Trade (GATT), 70, 219, 240
Generalized Preference Scheme, 236, 240–41
Generalized Tariff Preferences, 249–50
German Floor and Wall Tiles case, 87
Ghana, 227
Grain
  CAP, 118–19, 120–21
  prices, 136

Grants, CAP, 121
Greece, association, 222
Grundig-Consten case, 87, 88

Haferkamp, W., 35
Hague Summit, 29, 34, 178
Hartley Report, 151
Heath, E., 225
Heath–Pompidou meeting, May 1971, 232
Hillery, P., 35
Hong Kong, 227
Howard, D., 189

Ice-cream standards, 98–9
Iceland, 29
Incomes, average, 182–3
India, 227
Indirect taxes, 89–94
Industrial policy, 211–18
  anti-trust problem, 79–80
  cross-border mergers, 214–17
  research and development, 212, 217–18
  size of firms, 212
  structure and research and development, 212
International Monetary Fund, 70, 198
International Ruhr Authority, 19
Iran, Association, 224
Ireland, incomes, 182
  unemployment, 182
Irish Republic
  capital liberalization, 111
  membership, 225

Israel, association, 224
Italy
  devaluation, 133
  incomes, 182
  Mezzogiorno problem, 167

Josling, T., 243, 244–5
  Josling proposal, 138

Kennedy, J. F., 238
Kennedy Round, 238–40
Kenya, 224
Kissinger, H., 164
Korean War, 20

Labour
  discrimination, 107
  free movement, 105–9
    statistics, 108–9
  migrant, 107, 108, 183, 192
  social security, 107
Labour Committee for Europe, 249–50
Latin American states, 221
Luxembourg Agreement, 124
  compromise, 42
  devaluation, 133
  national corporation taxes, 113

Macleod, I., 231
Macmillan, H., membership application, 225
Macro-economic policy, 195–207
  Barre plan, 201
  basis, 195–6
  Budgetary Committee, 199

Commission's role, 199
Committee of Central Bank Governors, 199
Committee on Short-Term Economic Trends, 198
co-ordination, 198–200
devaluation, 206
economic and monetary union, 205–7
Medium-Term Economic Policy Committee, 199, 211
Monetary Committee, 198–200
Monetary Co-operation Fund, 205
Monetary integration, 200–205
Treaty rules, 197–8
Mansholt Plan, 128, 133
Mansholt, S., 120
Marshall-Edgeworth offer curve analysis, 74
Marshall Plan, 16, 20
Meade, J., 51
Medium-term policy, 208–11
Action programme (1962), 208, 210
Medium-Term Economic Policy Committee, 199, 211
origins, 208
planning, 209–11
programme, 208–11
Mendès-France, P., 22
Mergers, 83
cross-border, 214–17
Messina Conference, 24
Migrant workers, 183, 192

discrimination, 107
families, 108
housing, 108
social security, 107
Milk subsidies, 95
Mill, J. S., 74
Miller, M. H., 243, 244–5
Monetary Committee, 110, 198–200
Monetary Co-operation Fund, 205
Monetary integration, 200–205
Barre Plan, first, 200–201
Barre Plan, second, 203
Schiller Plan, 202–3
Werner Group, 203–5, 206
Monnet, J., 19
Monopolies, 102–4
Mugnozza, C., 35

National standards, 98–9
harmonization, 99–100
Naumann, F., 13
Negotiations and terms, UK membership, 231–7
Netherlands, the
common transport policy, 146, 147
devaluation, 133
incomes, 182
national corporation taxes, 113
oil crisis, 159
Neumark Committee, 109
New Zealand, 225, 226, 227, 232, 235
Nigeria, 227
association, 223

Nixon Round, 240–41
Non-tariff barriers, 79–104
North Atlantic Treaty Organization (NATO), 15
Norway, 225, 228, 231
Notification of agreements, 84

OEEC, *see* Organization for European Economic Co-operation
Ohlin Report, 187
Oil, 155, 157–8
    crisis, 1973, 159–65
        Copenhagen Summit communiqué, 162
        'low profile' policy, 160
        supply cuts, 160
O'Neill, Sir Con, 231
Organization for European Economic Co-operation (OEEC), 15–18
Organization of Petroleum Exporting Countries (OPEC), 159, 164–5
Ortoli, F.-X., 35
Overseas territories, 219–22

Pakistan, 227
Palmer, M., 20, 23, 198, 228
Paris Summit, 30, 31, 32, 34, 38–40
Part Four Association, 219–22, 236
Penn, W., 13
Pléven, R., 21
Pompidou, G., 231, 232
Portugal, 29, 225
Prebisch, R., 221

Presley, J. R., 203, 206
Proudhon, P. J., 13
Public purchasing, 100–102
Public works contracting, 101

Quinine case, 86

Regional Development
    aid schemes, 173–7, 179, 183, 248–9
    average incomes, 182
    and CAP, 173
    emerging problems, 167–8
    European Social Fund and EIB, 174
    factor price equalization, 170, 180
    industrialized areas, 168
    instruments under Rome Treaty, 172–7
    integration problems, 168–70
    Memorandum, 178
    migration, 183
    policy, 247, 248–9
    Regional Development Rebate Fund, 178, 181
    Regional Development Fund, 163, 181, 248, 249
    Thomson Report, 181, 182
    unemployment, 182
    Werner Report, 178, 180
Relance, 23–5
Renegotiation, 246–50
Research and Development (R & D), 212, 217–18
Restrictive practices, 87
Ricardo, D., 51, 58

Right of establishment, 114–15
Rippon, G., 231, 242
Rome Treaty, 35
  decisions, 3, 8, 35, 37–8
  tariff disarmament and
    trade expansion, 70

Saar problem, 20
Sandri, L., 167
Sanders, P., 215
Schaus Memorandum, 140
Schiller Plan, 202–3
Schumann Plan, 19, 20, 202–3
Second World War, 14, 16
Segré Report, 112
Select Committee on Nation-
    alized Industries, 101
Simonet, H., 35
Sirena-Eda case, 88
Smith, A., 13
Soames, Sir C., 35
Social policy, 184–94
  European Social Fund, 190–
    93
  free movement of labour,
    184–5
  harmonization of law on dis-
    missal, 194
  harmonization of social
    charges, 187–9
  harmonization of social
    standards, 185–7
  living standards, 184–5
  migrant workers, 107, 108,
    183, 192
  progress, 193
Spaak Committee, 24
Spaak, P.-H., 19, 24

Spain, association, 224
Spencer, J., 243, 244–5
Standards, harmonization, 104
State aids, 95–8, 141
State monopolies, 102
Sterling, 236
Stockholm Convention, 27, 48
Strange, S., 230
Sugar, 232, 235–6
Sugar case, 86
Sully, Duc de, 13
Supra-nationalism, 17–18, 22,
    31, 32, 225
Sweden, association, 29, 225
Switzerland, association, 29,
    225

Tanganyika, 227
Tanzania, 224
Tariff barriers. 48–78
  ad valorem, 62
  disarmament and trade ex-
    pansion, 70
  dynamic, 68–70
  effect on economic welfare,
    54–67
  elementary analysis, 51
  external tariff, 72, 226, 237
  free trade, 48–50
  internal tariffs, 73
  specific, 62
  theoretical analysis, 63
  trade creation and trade di-
    version, 51–4
Taxes
  cascade, 89, 91
  cases against Italy and Bel-
    gium, 93

Taxes–*contd*
harmonization, 91, 92
and industrial policy, 213
national corporation, 113
Thomson Regional Fund, 183–4
Thomson, G., 35, 183
Thomson Report, 181, 182
Trade creation and trade diversion, 51–4
Transport, *see* Common transport policy
Turkey, association, 222–3
TVA, *see* Value added tax

Uganda, 224
Unemployment, 182–3
UNICE, 33
United Kingdom
CAP, 118
grain prices, 136
capital liberation, 111
and common external tariff, 226
and commonwealth problems, 226
and EDC, 21
and EEC budget proposals, 233–4
and EEC negotiations (1961–3), 28, 29–31, 224–6
and EEC negotiations (1970–71), 226–31, 231–7
and EEC Parliamentary vote, 232
and EFTA, 28–9
and EPC, 21
and free trade area proposal, 25–8
incomes, 182
membership application, 225
issues involved, 226–31
refused, 226
national corporation taxes, 113
oil crisis, 160, 163
and Schumann Plan, 20
and Spaak Committee, 24
and supra-nationalism, 17–18; *see also* Supranationalism
unemployment, 182
value added tax, 89–90, 92, 93, 125, 233
and WEU, 23–4
United Nations Conference on Trade and Development (UNCTAD), 219, 221, 240, 241
U.S.A., 238–40
and oil crisis, 164–5
Marshall Plan, 16–17
Uruguay, association, 224
U.S.S.R., and Marshall Plan, 16

Value added tax, 89–90, 92, 93, 125, 233, 247, 248
Van den Tempel, A. J., 114
Vertical integration, 91–2
Viner, J., 51

Wageningen Memorandum, 136
Warsaw Pact, 23

Werner Committee, 178, 180
Werner Group, 203–5, 206
West Germany
  CAP, 116
  Corporation tax, 113
  devaluation, 132–3
  grain prices, 120
  incomes, 182
  and medium-term policy, 210
  revival after war, 19
Western European Union, 23, 24
West Indies, 227
Williamson, J. H., 243, 244–5
Wilson, H., 229

Yaoundé Convention, 221
  new, 227
Yom Kippur War, 1973, 159
Yugoslavia, association, 224

Zoja-Commercial Solvents case, 88

**More about Penguins
and Pelicans**

Penguinews, which appears every month, contains details of all the new books issued by Penguins as they are published. From time to time it is supplemented by *Penguins in Print*, which is our complete list of almost 5,000 titles.

A specimen copy of *Penguinews* will be sent to you free on request. Please write to Dept EP, Penguin Books Ltd, Harmondsworth, Middlesex, for your copy.

In the U.S.A.: For a complete list of books available from Penguins in the United States write to Dept CS, Penguin Books, 625 Madison Avenue, New York, New York 10022.

In Canada: For a complete list of books available from Penguins in Canada write to Penguin Books Canada Ltd, 41 Steelcase Road West, Markham, Ontario.

Books on Economics published by Penguins

Economic Systems and Society   *George Dalton*

Economics of the Real World   *Peter Donaldson*

Guide to the British Economy   *Peter Donaldson*

Worlds Apart   *Peter Donaldson*

Land Reform and Economic Development   *Peter Dorner*

International Investment   *John H. Dunning (Ed)*

The Energy Question   *Gerald Foley*

The Economics of Industrial Innovation
   Christopher Freeman

The New Industrial State   *J. K. Galbraith*

Economics and the Public Purpose   *J. K. Galbraith*

Economics, Peace and Laughter   *J. K. Galbraith*

Japanese Imperialism Today
   Jon Halliday and Gavan McCormack

Capital and Growth   *G. C. Harcourt and N. F. Laing (Ed)*

The Principles of Development Aid   *E. K. Hawkins*

Critique of Economic Theory
   E. K. Hunt and Jesse G. Schwartz (Ed)

Books on Economics published by Penguins

The Theory of the Firm   *G. C. Archibald (Ed)*
Unequal Shares: Wealth in Britain   *A. B. Atkinson*
Wealth, Income and Inequality   *A. B. Atkinson*
Inflation   *R. J. Ball and Peter Doyle (Ed)*
A Dictionary of Economics
   Graham Bannock, R. E. Baxter and Ray Reese
Monopoly Capital: An Essay on the American Economic
   and Social Order   *Paul A. Baron and Paul M. Sweezy*
Economics of Imperialism   *Michael Barratt-Brown*
Wealth   *Charles Carter*
The Economic History of World Population
   Carlo M. Cipolla
The City in the World Economy   *William M. Clarke*
Monetary Theory   *R. W. Clower (Ed)*
Poverty: The Forgotten Englishmen
   Ken Coates and Richard Silburn
Health Economics
   Michael H. Cooper and Anthony J. Culyer
The Complete Guide to Investment   *Gordon Cummings*